THE INTELLIGENCE OF INTUITION

People often confuse intuition with a sixth sense or the arbitrary judgments of inept decision-makers. In this book, Gerd Gigerenzer analyzes the war on intuition in the social sciences beginning with gendered perceptions of intuition as female, followed by the opposition between biased intuition and logical rationality, popularized in dual-system theories. Technological paternalism amplifies these views, arguing that human intuition should be replaced by perfect algorithms. Contrary to these beliefs, this book proposes that intuition is a form of unconscious intelligence based on years of experience that has evolved to deal with uncertain and dynamic situations where logic and big data algorithms are of little benefit. Gigerenzer introduces the scientific study of intuition and shows that intuition is not irrational caprice, but is instead based on smart heuristics. Researchers, students, and general readers with an interest in decision-making, heuristics and intelligence, cognitive psychology, and behavioral public policy will benefit.

GERD GIGERENZER is Director of the Harding Center for Risk Literacy at the University of Potsdam and Emeritus Director of the Max Planck Institute for Human Development, Germany. He trains federal judges, physicians, and managers in decision-making and has written award-winning books, including *Calculated Risks, Gut Feelings, Risk Savvy*, and *How to Stay Smart in a Smart World*, which have been translated into more than 20 languages. The Swiss Duttweiler Institute has distinguished him as one of the top 100 Global Thought Leaders worldwide.

THE INTELLIGENCE OF INTUITION

GERD GIGERENZER

Max Planck Institute for Human Development

CAMBRIDGE
UNIVERSITY PRESS

Shaftesbury Road, Cambridge CB2 8EA, United Kingdom

One Liberty Plaza, 20th Floor, New York, NY 10006, USA

477 Williamstown Road, Port Melbourne, VIC 3207, Australia

314–321, 3rd Floor, Plot 3, Splendor Forum, Jasola District Centre, New Delhi – 110025, India

103 Penang Road, #05-06/07, Visioncrest Commercial, Singapore 238467

Cambridge University Press is part of Cambridge University Press & Assessment, a department of the University of Cambridge.

We share the University's mission to contribute to society through the pursuit of education, learning and research at the highest international levels of excellence.

www.cambridge.org
Information on this title: www.cambridge.org/9781009304863

DOI: 10.1017/9781009304887

© Gerd Gigerenzer 2023

This publication is in copyright. Subject to statutory exception and to the provisions of relevant collective licensing agreements, no reproduction of any part may take place without the written permission of Cambridge University Press & Assessment.

First published 2023

A catalogue record for this publication is available from the British Library.

Library of Congress Cataloging-in-Publication Data
NAMES: Gigerenzer, Gerd, author.
TITLE: The intelligence of intuition / Gerd Gigerenzer, Max Planck Institute for Human Development.
DESCRIPTION: Cambridge, United Kingdom ; New York, NY : Cambridge University Press, 2023. | Includes bibliographical references and index.
IDENTIFIERS: LCCN 2023005663 (print) | LCCN 2023005664 (ebook) | ISBN 9781009304863 (hardback) | ISBN 9781009304894 (paperback) | ISBN 9781009304887 (epub)
SUBJECTS: LCSH: Intuition. | Decision making.
CLASSIFICATION: LCC BF315.5 .G543 2024 (print) | LCC BF315.5 (ebook) | DDC 153.4/4–dc23/eng/20230415
LC record available at https://lccn.loc.gov/2023005663
LC ebook record available at https://lccn.loc.gov/2023005664

ISBN 978-1-009-30486-3 Hardback
ISBN 978-1-009-30489-4 Paperback

Cambridge University Press & Assessment has no responsibility for the persistence or accuracy of URLs for external or third-party internet websites referred to in this publication and does not guarantee that any content on such websites is, or will remain, accurate or appropriate.

for Raine

Contents

List of Figures and Tables	*page* viii
Preface	ix
Acknowledgments	x
1 We Know More Than We Can Tell	1

PART I THE WAR ON INTUITION

2 Female Intuition Versus Male Reason: The Battle for Intelligence	21
3 Biases: Mistaking Intuition for Irrationality	42
4 Governmental and Technological Paternalism	68

PART II INTUITION AND ITS INTELLIGENCE

5 Heuristics: The Tools of Intuition	91
6 Embodied Heuristics	109
7 Moral Intuition	125
8 Simple Heuristics to Run a Research Group	141
References	154
Index	172

Figures and Tables

Figures

1.1	Fluency heuristic	*page* 5
3.1	Risk versus uncertainty	46
3.2	Which glass is half full, which half empty?	49
3.3	Throwing a fair coin four times	53
3.4	The special case where the length of the string (here three) is the same as the length of the sequence ($k = n$)	54
3.5	Citation bias in favor of articles reporting that people have biased statistical intuitions	62
4.1	An example of boosting: fact box for ovarian cancer screening, based on randomized studies with 200,000 women	73
5.1	A model of Elon Musk's one-good-reason heuristic for hiring	98
5.2	A model of Jeff Bezos's sequential decision process for hiring	99
5.3	Ecological rationality	101
5.4	Balancing false positives and misses	102
5.5	An illustration of the ecological rationality of the recognition heuristic	105
6.1	Gaze heuristic	114
6.2	Predators (dark hawks) pursuing prey (white ducks)	120
6.3	British controllers' reliance on the gaze heuristic to direct fighter planes to intercept German bombers	122

Tables

6.1	The as-if trajectory calculation model and the gaze heuristic compared	*page* 115
7.1	A four-card problem: A social contract with a perspective change	131

Preface

Intuition is an ultimate experience, beyond words: We know more than we can tell. This phenomenon upsets those who believe in rationality as a purely conscious activity. Its detractors tend to dismiss intuition as crazed superstition, while others have confused it with God's voice. *The Intelligence of Intuition* extends the argument for the rationality of intuition made in my book *Gut Feelings* (2007) with a deeper scientific analysis. I locate intuition in its larger societal context and argue that intuition is based on the unconscious use of adaptive heuristics. These simple rules make intuition smart.

Part I looks at the war against intuition. This battle began centuries ago to justify male paternalism by placing female intuition in opposition to male reason. With rising gender equality, this opposition was tailored to justify governmental paternalism by opposing female *and* male intuition to logical reasoning. In addition, the claim emerged that artificial intelligence (AI) will soon be, if it is not already, superior to human intuition, thereby justifying technological paternalism. All these clashes overlook that, like nature and nurture, intuition and deliberate reasoning act hand in hand. They are not antagonistic, nor is one of the partners superior. The false dichotomy serves obscured goals to exercise power over others.

Part II provides a closer view of the nature of intuition. Intuition is neither caprice nor irrationality, but unconscious intelligence based on long experience. The theoretical framework for understanding its nature is that of ecological rationality – the study of how mental processes are adapted to their environments. It is based on Herbert Simon's notion of bounded rationality, that is, how people make decision-making under uncertainty – in situations where the future is uncertain and the best action cannot be calculated. Good intuitions rely on adaptive heuristics that are not logically, but ecologically, rational. In this book, I weave together new chapters with previously published papers, which have been revised, updated, and integrated into a coherent structure.

In a nutshell, *The Intelligence of Intuition* explores the myth of intuition's fallibility by positioning it as a unique form of intelligence that complements rather than opposes rationality.

Acknowledgments

Although single-authored, the ideas in this book emerged from years of collaboration with my graduate students, post-docs, and colleagues, including the members and guests of the ABC Research Group at the Max Planck Institute for Human Development in Berlin, and previously at the Max Planck Institute for Psychological Research in Munich. Many of them kindly commented on the chapters and ideas in this book. My thanks go Colin Allen, Hal Arkes, Florian Artinger, Will Bennis, Sonja Bißbort, Edward Cokely, Leda Cosmides, Adam Feltz, Nadine Fleischhut, David Funder, Wolfgang Gaissmaier, Mirta Galesic, Andrew Gelman, Daniel G. Goldstein, Jonathan Haidt, Robert P. Hamlin, Reid Hastie, Ralph Hertwig, Ulrich Hoffrage, Perke Jacobs, Linnea Karlsson, Konstantinos V. Katsikopoulos, Gary Klein, Shenghua Luan, Laura Martignon, Björn Meder, Joshua B. Miller, Shabnam Mousavi, Jonathan Nelson, Hans-Jörg Neth, Andreas Ortmann, Ernst Pöppel, David Preiss, Markus Raab, Lael Schooler, Jan-Gerrit Schuurman, Özgür Simsek, Robert Sternberg, Jeffrey R. Stevens, Joline Tan, Peter M. Todd, John Tooby, Elisabetta Versace, Riccardo Viale, Kirsten Volz, Odette Wegwarth, and Tom Wells. I am grateful for the intellectual and emotional support of my wife, Lorraine Daston, and for her help in directing my way through the stacks of Cambridge University Library to search for material on the idea of a peculiarly female intelligence. My special thanks go to Rona Unrau, who edited the entire manuscript and helped me to improve the first drafts. Christel Fraser went over the final draft and edited footnotes and references, and Sarah Otterstetter helped with the figures. I am lucky to have had the generous and unique support of the Max Planck Society and to profit from its intellectual and interdisciplinary atmosphere. It's research paradise.

CHAPTER I

We Know More Than We Can Tell[*]

> The heart has its reasons of which reason knows nothing.
> *Blaise Pascal*[1]

> Intuition is a very powerful thing, more powerful than intellect.
> *Steve Jobs*[2]

After years of conducting research as a cognitive psychologist, I remain fascinated by the power of intuition – the ability to know more than we can explain. Most people recognize a face without being able to specify its features. An experienced physician can sense in a blink of an eye when something is wrong with a patient, without being able to articulate why. Chess masters such as Judith Polgár and Magnus Carlson report that their intuitive play is the secret of their success. Intuition emerges from years of experience and is a form of unconscious intelligence.

Intuition and reason are no opposing war parties. The physician's hunch initiates a deliberate search for the ailment. A musician's conscious and meticulous practice is the very basis from which those precious moments of flow emerge, where improvisation progresses without conscious guidance. Similarly, the majority of 17 Nobel Laureates explained in an interview that their "big leap" had occurred by them switching back and forth between intuition and analysis.[3] This interplay has enabled generations of scientists and engineers to create technology. Blaise Pascal, the French mathematician whose beautiful words are cited in this chapter's epigraph, was also one of the inventors of the calculus of probability. Intuition and reason not only go together, they depend on each other. Without reason, there would be no mathematics. Without intuition, there would be little innovation.

---

[*] The phrase is from Michael Polanyi (1966/2009), p. 4.   [1] Pascal, B. (1669/1995). *Pensées*.
[2] Cited by his biographer, Walter Isaacson, in his book *Steve Jobs* (2011).
[3] Dörfler & Eden (2019).

Nevertheless, intuition is subject to increasing mistrust. People confuse it with God's voice or the arbitrary decisions of an inept political leader. Some psychological theories even portray intuition as suspect and reason as superior. Representatives of tech companies at popular artificial intelligence (AI) events contrast dubious human feelings with trustworthy algorithms in their efforts to convince us that we should be anxious to give away our private data and let machines make our personal decisions. However, this mistrust was not born in the digital age. Albert Einstein already noted it when he said:[4]

> The intuitive mind is a sacred gift and the rational mind is a faithful servant. We have created a society that honors the servant and has forgotten the gift.

Einstein was so right. Whereas calling something *intuitive* indicates great respect in the hard sciences, the term is often used to indicate irrationality in the social sciences as something generally inferior that should be avoided whenever possible. As we will see, this disrespect of intuition has a history. But first, let us be clear about what intuition is.

What Is Intuition?

Thomas Aquinas and other medieval philosophers believed that angels are endowed with intuition.[5] Angels have no bodies and thus no sensory organs that could deceive them; therefore, they can intuit the truth directly with impeccable clarity. Similarly, philosophers, including René Descartes and Immanuel Kant, were looking for certainty beyond mere experience. Intuition could make us "see" the self-evident truths in mathematics, morals, or God.[6] While philosophers have debated the function of intuition, they themselves widely hold that they rely on it. The link between intuition and certainty was disentangled in the sciences when the great 19th-century physiologist Hermann von Helmholtz spoke of *unconscious inferences* and the 20th-century psychologist Egon Brunswik spoke of the mind as an *intuitive statistician*.[7] They were not the first; the idea that intuition is uncertain inference rather than direct knowledge of truths had been anticipated by David Hume and others before him. Unlike angels, mortals cannot perceive the world directly and have to rely on cues to infer

---

[4] Calaprice (2011), p. 477, lists this quote as "possibly or probably by Einstein."   [5] Goris (2012).
[6] Kant's word for intuition was "Anschauung," which derives from seeing ("schauen"). For an excellent introduction into the highly diverse philosophical views about intuition, see Osbeck & Held (2014).
[7] Brunswik (1955). Brunswik, following Helmholtz, focused on the intuitive nature of perception.

their world. Similarly, the idea that intuition would not need experience became dispelled. Unlike Kant who was looking for certainty independent of experience, Helmholtz and Brunswik understood intuition as a result of experience. In this way, intuition eventually became divorced from (the illusion of) certainty and wedded to learning from experience.

Nevertheless, those philosophers who think of intuition as directly providing certain knowledge, and those psychologists who think of it as uncertain inference based on experience, share one important belief. Both assume that intuition is a form of intelligence. For Descartes, intuition was the most fundamental of the two routes to knowledge, the other being deduction.[8] For Helmholtz, unconscious inferences enable the amazing intelligence of perception and, at the same time, explain perception illusions. Following this tradition of unconscious inferences, I understand intuition as unconscious intelligence.

In this book, I use a working definition:[9]

An intuition is a feeling:

1. based on long experience,
2. that appears quickly in one's consciousness, and
3. whose underlying rationale is unconscious.

The emphasis on experience contrasts with the idea that intuition is arbitrary, a sixth sense, or God's voice. The cases of the doctor and the chess masters emphasize the role of experience. The learning of one's first language is another case in point. Consider the sentence "I could not agree to you." A native speaker would sense immediately that something is wrong with that sentence without necessarily being able to say what rules of grammar are violated. Someone with another mother tongue who hasn't mastered the language cannot depend on intuition in the same way.

Learning from experience requires feedback, meaning that having good intuitions in one domain does not guarantee having good intuitions in others. Intuitions are domain-specific. Professional tennis players may have excellent intuitions about the perfect forehand, but not about investing their money. Be it acting, driving, dancing, programming, or playing bridge and chess – the superior intuitions of experts require extensive training, with elite performance estimated at some 10,000 hours of

---

[8] See Osbeck & Held (2014) for a more detailed analysis.
[9] See Gigerenzer (2007). Similar definitions have been used by Bruner (1973) and, more recently, Hogarth (2001), Gladwell (2007), and Klein (1998/2017).

deliberate practice.[10] The importance of experience also contrasts with rational choice theory, whose axioms are about being consistent and where experience plays little role.

The second aspect, "appears quickly in one's consciousness," provides a first indication of why intuition is indispensable. When fast decision-making is required, people have to act within the constraints of time. In life-and-death situations, deliberating all possible options can be fatal. Similarly, soccer players have to decide in a fraction of a second where to pass the ball. They may occasionally err, but would otherwise always miss opportunities if they deliberated extensively during a game. That limit of thinking too long is well known and time pressure is often considered a regrettable circumstance. However, the scientific study of intuition has revealed a stunning phenomenon: If players had more time to make a decision, their performance would not necessarily improve. Thinking deliberately can actually decrease performance. For an experienced player, intuition is guided by a simple rule:

Fluency heuristic: Choose the first option that comes to mind.

Studies with expert handball and golf players show that options come to mind *in the order of their validity*. That is, the first option is typically the best, the next option second-best, and so on (Figure 1.1). This explains why following one's first hunch is likely the best decision. If the first option cannot be carried out in the situation at hand, then following the second impulse is probably the best decision. In an experiment, experienced handball players were shown 10-second video sequences from top games. Then the sequences were frozen and the players had to say what option they would take, such as throw at the goal or pass to the right.[11] After their immediate and intuitive response, they were given another 45 seconds to deliberately inspect the frozen image and asked once again what they now thought the best option was. In about 40 percent of the cases, the players changed their minds. Yet, more time did not lead to better choices. Most of the time, the first intuitive choice was better than the action chosen after reflection. Similarly, when experienced golfers were given only 3 seconds to make their put, they were more successful in getting the ball into the hole than when given unlimited time.[12] Novices, in contrast, have not yet developed good intuitions and perform better when granted more time. They need deliberation because they lack

---

[10] See Ericsson et al. (1993); Cokely & Felz (2014).   [11] Johnson & Raab (2003).
[12] Beilock et al. (2004).

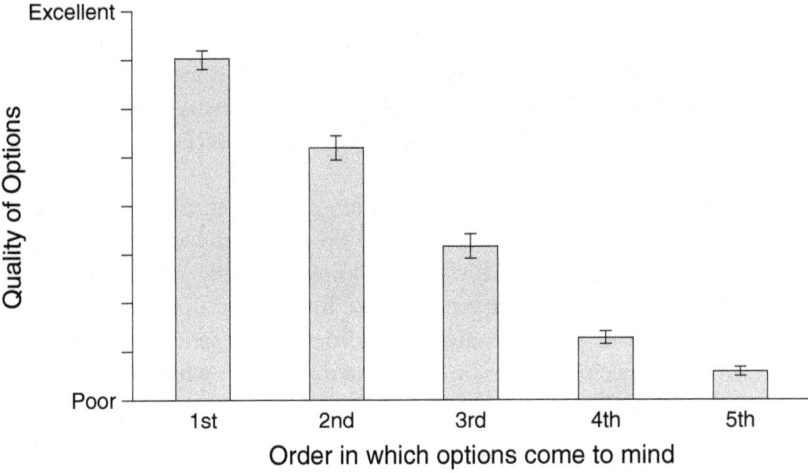

Figure 1.1. Fluency heuristic. For expert players, the quality of options decreases with the order they come to mind (adapted from Johnson & Raab, 2003). Thus, relying on the fluency heuristic enables not only fast but also accurate decisions. Note that this heuristic requires expertise and does not work as well for novices.

experience. The fluency heuristic is one illustration of how intuition is aided by heuristics.

Studies with chess players showed similar results: The first option that came to mind to chess masters (grand masters and international masters) was nearly always the best one.[13] Moreover, under time pressure, their decisions did not suffer, whereas less experienced chess players then chose inferior moves. The higher the expertise, the more the chess players trust their intuition and the more often they are right in doing so.

Thus, the first two aspects of intuition form a close couple: The more experience in a domain, the more likely that what quickly comes to mind is actually the best option. Note that this finding contradicts the hypothesis of a general speed–accuracy trade-off, where less time leads to less accurate decisions. As we have seen, this trade-off holds for novices, but not necessarily for experts. Fast decisions are not automatically inferior to slow decisions. How then did fast thinking come to be associated with errors and slow thinking with rationality?[14] Psychological experiments mostly

---

[13] Medvegy et al. (2022). Forgetting aids the fluency heuristic, see Schooler & Hertwig (2005).
[14] The opposition between fast, intuitive decisions that are prone to error and slow, rational decisions that avoid error is commonly made in dual-system theories, specifically in Kahneman's (2011a) version. Despite the vagueness of these theories, there is little evidence that the attributes of

enlist undergraduates or crowdworkers who have no experience with the task at hand or confront them with artificial tasks they have never seen before. In this situation, the speed–accuracy trade-off does exist. The story of fast, intuitive decisions that are often wrong versus slow, reasoned decisions that are generally better is an overgeneralization based on the study of nonexpert undergraduates.

The third defining feature of intuition is crucial: that the process underlying an intuition is unconscious. To repeat the words of Pascal, "the heart has its reasons of which reason knows nothing." A skillful player is unaware of the process that generates the first option that comes to their mind. Unconscious processes are not oddities, but essential for cognitive functioning. Conscious attention is a limited resource, which is the reason why multitasking is difficult:[15]

> If one simultaneously performs two tasks that require deliberate attention, one's performance on each of the tasks deteriorates.

Human attention can fully focus on one task alone, meaning that multitasking leads to a decrease in performance on the task(s) that demand focus. Our brain's solution is to perform as many tasks as possible unconsciously. If all of its tasks, including breathing and walking upright, needed to take place consciously, they would interfere with each other. In the words of the Portuguese poet Fernando Pessoa, "Could it think, the heart would stop beating."[16] Once a process is unconscious, it no longer interferes with attention. Breathing while driving does not interfere with driving safety; texting while driving does.

Nevertheless, the unconscious has not received much appreciation in consciousness-centered philosophy, particularly in the 20th-century analytic tradition. In psychology, the unconscious has similarly met with suspicion. Sigmund Freud's revelation that our behavior is heavily influenced by unconscious processes has been hailed as the third blow dealt to the human ego – after Copernicus and Kepler demonstrated that the Earth is not the center of the solar system, and Darwin found that humans and animals have common ancestors. Freud's unconscious processes were discovered when studying hypnosis and hysteria, which he investigated mostly in women. While unconscious influences, as embodied in the term

---

cognitive processes actually cluster into two poles, but substantial evidence against it (Keren & Schul, 2009; Melnikoff & Bargh, 2018; Rizzo & Whitman, 2020).

[15] Tombu & Jolicoeur (2004). [16] Pessoa, F. (1996).

Freudian slips, are now common wisdom, accounts of them are mostly negative and refer to unintentional influences that cannot be controlled and should better not happen.

The supposed link between unintentional and unconscious is, however, a misconception. Unconscious processes are typically initiated by intention. For instance, an experienced driver drives intuitively, but intentionally. An experienced scientist may have a sudden hunch while pondering a puzzling finding, but the hunch is motivated by conscious intention. Similarly, when typing, we do not move our fingers consciously, but typing is nevertheless an act of intention. These unconscious, but intentional, processes are the subject of psychological research on the automaticity of higher mental processes.[17] The general lesson is: The fact that much of what we do is unconscious does not mean that it is irrational or unintentional. Unconsciousness is a necessary condition for a rational being.

Fear of Admitting Gut Decisions

Not being able to explain one's intuitions has led philosophers and psychologists to mistrust intuitive decisions. Those who cannot explain their actions are subject to suspicion. Mistrust of intuition fuels a culture of post hoc justification, motivated by fear of liability. In large corporations and administrations, justification and self-protection have become the primary motive in place of achievement. In this world, intuition is not talked about openly, but relied on surreptitiously.

In a series of studies, I asked hundreds of executives from half a dozen international corporations how often an important professional decision they made or participated in was ultimately a gut decision (their term for intuition). That is, if the available data did not provide a clear answer, which often happens in the uncertain world of business, how frequently did they rely on their intuitions? On average, the answer was for 50 percent of important decisions.[18]

Yet, the majority of the same executives would never admit to this practice in public. Many executives were unwilling to take personal responsibility for their decisions. They feared making errors and being blamed if they were unable to explain an intuitive decision.

---

[17] Bargh & Morsella (2008).   [18] Artinger et al. (2019); Gigerenzer (2014a).

The Business of Justifying Decisions Post Hoc

I have observed two ways in which managers cope with this anxiety. The first is to hire a consulting firm to justify the intuitive decision after the fact. Curious about how often this happens, I asked the principal of one of the largest consulting firms worldwide what proportion of their customer contacts involved justifying decisions post hoc. On the condition of anonymity, he disclosed that it was more than 50 percent. That gives a rough idea of the time, resources, and intelligence spent on concealing intuitive decisions and avoiding responsibility. In these cases, the function of reasoning and argumentation is to rationalize intuitive decisions and to hide them from view.

A second strategy is even more expensive for the companies: defensive decision-making. It occurs when a manager feels that option A is the best for the company, yet nevertheless recommends and pursues a second-best option B that is less risky for their own career if something goes awry. In my studies with managers from large corporations, the majority admitted to such practices for an average of 30–40 percent of all their important professional decisions.[19]

Both strategies to camouflage intuitive decisions – hiring consulting firms or choosing second-best decisions – are costly. For every 1 percent loss in corporate income due to defensive decisions, a rough estimate is that, in highly industrialized countries such as Germany, large corporations lose billions of dollars each year.[20] In family-owned businesses, by contrast, there is much less fear of admitting to following one's intuition; after all, it is their own money that is at stake, and most plan a generation ahead rather than up to the next quarterly report. If there is skin in the game, good intuitions are welcome. Wasting one's own money to cover these up would be a poor business strategy. Independent of whether leaders admit or deny gut decisions, both the analysis of data and intuition are required. Intuition and reasoning work with, not against, each other.

Reasoning and Intuition: Two Sides of the Same Coin

Intuition is based on experience. There are two ways in which experience is gathered: by *implicit* or *explicit learning*.[21] In implicit learning, also called

---

[19] Gigerenzer (2014a).   [20] Artinger et al. (2019).
[21] Reber (1989) identified intuitive thought as the product of implicit learning. Yet, intuition can also be the product of explicit learning.

incidental learning, a person is not aware of the process (such as a heuristic or a grammar) underlying an intuition. The learning of one's first language proceeds in this way without being aware of the rules of grammar underlying one's speech. Second languages, in contrast, are typically taught by making the rules of grammar (and their exceptions) explicit. Similarly, in order to catch a fly ball, baseball outfielders rely on the gaze heuristic without being fully aware of it (see Chapter 6). Yet, ever since research figured out the heuristic process, it can be explicitly taught to novices. The important point is that the *same* heuristic rules, such as those of grammar and of catching a ball, underlie both intuition and deliberate reasoning.

Intuition can also start out as deliberate reasoning, that is, by explicit learning. Tying shoelaces is learned consciously, as a sequence of movements, but, with experience, it becomes unconscious. Once this state is achieved, the process works fast and flawlessly. At that point, consciously thinking about the sequence of movements can actually disrupt one's ability to tie the laces. Similarly, a difficult piece on the piano is learned consciously by paying attention to the right sequence and timing of fingers, but true music starts when piano players are no longer conscious of what their fingers are doing. Many skills have passed through this trajectory from deliberate to intuitive. Alfred Whitehead, the English mathematician who coauthored the *Principia Mathematica* with Bertrand Russell, emphasized this trajectory to counter the axiom that deliberate thinking is all that matters:[22]

> It is a profoundly erroneous truism, repeated by all copy-books and by eminent people when they are making speeches, that we should cultivate the habit of thinking of what we are doing. The precise opposite is the case. Civilization advances by extending the number of operations which we can perform without thinking about them.

Contrast Whitehead's statement with the belief that free will denotes always consciously deciding before acting. In the widely discussed experiments by the American neuroscientist Benjamin Libet, for instance, a change in participants' electroencephalogram (EEG) signals occurred before the participants actually reported their decision to act (a simple motor action).[23] The conscious decision thus did not appear to cause the action, a finding that has been interpreted by others as proof that free will is illusory. Yet that conclusion assumes volition and intention to be unremittingly conscious, and it overlooks the fact that intuitive processes

---

[22] Cited in Egidi & Marengo (2004), p. 335. [23] Libet (2004).

guide many of our decisions. Our unconscious is every bit part of our identity. We would get nowhere by deliberating all day long, leaving our body to wait patiently for orders.

Einstein's concern that we have forgotten the gift of intuition is as timely today as it was then. And the campaign against intuition has a history.

The War on Intuition

Even into the 20th century, prominent psychologists were convinced that men are rational and women intuitive and that only men could master abstract thought. It was asserted as a scientific fact that women's concrete and intuitive thinking prevented them from grasping abstract moral principles, going so far as to claim that women who lied were simply incapable of comprehending that their actions were evil. According to this line of reasoning, women needed men's guidance and should be kept out of politics, economics, and other important decision-making domains. In Chapter 2, I tell the story of this peculiar idea of women's intuitive intelligence and how the opposition of female intuition and male reason faded away due to the emerging concept of a single intelligence shared by both sexes. Women and men were eventually deemed equal partners, but intuition and rationality were kept unequal.

In spite of these changes, women continue to be associated with intuition today. For instance, when asked whether women recognize emotions better than men, women and men responded in the affirmative, a result also consistently obtained in self-report questionnaires on emotional intelligence. However, when actually testing people's abilities, studies did not find a difference for strong expressions of emotions; for emotional expressions of lower intensity, the results are inconsistent.[24] In one study, 5,000 participants were shown 24 faces with emotional expressions, either at a high or low intensity, and were asked to rate these on each of six emotions: anger, disgust, fear, happiness, sadness, and surprise. Both genders rated the target emotions equally correctly, regardless of whether the expression was intensive or subtle. There was no evidence that women have better intuitions than men about others' emotional expressions.[25]

Beginning in the 1970s, a group of psychologists and behavioral economists began a new war on intuition, pitting it once again against rationality. This time, the target of attack extended beyond female intuition to

---

[24] Hoffmann et al. (2010); Montagne et al. (2005). [25] Fischer et al. (2018).

include everyone's intuition. The key message, spread by bestselling books such as Ariely's *Predictably Irrational* (2008), Kahneman's *Thinking, Fast and Slow*, (2011a), or Thaler and Sunstein's *Nudge* (2008), is that only the abstract logic of rational choice theory is worthy of trust. Just as female intuition had been opposed to male reason, two antagonistic systems were posited, one fast, intuitive, inconsistent, and often wrong, and the other slow, rational, and apparently always right. Humans err if the rational "System 2" does not pay sufficient attention and fails to correct what the intuitive "System 1" gets wrong. The similarity of this new opposition with that of female intuition versus male reason may not be entirely coincidental. It is based on a philosophical and psychological tradition that differs strongly from the angelic view of intuition. From the 19th century to the first half of the 20th century, it was not uncommon that psychologists contrasted what they believed to be the intuitive, primitive, and fast judgments of children, women, and the mentally retarded, with the slower and more deliberate rational judgments of male adults.[26] In the more current view, everyone's intuition is riddled by dozens of cognitive biases, many of which have become household words.

The new target is a specific kind of intuition, namely, understanding chance and randomness, at which humans are claimed to be miserably incompetent. This dismal picture, however, is surprising. Prior to the 1970s, two decades of psychological research concurred that human intuition about chance and randomness is fairly accurate – at least by age 12 or so, as Swiss psychologists Jean Piaget and Bärbel Inhelder were the first to conclude in 1951. Why did people show fairly good intuitions about chance before the 1970s and shoddy ones thereafter? The 1970s brought the Watergate scandal, the end of the Vietnam War, and the death of Elvis Presley. But how would such events explain a decline in our intuition?

Weapons of Destruction

I argue that there was no such decline in intuition in the first place. Rather, three measures were taken to make human intuition look wanting. For one, quite a few researchers bore a "bias bias," that is, a tendency to spot cognitive biases even when there were none. This led them to mistake what were, in fact, people's intelligent intuitions for persistent irrationality. Second, studies demonstrating biases introduced a new kind of classroom and online experiment that produces data in a few minutes and does not

---

[26] For an overview, see Osbeck & Held (2014).

allow participants to learn from experience. Pre-1970s psychological experiments, by contrast, gave participants the opportunity to learn. When people can learn from experience, their intuitions about chance, randomness, and risk are not perfect, but fairly good. It was only recently understood that this change in experimental practice was one of the factors that made intuitions suddenly appear to be infected with biases.[27] Strikingly few people are even aware of research unveiling the marvels of intuition. This blind spot is fueled by a third measure, a conspicuous citation bias: Studies reporting good intuitions are rarely mentioned and cited, whereas those reporting biases are highly popularized.[28] The bias bias and the lack of learning opportunities were crucial in producing the new negative view of intuition, and the massive citation bias, now and then, makes the untrustworthiness of intuition appear to be a hard, scientific fact.

These three weapons in the war against intuition have created a distorted picture of intuition and reinforced the misleading idea that intuition is hostile to reason. This war, eventually called the *great rationality debate*, or *rationality war*,[29] spilled over into politics. If ordinary people's intuitions are riddled with biases, citizens cannot make appropriate decisions by themselves and therefore need steady guidance by experts and governments. Governments, so the argument continues, know better what their citizens really want and should nudge them along that path.[30] This new paternalism is reminiscent of the male paternalism of the past, where women were seen as irrational and in need of male guidance. Now the verdict is on people's intuition across the board, and governments have a scientific blueprint to nudge their citizens into "proper" behavior. Once again, intuition has been discredited in the name of science.

The Bias Bias in the Service of Governmental Paternalism and Reckless Companies

Male paternalism is, of course, not the same as governmental paternalism, even if both have been justified by attacking intuition. Yet there are striking parallels. Female intuition had been linked to moral flaws, while

---

[27] Lejarraga & Hertwig (2021).
[28] See Christensen-Szalanski & Beach (1984); Lejarraga & Hertwig (2021); and Chapter 3 of this volume.
[29] Gigerenzer (1996); Kahneman & Tversky (1996); Tetlock & Mellers (2002); Stanovich et al. (2011); Sturm (2012).
[30] Thaler & Sunstein (2003, 2008).

in the 21st century, intuition was linked to individual moral weaknesses and considered the cause of individual wrongdoings such as failure to take care of one's health, to use condoms as protection from AIDS, and to save money for the future. Moreover, intuition was increasingly seen to be at the root of social problems, causing more than individual damage. Obesity was suspected to result from a "present bias" (overweighting the present moment), addictive gambling from wrong statistical intuitions, and the financial crisis of 2008 from traders' overconfidence bias. Once again, governments were called to step in and nudge their citizens in order to protect them – not from criminals, but from themselves. As we will see, these brash claims were rarely based on independent evidence. In fact, when my colleagues and I reviewed over a thousand studies, we found little reliable evidence that so-called biases of intuition are associated with loss of wealth, health, happiness, or any other measurable costs.[31] Yet, blaming intuition for society's ills has become a story too powerful to be disturbed by facts.

Attributing obesity or financial crises to a failure of the brain's rational part to prevent its intuitive part from irrational action amounts to a one-sided, individualistic view of responsibility. This internal narrative deflects attention from some of the real culprits in the external world. The food industry earns billions from advertising and selling unhealthy food, the gambling industry has deliberately designed personalized slot machines to make people addicted, and legal systems allow bankers to profit from taking undue risks and letting taxpayers pick up the bill.[32] In this way, the war against intuition can serve quite a few parties' interests. For instance, the House of Lords criticized the UK government under former prime minister David Cameron for nudging citizens to avoid obesity instead of considering more efficient solutions such as prohibiting the television advertising of products high in sugar, salt, and fat.[33]

Focusing on systematic errors made by human intuition is also of interest for companies that severely pollute the environment, as the 1989 Exxon Valdez oil spill in Alaska illustrates. In 1994, an Alaskan federal jury awarded $5.3 billion to fishermen and others whose livelihoods had been devastated by the spill. When Exxon waged its appeal, a new line of research emerged that used studies with mock juries to question jurors'

---

[31] Arkes et al. (2016).
[32] On the design of addictive slot machines, see Schüll (2012); on the reckless practices of banks, see Admati & Hellwig (2013).
[33] House of Lords (2011).

intuitions. Without mentioning that it had funded the research, Exxon argued "that jurors are generally incapable of performing the tasks the law assigns to them in punitive damage cases."[34] The results served Exxon well in court. This new line of research on jurors' intuitions eventually became part of a new field known as *behavioral law and economics*. Its key program is to show how intuition fails in legal contexts.

By no means do I defend intuition for its own sake. A "war on reason" would be equally dangerous. The scientific method has struggled for centuries to promote fact over opinion and encourage people to look at the evidence rather than to defend their favored theories. Today, we witness new versions of this long-standing struggle, amplified by the rapid dissemination of fake news by social media. The international Programme for International Student Assessment (PISA) study reported that over 90 percent of 15-year-olds worldwide do not know how to distinguish facts from mere opinion or fake news.[35] Even worse, many do not seem to be motivated to do so in the first place. Social scientists and philosophers themselves struggle to respect the evidence if it does not validate their theories, as the accounts of female intuition versus male reason and of the bias bias illustrate.

This struggle has a long history. In the early 17th century, disputes among scholars grew so fierce and insults so intolerable that the Royal Society of London prevented scholars from publishing their pet theories and focused on oddities of nature instead. For about half a century, the annals were filled with striking observations for which no theories existed, such as double-headed calves, blood rain in Bavaria, and cold light. Francis Bacon, one of the spearheads of the movement, complained that observations are too often contaminated with arbitrary dogmas.[36] Looking at strange facts helped to reduce the avalanche of personal insults.

Common Sense, Freedom, and Dignity

The war on intuition, be it on female's or everyone's intuition, intersects with the struggle for freedom and dignity of a group of people and the effort of others to control them. Thomas Paine's *Common Sense*, written in 1776 against the rule of authority – about the then king of Great Britain and his injustices to American colonists – exemplifies the ideal that people should be free and trust their own senses to rule themselves. *Common Sense*

[34] Zarembo (2003). [35] OECD (2019). [36] Daston & Park (1998).

swept through the colonies like a firestorm, selling half a million copies and fueling the American War of Independence.

Today, digital technology is being misused to convince people that they should submit to a new rule of authority, technological paternalism. We are told that Google knows us better than we ourselves do and that we would be better off following the recommendations of algorithms rather than our own intuition. Underlying technological paternalism is the idea that algorithms will soon outperform human intelligence in all respects, if they have not done so already, and it is thus only prudent to stop making decisions on our own and defer to AI. In this view, AI is seen not as a complement to human intuition, but as an authoritative superintelligence that is immune to the errors we make. Yet, the evidence to back such technological paternalism is as scarce as for the claim that women are intuitive and men rational.[37] What drives this narrative is marketing hype and techno-religious faith. Statistical machines such as deep artificial neural networks are excellent for some tasks, but incorporating intuition and common sense into AI remains an enormous challenge.

Toward a Science of Intuition

To develop a scientific perspective on intuition, we first need to dispense with the old and misleading dualistic opposition of intuition and reason that has survived in many psychological theories. Instead, intuition and reason go hand in hand: In the case of the doctor who feels that something is wrong with a patient, intuition comes first, followed by a deliberate search for what is wrong. Even in abstract disciplines such as mathematics, both intuition and reasoning are needed. As George Pólya emphasized, finding a problem or discovering a proof requires intuition and heuristics; checking whether the proof is correct requires logic and analysis.[38]

Accordingly, psychological studies do not support the polarization of intuition and reason. If intuition and analysis were exclusive poles, their use would be negatively correlated (either the one or the other). An evaluation of 75 studies, however, showed that intuition and analysis were uncorrelated.[39] Nor is the alignment of intuition with heuristics and biases in popular dual-systems theories supported by evidence. Every heuristic

---

[37] Gigerenzer (2022a).
[38] Pólya (1945/1988). See also Mercier & Sperber (2011) on the close relation, not opposition, between intuition and deliberate argumentation.
[39] Wang et al. (2017).

can be used both intuitively (unconsciously) and consciously; intuition can lead to errors, but so can deliberate reasoning, logical argument, and big data.[40] Although the dichotomies in dual systems are quite vague, it is easy to see that they do not even align. Rather, they reflect the centuries-old view that pits reason against intuition, with reason as the dominant force. Instead of simply positing value-laden polar opposites, it is more fruitful to empirically study the nature of intuition and its relation to reason.

To get there, we also need to dispose of the bias bias, that is, the preoccupation with showing that people's intuition is flawed, even when evidence of that is scarce or nonexistent. For instance, at the beginning of the Covid-19 pandemic, *Bloomberg* published an article entitled "The Cognitive Bias That Makes Us Panic About Coronavirus." The author confidently asserted that "most people in North America and Europe do not need to worry much about the risk of contracting the disease" and are "more scared than they have any reason to be."[41] People's fear of getting infected was attributed to a bias of intuition, *probability neglect*. This means that people *overestimate* the danger because they fixate their attention solely on the potentially severe consequences of Covid-19 and neglect the low probability of these actually happening. At that time, however, nobody could know whether the probability was low or high, or how the pandemic would develop. When, during the following months, hundreds of thousands of people became infected with the virus and died, it became clear that people's intuitions were not so wrong. Other fighters in the war against intuition now blamed people for *underestimating* how quickly the virus spreads. People were said to suffer from an *exponential growth bias*, that is, a flawed understanding of the virus's exponential growth.[42] Many people have never been taught exponential functions and, thus, may indeed have difficulties in understanding them, but that is not the point. As it turned out, the spread of the virus was not exponentially increasing, but instead came in waves, growing and fading. The Covid-19 pandemic was a situation of uncertainty, not calculable risk, where no one could know the ever-changing probabilities and ups and downs, which left both experts at the World Health Organization (WHO) and ordinary people in the dark.[43]

---

[40] Gigerenzer et al. (2011); Kruglanski & Gigerenzer (2011).   [41] Sunstein (2020).

[42] Understanding experimental growth does indeed appear to be a problem, both for researchers and their subjects. Hamann (2022) shows the lack of understanding of exponential growth among the authors (not only the participants) of a classic experiment on the perception of exponential growth.

[43] Many physicians had originally hoped that the virus's harm would be comparable to that of the swine flu, which governments had overestimated. For instance, the British government announced

Thus, there are two indispensable preconditions for a mature science of intuition. First, one needs to eliminate the opposition between intuition and reason, both of which are needed for human intelligence. Second, one needs to eliminate the bias bias. Only by taking both intuition and reasoning seriously can we find out how they work, how they relate to each other, and when they each err.

What Follows

Part I of this book deals with the widespread mistrust of intuition. It begins with the opposition of female intuition versus male reason in the context of ideas about female intelligence. This chapter not only presents the history of the idea of a peculiarly female intelligence but also provides a larger context for the struggle to understand the mystery of intelligence and for the historical bias against women masked as science. It shows how the polarity eventually became resolved, even though beliefs in male superiority have not yet been fully extinguished. However, the opposition between intuition and reason has survived in present-day dual-systems theories of reasoning, which wage a new war against intuition. I make the case that there is little evidence for this opposition, even after it was cleansed of its problematic association with gender. The last chapter in Part I shows, in more depth, how the war against intuition has not only fueled male paternalism but also governmental and technological paternalism.

In Part II, I address the question of the nature of intuition. I argue that intuition is guided by the unconscious use of adaptive heuristics. These heuristics are ecologically rational and can lead to better decisions with little to no deliberate thinking. The fluency heuristic is an example. Heuristics can be embodied, that is, enlist motor and perceptual abilities without awareness. I also show how professional intuitions can be explicated by models of heuristics, such as the heuristics that Elon Musk and Jeff Bezos have used for hiring. The final chapter looks at the social world of science: How can one establish and maintain an environment that fosters successful collaboration in a research group? Using my 20 years of experience in directing a research group at the Max Planck Institute for Human Development in Berlin as a case study, I illustrate how heuristics shape the intellectual and social climate of research and how they influence

that as many as 65,000 citizens might die from swine flu, while, in the end, fewer than 500 had died. But there was no way to know where and how fast the new virus would spread.

whether a group culture can become more or less open, more or less formal, and more or less inclusive.

The important point is that intuition and adaptive heuristics can deal with situations of uncertainty (where we cannot know all possible future states and their consequences), with situations of intractability (where no computer can find the best solution), and with incommensurability (where there is no common currency). Rational choice theory cannot deal with these situations and is forced to reduce uncertainty to risk (where one knows everything that can happen in the future), to ignore intractability, and to exclude all problems where a dollar value cannot be attached to each option.

PART I

The War on Intuition

> Intuition was more or less a casualty of early 20th-century psychology's efforts to purge itself of metaphysical baggage.
>
> *Lisa M. Osbeck and Barbara S. Held*[1]

---

[1] Osbeck & Held (2014), p. 8.

CHAPTER 2

Female Intuition Versus Male Reason
The Battle for Intelligence[*]

> Her philosophy is not to reason, but to sense.
> *Immanuel Kant (1764)*

> Her logical thought is slower, but her associations quicker than those of man, she is less troubled by inconsistencies, and has less patience with the analysis involved in science and invention.
> *G. Stanley Hall (1904)*

Immanuel Kant's conviction that women's nature is sense rather than reason surprised few scholars during the Enlightenment. Learned ladies, Kant believed, were worse than useless, and the very thought of women intellectuals interested in Greek philosophy or the foundations of mechanics seemed almost comical in his eyes.[1] Kant stood in a long and tenacious tradition of scholars convinced that the mind of a woman differs from that of a man. It can be traced back to Aristotle's influential contention that "the female is softer in disposition, is more mischievous, less simple, more impulsive, and more attentive to the nurture of the young; the male, on the other hand, is more spirited, more savage, more simple and less cunning ... She is, furthermore, more prone to despondency and less hopeful than the man, more void of shame, more false of speech, more deceptive, and of more retentive memory."[2] At the beginning of the 20th century, psychology reiterated the idea that women are qualitatively different. The founder and first president of the American Psychological Association, G. Stanley Hall, held that women are intuitive and emotional, slow in logical thought, better at mental reproduction than production, and too impatient for analysis and science:[3]

---

[*] This chapter is a slightly revised and shortened version of Gigerenzer (2022c).
[1] Kant (1764/2011). [2] Aristotle (350 BCE/1984), pp. 948–949.
[3] Hall (1904/1976), pp. 565, 651.

> She works by intuition and feeling; fear, anger, pity, love, and most of the emotions have a wider range and greater intensity. If she abandons her natural naiveté and takes up the burden of guiding and accounting for her life by consciousness, she is likely to lose more than she gains, according to the old saw that she who deliberates is lost.

Hall, then president of Clark University, consequently opted against coeducation. Like Clark University, Harvard set up a female institution in the 1890s, Radcliffe College, next to the all-male Harvard College. But even there, women were treated differently. Not until 1967 did Harvard's Lamont Library open its doors to female students, an opening vehemently opposed by the administration and the majority of male undergraduates, on the grounds that females would distract male students and that there weren't even bathroom facilities for women.[4] It took yet another 10 years before Harvard terminated its policy of admitting only one female student for every four male students.

Hall expressed what psychologists at the time held to be a law of nature, traces of which can be found in people's thinking today. When my colleagues and I asked representative samples of 21st-century Germans and Spaniards about gender differences, the result was surprising – or perhaps not. The vast majority of women and men, young and old, believed that women had better intuitions than men about personal affairs, but not about science and finance.[5] And the rejection of learned ladies persists: Most contemporary American men in search of a partner on online dating sites find women with a Master's or PhD degree unattractive and prefer those with lower education.[6]

This chapter is a case study on how the lack of theory about the nature of intelligence enabled cultural biases about women to be presented as science by major psychologists. A discipline that is unaware of the errors in its history is potentially hazardous: "Those who cannot remember the past are condemned to repeat it."[7] I reconstruct the history of the idea of a peculiarly female intelligence in three overlapping views. In the first view, from Aristotle through to the mid-19th century, the idea of intelligence as we encounter it today – as a general ability that is measurable and is largely independent of personality and moral character – did not exist. Instead, the difference between men and women was understood in terms of polarities that were a mixture of intellect, personality, and moral character, such as men's reason versus women's intuition. The notion of these

---

[4] Masters (1986). [5] Gigerenzer et al. (2014). [6] Bruch & Newman (2018).
[7] Santayana (1905).

polarities wore away in the mid-19th century and was supplanted by the concept of an inherited "natural ability" (soon to be named *intelligence*), mainly through the writings of the English polymath Francis Galton. As a consequence, in this second view, men and women no longer differed in quality, but in quantity: On average, it was thought, women had inherited a smaller share of intelligence. The psychologist Lewis Terman put an end to this view by eliminating particular test items from his test (the Stanford-Binet test, which I discuss in the section "Binet's Intelligence Test Crosses the Atlantic and Becomes Seen as a Test of Genetic Ability") and balancing the rest so that girls and boys had the same mean IQ. The eliminated items landed in a personality scale called "masculinity-femininity" (see the section "How Differences in Intelligence Become Differences in Personality"), which illustrates the arbitrariness of what counted as a measurement of intelligence rather than of personality. What remains debated to the present day is the third view, promoted by sexologist Havelock Ellis (1859–1939). It alleges that men's intelligence varies more than that of women, implying the existence of more male idiots and geniuses.

Whatever the hallmark of a peculiarly female intelligence has been – polarities, lower average, or lower variability – it has served the dubious purpose of justifying men's dominant role in society. Similarly, whatever the supposed mental differences were, these became presented as part of the natural order, expressed in the female body and women's reproductive function.[8]

Before Intelligence: Female Intuition Versus Male Reason

Intelligence, as we know it from IQ tests, refers to a general ability that can be measured by a single number and is assumed to be largely independent of personality and moral character. IQ tests have been given to millions of children, recruits, and job applicants, and continue to influence access to education and jobs. The IQ has often been presented as a hard fact, and debates have raged over how much of its variability is due to nature or nurture. These debates ignored the fact that intelligence as we know it was "invented" in the late 19th and early 20th centuries.

Before that time, what we now call the intellect was considered neither as a single general ability nor as largely unrelated to moral and personality traits. Rather, psychological theories conceived the mind as a collection of

---

[8] Daston (1992).

faculties or talents. For instance, the key concept of *sensibility* in early 18th-century psychology encompassed both perceptual and emotional sensitivity as the precondition for empirical knowledge and the emotions of charity and compassion.[9] Reason was even more closely identified with morality because the light of reason enabled one to recognize all forms of truth, including the distinction between good and evil. No single one of these faculties or a combination thereof corresponds to the contemporary concept of intelligence.[10]

The prototypical male and female occupied opposite poles on the spectrum of these faculties. For instance, men were characterized by judgment, abstract thought, and genius, while women were considered to lack these and, instead, excel in intuition, concrete thought, and retentive memory. Male strength was opposed to female delicacy or bodily and mental weakness. This supposed weakness was, in turn, seen as evidence that nature intended women to confine themselves to the home and subordinate themselves to men. It was reasoned that because men's thought was abstract, they could comprehend truth, including moral truth, while women's concrete thinking prevented them from grasping abstract moral principles. Hence, women who lied or stole were considered incapable of understanding that their actions were evil. When Hall, in 1904, wrote that women, guided by intuition and feeling, were unfit for science and invention because they lacked patience, he was simply reiterating the timeworn conviction that women did not have the necessary self-discipline and stamina to reason by following a lengthy chain of argument.

Women's and men's virtues were also seen as diametrically opposed. For centuries (and in many contexts even today), chastity was considered the chief female virtue and its violation a cardinal sin for women alone. Timidity, in contrast, was a cardinal sin for men, but easily excused in women.[11] The view that women's intellect, character, and moral traits are intimately connected to their biology survived in various forms into early 20th-century philosophy. Consider the controversial Austrian philosopher Otto Weininger, hailed by Freud and Wittgenstein as a great genius.[12] In his book *Sex & Character*, Weininger drew on a wide range of philosophers and psychologists to assert that reasoning and feeling are equivalent in women who, as a consequence, are prone to suggestibility, hypnosis, and hysteria, as documented by Freud. These alleged flaws correspond to Aristotle's view that women's memory is easier to imprint. From biologists Sir Patrick Geddes and John Arthur Thomson, Weininger borrowed the

---

[9] Rifkin (2002).   [10] Daston (1992).   [11] Ibid.   [12] Dury (1984); Weininger (1906).

conviction that each cell in a woman's body is sexually marked to make the female in every respect passive, submissive, and lacking in personality.[13] Unlike man, he wrote, "woman is non-logical and non-moral."[14] Faced with the fact that more men stand trial for crimes, he argued that behind every lawbreaker is a woman who proposes the crime and profits from it. Weininger gained great popularity when he killed himself at the age of 23 at a spectacular site, the room in which Ludwig van Beethoven had died. This dramatic finale led to huge book sales and an enthusiastic reception by many contemporaries, including the Swedish playwright and novelist August Strindberg, who claimed that Weininger's book had finally solved "the problem of women."[15]

In sum, for millennia, a fairly consistent view reigned about women's intellect as differing fundamentally from that of men. My brief account does scant justice to the variations of this view among scholars and centuries. Yet, the common denominator between them is that there was no concept of a general intelligence, which was, instead, defined by a number of diametrically opposed polarities attributed to the prototypical male and female, a combination of what were only later separated into intelligence, personality, and moral traits. While the specific descriptions of the female and male attributes varied, they revolved around the poles of female intuition and male reason. This opposition, allegedly handed down by nature, was so manifestly true to psychologists and philosophers that evidence could not compromise the narrative. It was driven by motives outside of science, in particular the attempt to defend male's intellectual and moral dominance over females as part of the natural order. That is history, one might contend, and will not repeat itself. Yet, Chapter 3 shows that, in the 21st century, the opposition between intuition and reason has been resurrected in psychology and once again embraced as a persuasive narrative that is held to be self-evident.

The Invention of a General Inherited Intelligence

The idea of mental faculties was slowly abandoned in the late 19th century for that of a single overarching intelligence. However, the associated idea that this intelligence combines cognitive abilities, personality, and moral traits did not fade away until the early 20th century. The transition from multiple mental faculties to a single intelligence was driven not by data or by experiment, but by concerns outside the realm of science, chief among

---

[13] Geddes & Thomson (1890).   [14] Weininger (1906), p. 297.   [15] Abrahamsen (1946).

them being Francis Galton's interpretation of evolutionary theory, his fascination with measurement, and his involvement with the fateful eugenics program.

Women Are Granted the Same Kind of Intelligence As Men, but Less of It

Galton, a cousin of Charles Darwin, promoted a strict distinction between nature and nurture, which had not been considered mutually exclusive before his time.[16] This artificial distinction later led to a flood of psychological research seeking an answer to the (wrong) question of what percentage of the variation in intelligence is due to nature and to nurture (as opposed to asking how genes and environment interact, as in epigenetics). For Darwin's theory of evolution to work, it was clear that something must be passed on to the next generation and inherited by both boys and girls. In *Hereditary Genius*, Galton called this something *natural ability* (later known as *intelligence*).[17] As he saw it, evolution implied that men and women must have the same kind of natural ability and also that this ability shows variability between individuals, given that variation is a driver of evolution. Men and women were assumed (no measurements or tests were involved) to exhibit the same bell-shaped ("normal") distribution of intelligence, an assumption Galton justified by analogy with height. Using the same analogy, he assumed the female distribution to have a lower average. Consequently, in *Hereditary Genius*, women feature solely as the mothers or wives of male geniuses.

Galton maintained the view that natural ability is a combination of intellect, personality, and moral traits, such as capacity, zeal, and the power to do laborious work. With respect to morals, he wrote that it is the nature of all of us to believe blindly in what we love, rather than in what we think most wise:[18]

> We are indignant when others pry into our idols, and criticize them with impunity, just as a savage flies to arms when a missionary picks his fetish to pieces. Women are far more strongly influenced by these feelings than men; they are blinder partisans and more servile followers of custom.

The invention of a single, general form of intelligence, or natural ability, allowed Galton and his followers to compare men and women on a single dimension, similar to how he compared humans of different racial categories and even animal species. For instance, he conjectured that what he

---

[16] Daston (1992). [17] Galton (1869/1979). [18] Ibid., p. 196.

called the "negro race" differed from the "Anglo-Saxons" in their lower mean, not in the nature of their intelligence, and that certain gifted dogs had superior intelligence to some human "idiots and imbeciles."[19]

Today, the idea of a general kind of intelligence is mostly related to Charles Spearman's "g" factor.[20] In fact, Spearman was strongly influenced by Galton, and his main statistical tool was correlation, developed by Galton. Like Galton, he thought that high-sensory discrimination and high intelligence are part of the same universal intellectual function. Unlike Galton, however, Spearman steered clear of prejudices about women or non-whites being genetically inferior in their intelligence.

The Failure to Measure Intelligence

After Galton had invented the concept of general intelligence, he tried to measure it in his Anthropometric Laboratory in London, which opened in 1884. He started with the hypothesis that intelligence, being inherited, can be found in the mind and body – in the entire nervous system. From that perspective, greater sensory acuity would be the external sign of higher intelligence. Inspired by Galton, James McKeen Cattell established another anthropometric laboratory at Cambridge University, which also focused on sensory acuity. However, a student of Cattell's, Clark Wissler, could not find a clear relationship between sensory acuity and mental ability when looking at college freshmen's grades.[21] Moreover, the various acuity measures did not appear to correlate with each other.[22] Rather than acknowledging this failure as an invalidation of his hereditary theory of intelligence, Galton assumed a need for better measures of innate ability. His quest failed.

The key to measuring intelligence was found later in the work of Alfred Binet and Théodore Simon in France. In contrast to Galton and his followers, however, neither Binet nor Simon conceived intelligence as fixed or inherited, and Simon protested against the misuse of their test in England and the USA for measuring an allegedly inherited ability.[23]

How Women's and Men's Average Intelligence Were Made Equal

Binet, a member – and, later, director – of the Free Society for the Psychological Study of Children, was concerned about the unreliable

---

[19] Ibid., p. 338 (on race); p. 36 (on "idiots"). [20] Spearman (1904). [21] Wissler (1901). [22] See Blum (1978); Sternberg (1990). [23] Wolf (1973).

diagnoses of children with intellectual disabilities in France. One and the same child might be classified according to the categories back then as "imbecile," "idiot," "feeble-minded," or "degenerate" in different certificates.[24] Around 1899, Binet set out to classify these children in an objective way with scientific precision. His goal was to place children with intellectual disabilities in special schools geared to improve their abilities, as in the German school system at the time, and also to ensure that children without any intellectual disabilities would not be placed in special classrooms solely because they were behaviorally challenging. But Binet had no coherent idea how to measure intelligence. Like Galton, he searched in vain for correlations with sensory acuity and tried almost everything else that seemed viable, including assessing intelligence on the basis of facial features (physiognomy), measurements of the head (cephalometry), and handwriting (graphology). For instance, he presented handwriting samples from convicted murderers mixed with those from normal citizens and asked expert graphologists for character assessments, only to find out that even the most eminent experts arrived at disastrously false assessments.[25] The results were consistently disappointing. It remained a mystery what intelligence was and how to measure it.

Eventually, however, Binet and Simon found an ingenious answer to the question of finding a test that correlated with teachers' assessments. They developed questions about subjects that mirrored what was taught at school, such as reasoning skills, knowledge, memory, and attention. Children's answers to these questions now correlated with their school grades as well as with teachers' evaluations. By 1905, Binet and Simon had their first test of intelligence for classifying intellectually challenged children into several levels of developmental delay; in 1908, the test was revised and called a test of the "development of intelligence among children." Note that the test was intended to sort children into categories, not to assign them a single number such as an intelligence quotient. It was also not intended to measure innate intelligence, but to replace teachers' and physicians' unreliable diagnoses of children with intellectual disabilities, as a "means of prophylaxis, a means of escaping conscious and unconscious error."[26]

Binet and Simon's test questions still reflected the meaning of intelligence as a combination of intellect, character, and moral traits. For instance, the test included questions such as: "If you are late for school, what would you do?" and "Why should one judge a person by his acts

[24] Binet & Simon (1905/1973).   [25] Wolf (1973).   [26] Binet & Simon (1907/1914), p. 10.

rather than by his words?" Today, one might call this social intelligence, but Binet and Simon thought of social judgment as inseparable from intelligence. Now they had a test, but without a theory of intelligence, apart from a loose definition of intelligence as "judgment, otherwise called good sense, practical sense, initiative, the faculty of adapting oneself to circumstances. To judge well, to comprehend well, to reason well, these are the essential activities of intelligence."[27] Shortly before his death, Binet (1911) wrote: "Thus we return to our favorite theory: intelligence is marked by the best possible adaptation of the individual to his environment" and "to this we really do not want to add another thing."[28] To which his biographer Theta H. Wolf added: "How strikingly inept is such a pronouncement if we think of the excellent 'adaptation' to their environment of mice and moose!"[29] Measuring without precisely knowing what one is measuring has been, and still is, one of the striking features of research on intelligence. This feature conveniently allowed researchers to adjust the facts about female intelligence.

Binet's Intelligence Test Crosses the Atlantic and Becomes Seen As a Test of Genetic Ability

After obtaining his PhD under G. Stanley Hall at Clark University, Lewis Terman joined the faculty at Stanford University and gained a reputation as *the* leading US researcher on intelligence. Terman was more interested in gifted children than in intellectually challenged ones. In line with Hall and Galton, he firmly believed that intelligence was inherited. He translated Binet and Simon's test into English, added and deleted some questions, and published the product in 1916, which became known as the *Stanford-Binet Intelligence Scales*.

Yet, Terman had made important alterations that went largely unnoticed in the USA, but were to have damaging implications. He named the test an *IQ test* (the term was originally introduced by the German psychologist William Stern), where IQ was the ratio between mental age and chronological age. He believed that whatever the test measured was fixed and inherited, or at least predominantly so. Whereas Binet and Simon thought of the test as a means to send children with intellectual disabilities to special schools so that they could ideally be channeled back into normal classrooms, Terman instead advocated for special institutions and the

---

[27] Binet & Simon (1905/1973), pp. 42–43.   [28] Binet (1911), p. 172.
[29] Wolf (1973), p. 210.

sterilization of the "mentally retarded."[30] Terman had a strongly biased vision of what would happen once his test was widely applied: "There will be discovered enormously significant racial differences in general intelligence, differences which cannot be wiped out by any scheme of mental culture."[31]

Under the leadership of Robert Yerkes, president of the American Psychological Association and a member of the Eugenics Record Office's Committee on the Inheritance of Mental Traits, the *Army Alpha and Beta Tests*, based on Terman's IQ test, were applied to 1.75 million men in World War I.[32] Yerkes and his staff were convinced that the test measured native intelligence, even though it included items such as "The Overland car is made in Buffalo/Detroit/Flint/Toledo."[33] They recommended about 8,900 men with low test results to be immediately discharged from service, many of whom were foreign born or illiterate. The Army officers disagreed with the psychologists, pointing out that these men would become good soldiers after training.[34] Nevertheless, Yerkes hailed the test a great success, despite little evidence that it had made recruiting more efficient or had contributed to winning the war. In fact, it was the war that helped to win publicity for mass testing – if only because the psychologists had shown that such testing could be accomplished. On that wobbly basis, IQ testing spread across the USA.

Binet did not live to see what happened to the Binet-Simon test once it crossed the Atlantic, but Simon did. He objected to the term *IQ* because it suggested a fixed, inherited mental age. In interviews with Binet's biographer Theta Wolf, Simon even called the term and its genetic interpretation a betrayal ("trahison") of their test's original objective.[35]

Men and Women Are Assigned the Same Mean Intelligence

Without much fanfare, Terman eradicated the idea that females have lower average intelligence. In his revised Stanford-Binet test, he deleted questions for which boys and girls had different success rates and balanced the rest so that, on average, girls ended up with the same IQ as boys. Terman was not particularly explicit about this correction, nor about its reasons. But his decision finally made women equal to men in terms of IQ, at least on average.

---

[30] Minton (1988), p. 149. [31] Terman (1916), p. 92. [32] Carson (2007).
[33] Minton (1988), p. 70. [34] Ibid., p. 73. [35] Wolf (1973), p. 203.

What was Terman's motivation? Terman and Maude A. Merrill later explained that they plotted the difficulties of each item against age groups "for the sexes separately as a basis for eliminating tests which were relatively less 'fair' to one sex than the other."[36] Moreover, "a considerable number of those retained show statistically significant differences in the percentages of success for boys and girls, but as the scales are constructed these differences largely cancel out."[37] The explanation of "fairness" appears strange in the face of Terman's intention to measure largely genetic differences in intelligence. And fair to whom? Were boys or girls originally better, and whose mean was upgraded? Terman and Merrill did not say.

Others proposed that Terman made the means equal to reckon with the fact that girls usually perform better in school or in response to pressure generated by the increasing women's movement of the period.[38] A third explanation is that Terman, working closely with a large number of women coworkers (according to his biographer, Henry Minton, sometimes too closely), was influenced by them. Yet, all three explanations assume that boys initially tested better than girls and that item deletion served to upgrade the girls' average. Who really did perform better in the original set of test, girls or boys?

It took me a while to find an answer in Terman's writings. It appeared years later, in a different context, in the study on gifted children by Terman and Melita Oden, hidden in a side remark on another topic, the question of why there were more boys than girls in the group of gifted children. Terman and Oden discussed the possibility of a nomination bias (teachers nominate more boys than equally gifted girls) and also the possibility of "a real average superiority of boys in the intellectual function tested."[39] They concluded that such a real average superiority is unlikely because for the 905 subjects on whom the 1916 Stanford-Binet test was standardized, the mean IQ was slightly higher in girls. In other words, Terman appears to have found that girls had higher average scores in his intelligence test than boys and then deleted items and balanced others to lower the mean of the girls to match the inferior mean of the boys!

One might ask what would have happened if girls had had the lower scores. Would Terman also have deleted items to even the averages out? If not, the test might have been standardized such that females' average IQ was a few points lower than that of males.

---

[36] Terman & Merrill (1937), p. 22.   [37] Ibid., p. 34.   [38] Blum (1978).
[39] Terman & Oden (1947), p. 13.

Terman's decision to make the average IQ of males and females equal put an end to the second idea of a peculiarly female intelligence. It also illustrates the deep problem of how to measure something in the absence of a theory, where there is wiggle room to make decisions about test items that produce the result one favors – for fairness or whatever other reasons. In principle, Terman could have designed a test in which women are superior to men or where certain cultures or races are superior or inferior to white Americans. The problem is this: One can measure whether women and men differ in a specific and clearly defined task, such as memory span. But if one has neither a clearly defined task nor a theory and, instead, selects dozens of test items and adds the points up to determine an IQ, there are many degrees of freedom that allow for tinkering with the test to fit its result with preconceived beliefs and biases.

This key problem of measuring IQ is not always acknowledged. Consider Hans-Jürgen Eysenck, who once was the most frequently cited living psychologist and one of the most controversial intelligence researchers. In his *The Intelligence Controversy* with Leon Kamin, he reified the equal averages, complaining that psychologists "are said to have selected items in such a way that equal scores are achieved regardless of whether there might or might not be genuine differences between the sexes. This accusation is false."[40] He continued: "Given that unselected items give the sexes equal IQ scores, it was only reasonable for other test designers to avoid bias in favour of one or the other sex." However, there is no such thing as "unselected" items in the absence of a theory of what intelligence is and how it can be measured. Terman himself occasionally reified the equality of mean IQ to support women's equality. In *Sex and Personality*, Terman and Catherine Cox Miles wrote: "Intelligence tests, for example, have demonstrated for all time the falsity of the once widespread prevalent belief that women as a class are appreciably or at all inferior to men in the major aspects of intellect."[41] All in all, Terman's IQ test ended the view that females have lower average intelligence than males so that men and women were finally seen as equally intelligent – at the expense of favoring racial prejudice.

How Differences in Intelligence Become Differences in Personality

In the introduction to *Sex and Personality*, Terman and Miles noted that it appears impossible to explain sex differences in behavior wholly in terms of

---

[40] Eysenck & Kamin (1981), pp. 40–41. [41] Terman & Miles (1936), p. 1.

biological factors and complained that the concepts of masculinity and femininity are even more vague than the 19th-century concepts of intelligence.[42] By way of example, they referred to the stereotype of the "occidental" woman whose moral life is shaped less by principles than by personal relationships and whose everyday behavior is more determined by emotion, submissiveness, and inferior steadfastness of purpose.

Nevertheless, Terman and Miles did not present a theory that replaced the vagueness and stereotypes to which they objected. How then could they measure personality differences between men and women? Terman and Miles came up with an ingenious solution, which was initiated as subtly as Terman's strategy to discard test questions had been. It turns out that the discarded questions ended up in their "masculinity-femininity scale." That action guaranteed differences between males and females on the new scale, which contained, among others, questions on interests such as movies and amusement, opinions such as "The unmarried mother deserves the scorn she gets" and "Blondes are less trustworthy than brunettes," and information such as "The most gold is produced in Alaska/NY/Tennessee/Texas." Once seen as items that measured inherited intelligence, these now served to measure personality and gender-specific knowledge. In the absence of a theory of intelligence that determines what questions are relevant, one-and-the-same item can be applied to measure sex differences in intelligence or in personality. In various forms, the masculinity-femininity scale remains in use and is still presented as measuring sex differences in personality.

Larger Variability in IQ Justifies Male Superiority

In 2006, Harvard president Larry Summers resigned from his position in the wake of a no-confidence vote by his faculty. Among the reasons cited by the faculty was a remark he had made regarding women's intelligence and ability. On the question of women's aptitude for science, Summers said: "It does appear that on many, many different human attributes – height, weight, propensity for criminality, overall IQ, mathematical ability, scientific ability – there is relatively clear evidence that whatever the difference in means – which can be debated – there is a difference in the standard deviation, and variability of a male and a female population."[43] From that he drew the conclusion that the greater variability of males

---

[42] Ibid., pp. v–vi.   [43] Summers (2005).

explains why top universities such as Harvard hired relatively few women as professors.

Summers' statement simply repeated a hypothesis discussed in psychological research for over a century: that the variability of women's physical and mental traits, including IQ, is smaller than that of men. This variability hypothesis both explains and justifies observations that there are more male geniuses than female ones and also explains why there are more male idiots at the other end of the IQ distribution.

After Galton replaced the first version of intelligence – that men's and women's mental abilities were at opposite poles, such as reason versus intuition – with one common intelligence, and Terman, in turn, put an end to the subsequent idea of average differences, the only possible remaining difference on the bell curve was the variability, or standard deviation, in IQ. After all, a bell curve has only two parameters, mean and standard deviation. The variability hypothesis became the third and last bastion for the idea of a specifically female intelligence, contributing to Summers' fall. Its origins seem to lie in an observation by Darwin in the second edition of *Animal and Plants Under Domestication* that male animals tend to be more variable than females, although Darwin himself devoted little attention to this issue.[44] Instead, the claim of greater male variability was promoted by the English sexologist Havelock Ellis.

The Variability Hypothesis

Ellis rebelled against the conspiracy of silence surrounding the sexes and decided to devote his life to their scientific study. For him, women and men were different, but complementary – in contrast to Galton, who did not see much usefulness in women's lower average natural ability. In the first edition of *Man and Woman*, Ellis wrote: "From an organic standpoint, therefore, men represent the more variable and the more progressive element, women the more stable and conservative element, in evolution. It is a metaphorical as well as a literal truth that the center of gravity is lower in women and less easily disturbed."[45] (In the fourth and fifth edition, Ellis left out the "progressive element," indicating second thoughts about the generalizability of biological variation, particularly to politics.) He wrote that women's smaller stature approximated that of humans' ancestors, and that women – as in witches and soothsayers – preserved ancient custom and methods of intuitive knowledge. Women had "an

---

[44] Darwin (1893), p. 457.   [45] Ellis (1894), p. 367.

organic tendency to stability and conservatism, involving a diminished individualism and variability."[46] To exemplify, he made the case that women had opposed the French Revolution, albeit also noting that the revolutionary movement of Christianity was, to a considerable extent, furthered by women. While acknowledging that the facts are very complex and that that the claim of absolute inferiority for either sex is untenable, Ellis nonetheless concluded: "It is undeniably true that the greater variational tendency of the male is a psychic as well as a physical fact."[47]

Man and Woman received scant attention when it first appeared.[48] Yet, this changed when the statistician Karl Pearson vigorously attacked Ellis' variability hypothesis.[49] Pearson was a committed socialist and promoted feminism and eugenics, both of which were considered progressive and revolutionary at the time. Pearson argued that the claim of greater male variability contradicts Darwin's theory of evolution by natural selection, which emphasizes variability as one of the driving forces of evolution, but postulates that the more intense the struggle is, the less is the variability. Therefore, he expected men, not women, to be less variable. Next, he criticized Ellis' inconclusive evidence, based almost entirely on pathological variation such as criminality and color-blindness. Finally, Pearson contended that measuring the variability of absolute variables such as the length of bones (as opposed to ratios such as cephalic index) by the standard deviation, as Ellis did, was an error. Instead, one needed to calculate the coefficient of variation, that is, the standard deviation divided by the mean. After all, women's bodies were smaller than men's and so, therefore, was the standard deviation of bodily measures. Pearson concluded from his own physical measures that the coefficient of variation is slightly larger for women, not smaller, reflecting their "slightly less severe struggle for existence."[50]

In an Appendix in *Man and Woman*, Ellis rejected Pearson's "hostile" criticism at length, which Pearson did not deem worthy of a response. Pearson's sole reaction was a footnote in an article unrelated to variability, in which he noted that Ellis' response required no reply as Ellis did not appear to understand that scientific evidence, not vague generalities, was what counted.[51] Afterwards, Pearson did not pursue the variability hypothesis any further.

Why did this bitter controversy over females' allegedly lower variability erupt? According to Ellis' biographer Phyllis Grosskurth, one likely reason

---

[46] Ibid., p. 369. [47] Ibid., p. 370. [48] Grosskurth (1980), p. 170. [49] Pearson (1897).
[50] Ibid., p. 297. [51] Pearson & Lee (1903), p. 372.

was personal resentment. Many women of the time found Ellis, who with his flowing beard resembled "a combination of archetypal Father and sensual Faun," irresistibly attractive.[52] The South African writer Olive Schneider was one of the women upon whom Ellis had a strong influence, before she fell in love with Karl Pearson. Whatever the motivation, Pearson's critique of the variability hypothesis in fact contributed to making the hypothesis popular.

Ever since, psychologists, biologists, and statisticians have debated the variability hypothesis. Whereas Ellis and Pearson related it to both physical and mental traits, psychologists have focused largely on intelligence. Quinn McNemar and Terman reported greater variability in boys on the Stanford-Binet and other tests, but, given the inconsistent evidence, were careful not to draw any general conclusions.[53] In 1932, Scotland undertook the ambitious project of testing all 11-year-old Scottish children with the goal of discovering the amount of mental deficiency in the country.[54] Because suppliers demanded too much money for the nearly 100,000 commercial tests, the Council used the *Morey House Test* in place of the Stanford-Binet test. The conclusion was that boys and girls did not differ in average IQ, but that the standard deviation of boys was one IQ point higher than that of girls. In 1947, the same project was repeated with all 11-year-olds at that time, and again the standard deviation was one point higher for boys. This appeared to support the hypothesis of both higher and lower male intelligence. Although this result was hailed as the most comprehensive demonstration of the greater variability of mental ability among males, the small difference in variability in the 1947 study was, in fact, mainly due to an excess of males with very low scores, not to male genius.[55] The primary impetus of the 1947 study (and that of 1932) was not variability, but rather the concern that the nation's intelligence would decline because people with lower mental ability tended to have more children. Yet, the children scored no worse than those studied 15 years earlier; in fact, their average IQ went up by about one point in boys and three points in girls.

Follow-ups of the Scottish children study have shown similar, inconclusive results. In 1939, the Council found no significant difference in variability between boys and girls; in 1949, it reported slightly larger standard deviations in boys; and in 1958, it reported a greater proportion

---

[52] Grosskurth (1980), p. xvi.   [53] McNemar & Terman (1936).
[54] Scottish Council for Research in Education (1933, 1939, 1949, 1958).
[55] Deary et al. (2009), pp. 21, 184–185.

of females than males at the lower end of the IQ scale. Thus, one could find support for or against the variability hypothesis in intelligence, depending on the age group and study. More fundamentally, findings about variability – like mean differences – always depend on how the test items are selected and weighted. Just as Terman made the means between males and females equal, one can select items to make the variability equal.

Outspoken advocates have presented greater male variability as a biological fact, possibly due to sex linkage, speculating that intelligence might be located on the X chromosome. According to this line of reasoning, intelligence in males can express itself without interference of a second X chromosome, thereby causing greater variability in IQ.[56] This ignores the fact that the same hypothesis could likewise be used to predict that females have higher average intelligence than men, thanks to their two X chromosomes, once again illustrating the utter arbitrariness of genetic explanations in the absence of a theory. Whereas the first two ideas about a peculiarly female intelligence had been conceived and debated virtually entirely by men, the variability hypothesis was challenged by an early generation of women scientists.[57] Helen Bradford Thompson conducted her own studies and criticized Ellis' conclusions.[58] Her critique of the variability hypothesis was widely read, yet had no equivalent impact. In the most systematic critique of the variability hypothesis at the time, Leta Setter Hollingworth reported no evidence of this in her review of the literature.[59] Beth Wellman found in her review slight support for greater variability in boys, which, however, depended on the measure of variability used, the selection of children, and other details.[60] The variability hypothesis remains a matter of discussion. In her 2012 review of the state of art in sex differences in cognitive abilities, the former president of the American Psychological Association, Diane Halpern, accepted it, concluding "that females and males are very similar when we consider the average performance, and they are highly dissimilar when we consider performance at the high and low extremes."[61]

As with the question of whether males and females differ in their average IQ, the absence of a theoretical understanding of what a test actually measures opens the door to including or excluding items that make the mean and variance of IQ equal or different.

---

[56] Johnson et al. (2009); Lehrke (1978).   [57] Shields (1982).   [58] Thompson (1903).
[59] Hollingworth (1914).   [60] Wellman (1933).   [61] Halpern (2012), p. 103.

Lessons Learned

In sum, the idea of a peculiarly female intelligence emerged in three different and unrelated versions: male–female polarities, female lower mean intelligence, and female lower variability. The idea that men and women occupy opposite poles on a continuum, such as analytic versus intuitive, is the oldest; it reigned for millennia. It began to fade away when Francis Galton invented intelligence (natural ability) as a single dimension, which later morphed into IQ or g (general intelligence), so that the minds of men and women now had the same quality, but with women having less of it. The idea that women have lower intelligence expired in the hands of Lewis Terman, who eliminated test items so that both males and females had the same average IQ – otherwise, female means would, in fact, have been higher. The third idea was that while the means are the same, woman's variability is smaller, resulting in more male geniuses and idiots. This variability hypothesis is still debated today. It remains the last bastion of those who cling to the idea of male supremacy.

Despite the differences in these three ideas about a peculiarly female intelligence, their justifications are strikingly similar, and the supposed nature of women features prominently in all three. A woman's mind was said to be determined by her reproductive biology, her body, her genes, and her naturally ordained functions. The first president of the American Psychological Association, G. Stanley Hall, staunchly believed that the female mind was created for nursing and motherhood, serving the production of men of genius and of daughters to bear future male geniuses.[62] Education, he felt, would damage women's reproductive organs, particularly coeducation in competition with men. Like many others at the time, Hall did not think of women as generally inferior, but instead idealized them. In his view, women who entered the men's world of education and business became innocent victims of man's evil nature, losing their purity and sainthood.[63]

The historian of psychology, Edwin Boring, famously said that intelligence is whatever the IQ tests measure. But that is precisely the problem. The idea of a peculiarly female intelligence is a striking case of measurement without understanding what one is measuring, paired with the hope that sophisticated correlation statistics and factor analyses could fill this theoretical void. From Galton to Binet to Terman, researchers variously believed that one could measure intelligence in terms of sensory acuity,

---

[62] Diehl (1986).   [63] Schofer (1976).

head size, facial features, handwriting, memory capacity, or knowledge of facts, or by asking questions about proper social behavior.

This absence of theory left too many points of entry for biases and preset convictions, to the detriment of many. Galton's vision was to promote the eugenics program: to detect the less well-endowed and prevent them from reproducing. Both Ellis and Pearson were early feminists but also proponents of eugenics, both of which were considered progressive movements at the time. Binet and Simon intended to give children with intellectual disabilities a second chance through special education. Yet, when adapted "to American conditions and needs," as the editor's introduction to the 1916 edition of Terman's *The Measurement of Intelligence* put it, their test came to serve the various goals of eugenics, sterilization, racism, feminism, and, last but not least, a multibillion testing industry.

Why Is History Relevant?

Knowing one's history provides an opportunity to learn from errors and to avoid repeating these. Differences between men and women, as well as their causes, have been an emotionally and politically charged topic for centuries. Firm convictions continue to be enforced in the guise of new technology. For instance, Diane Halpern warns that modern neuroscience is being misused to justify sex role stereotypes in how men and women think, a program dubbed "neurosexism."[64] Basing conclusions about human thinking and behavior on the firing of neurons or changes in blood oxygen levels entails a long leap in logic. Such leaps are not new; we have already seen one, for instance, in the argument that the smaller brain of females is responsible for woman's alleged intellectual inferiority. The stereotypes of the past also tenaciously survive in popular psychology bestsellers that present men and women as if they were alien species, as in *Men Are from Mars, Women Are from Venus*.[65] In a throwback to the view of women being submissive by nature, such books imply that a wife's role is to hide her intelligence, to admire and appreciate her husband, and to not offer him advice unless he asks. Online communities such as *Men Going Their Own Way (MGTOW)* and *TradWives* revive the traditional view that the position of men is above women.

What is the current consensus about differences in men's and women's cognitive abilities? According to Halpern, the list of differences is relatively small, and the similarities between the sexes are larger in number. Few of

[64] Halpern (2012), p. xi.   [65] Gray (1992).

the differences that have been claimed over the years are stable across age, task, and culture. Among the few exceptions are that women have better memories than men and excel in reading and verbal abilities, while males excel in science and mathematics.[66] What causes these differences is far from being understood.

This history of the idea of a peculiarly female intelligence can teach us several general lessons. The first is to beware of research that evaluates the sexes in terms of polarities and, in general, uses polarities as a means to understand the human mind. Second, beware of composite index numbers, such as IQ. Unless there is a strong theory, test items can be selected to verify any existing bias "scientifically." Third, keep in mind that intelligence is about cognitive processes. All in all, we would be well advised to replace polarities and IQ numbers with the study of the actual processes underlying intelligent behavior, a scientific research agenda that would also leave little room for individual and cultural biases.

Beyond Polarities and IQ: Intelligent Decision Processes

The history of the idea of a peculiarly female intelligence shows, in my view, that the field of sex differences in intelligence, and of intelligence in general, could benefit from a fresh start. Herbert Simon's and Alan Newell's work on heuristics and artificial intelligence (AI), which has inspired my own research on both intuitive and deliberative heuristic decision-making, offers such a new framework. Heuristics are strategies that help agents to make decisions and solve problems in an intelligent and efficient way.[67] After all, what we call intelligence manifests itself in the quality of the decisions we make. In Part II, I describe the research agenda in more detail, which centers on two questions: (i) What is the repertoire of intelligent strategies (such as heuristics) at a person's disposal for making decisions? And (ii) what is a person's ability to choose a proper strategy for the situation at hand? In this framework, intelligence has a very concrete meaning that connects cognitive abilities with behavioral strategies, namely, the "adaptive toolbox" of strategies available and the ability to choose a strategy wisely to achieve a particular goal.

Although the study of intelligent heuristics is well established, it has had a blind spot for sex differences in how males and females search for information, when they stop searching, and how they make or delay

---

[66] Halpern (2012); Halpern & Wai (2020), pp. 119, 126–127.
[67] Gigerenzer & Gaissmaier (2011); Gigerenzer et al. (2011).

decisions. One exception is the work of Joan Meyers-Levy and Barbara Loken, who reported that, in consumer choice, females search more extensively for information than males, while males are more selective in search and rely on faster stopping rules.[68] Moreover, they concluded that females are more sensitive to environmental cues, whereas men more often ignore these and rely on the same heuristics across contexts, indicating less ability in adaptive choice. As for social heuristics, they found that women are more likely to base decisions on trust and are more likely to be trusted. Note that these are preliminary findings, but they indicate a different kind of question to pursue: abandon studying polarities and differences in IQ test outcomes and, instead, ask whether there are concrete differences in the way males and females search for information and make decisions.

The Myth of Female Intuition and Male Reason

It is telling that quite a few smart men in the social, biological, and medical sciences insisted on female inferiority as a scientific fact, in terms of both intellect and morals. Many of the tribulations mankind has had to endure were attributed to Eve's weakness when facing the serpent. After females were allowed to attend schools and universities during the 20th century, it became evident that science had previously been informed by prejudice. The opposition between female intuition and male reason then disappeared from the social sciences and women were no longer accused of naivete, hasty conclusions, lack of logic, or low moral principles. Nevertheless, traces of these prejudices still surface occasionally. Why are so few females hired as professors in philosophy departments? Some male philosophers have argued that intuition is gendered, and that women have wrong philosophical intuitions more often than men.[69]

In the course of time, women and men have become increasingly equal partners – but not intuition and rationality.

---

[68] Meyers-Levy & Loken (2015).   [69] Tripodi (2015).

CHAPTER 3

Biases: Mistaking Intuition for Irrationality[*]

> Mental illusions should be considered the rule rather than the exception.
>
> *Richard Thaler*[1]
>
> Kahneman and Tversky are more responsible than anybody for the powerful trend to mistrust human intuition and defer to algorithms.
>
> *Michael Lewis, The Undoing Project*[2]

When psychology struggled for its independence from philosophy in the late 19th century, intuition was one of its casualties. In a radical turn from philosophers' and theologians' view of intuition as "direct" knowledge and as one of the highest intellectual powers, intuition became seen as a primitive, impulsive, and developmentally earlier mental process. Studies in the 1920s sought to show that children and those with cognitive impairments excel in making rapid, intuitive judgments of physical quantities; results were inconclusive.[3] Others tried to show that women's judgments of children's character are more intuitive than male's rational judgments, again without finding such a difference in comparison to the judgments of character made by children's teachers. Behaviorists such as B. F. Skinner did not even deem the study of intuition (and other nonobservable processes) worthy of rigorous science, distancing themselves from what they saw as unscientific mysticism. Between 1985 and 2004, an analysis of 2.1 million articles in the *PsychINFO* database found only 355 peer-reviewed articles that featured "intuition" in the title.[4] There are,

---

[*] This chapter is partly based on Gigerenzer (2018). [1] Thaler (1991).
[2] Lewis (2017). The quote is from the front flap.
[3] For an overview of early-20th-century studies on intuition, see Osbeck & Held (2014).
[4] Haidt & Kesebir (2008). The search included the words *intuition*, *intuitive*, and *intuitionist*. In a search conducted in 1978, Bastick (1982) reported only 91 studies with the word *intuition* in the title or abstract. It has been unusual for psychologists to study intuition for a long time.

however, notable exceptions to this general dismissal. Jean Piaget explained that his studies of the development of intuitions about time and motion were prompted by questions suggested by Albert Einstein, and his research in turn stimulated contemporary analyses of intuitive physics and intuitive psychology.[5]

By the 21st century, the association of intuition with women was dropped in psychology, albeit continuing in parts of the general public. Yet, after being stripped of gender, intuition has once again been opposed to reason and, like female intuition, has been classified as inferior. The polarity morphed into two supposed systems of reasoning, referred to as Systems 1 and 2. System 1 is said to be fast and unconscious, to work by intuition and heuristics, to lack rationality, and to be the source of error. System 2, in contrast, is said to be slow and conscious, to work by logic and statistics, and to make no apparent errors in reasoning.[6] At the same time, System 2, as mentioned in Chapter 1, is held responsible for the errors System 1 makes by failing to detect and correct these.[7] Just as men were once held responsible for preventing females from committing mistakes, a logical system is now assigned the paternalistic task of keeping the intuitive system in check. Logical reasoning is always rational, we are told, while intuition is not.

---

[5] See Gruber & Vonèche (1977), p. 548. On the origins of intuitive concepts, see Carey (2009).

[6] Dual-process theories come in many kinds, creating a scattered, moving, and blurred framework. The first dual-process models by psychologists Jonathan Evans and Peter Wason, published in the mid-1970s, made somewhat different claims. They included the idea that deliberative reasoning is typically used to rationalize a conclusion that has been arrived at by intuition, which was later mostly dropped (see Mercier & Sperber, 2018, pp. 43–48, for a history). Sloman (1996) and many others proposed different lists of oppositions, without emphasizing that one is superior to the other, while Evans & Stanovich (2013) had second thoughts and spoke of "Type-1 and Type-2 processing," dropping their earlier terminology of System 1 and System 2, in response to criticism (e.g., Gigerenzer & Regier, 1996). That change avoided the unrealistic implication that there were two different systems in the brain, but maintained two different kinds of processes. However, as we will see, the heuristic processes on which intuition and deliberate thinking is based are typically the same (Kruglanski & Gigerenzer, 2011). In this book, I refer to dual-systems theories which assume (i) an opposition between the two systems and (ii) the superiority of System 2, as popularized by Kahneman (2003, 2011a). It is default-interventist, meaning that "system 1 quickly proposes intuitive answers to judgment problems as they arise, and system 2 monitors the quality of these proposals, which it may endorse, correct, or override" (Kahneman & Frederick, 2005, p. 267). Let me point out that the opposition between intuition, heuristics, and unconscious on the one hand, and deliberate, rule-based (logic or probability) and conscious on the other hand, which appears to be the key part of most dual-process theories, is not shared generally in psychology. For instance, in Bayesian theories in cognitive science and cognitive neuroscience, unconscious processes are modeled by "optimal" statistical algorithms (Chater & Oaksford, 2008), and in theories of ecological rationality, heuristic processes are part of conscious decision-making (Gigerenzer et al. 2022a).

[7] Kahneman (2002), p. 471.

Logic Versus Intuition

Imagine a patient with a serious heart condition who is pondering whether or not to have a potentially risky surgery. They consult with their doctor regarding their prospects. The doctor informs them:

Five years after surgery, 90 percent of patients are alive.

The patient's intuition may tell them that the doctor is encouraging them to decide in favor of surgery, which they might do. But what if the doctor had said:

Five years after surgery, 10 percent of patients are dead.

In this case, the patient might infer that the doctor is presenting a warning and might think twice before forgoing the surgery. Studies show that more people are willing to agree to a medical treatment if the doctor uses a *positive frame* (90 percent alive) than a *negative frame* (10 percent dead).[8] This phenomenon is known as the framing effect – people listen to how a message is framed and may change their decision.

Should a patient listen to how the doctor frames a message? Economic theory has traditionally not considered psychological factors such as making implicit recommendations by framing a message. However, an influential group of behavioral economists, led by psychologists Daniel Kahneman and Amos Tversky, took logic and Homo economicus more literally than many economists and went a step further. Any difference between human judgment and abstract logic was perceived as a fault in human intuition.[9] Accordingly, patients should not listen to how a doctor frames the message because the positive and negative frames are logically equivalent. Patients who decide for or against surgery on the basis of the frame are said to lack rationality and suffer from a cognitive bias.

Commenting on the surgery problem, behavioral economist Richard Thaler and legal scholar Cass Sunstein concluded that "framing works because people tend to be somewhat mindless, passive decision makers" and framing thus offers a "brief glimpse at human fallibility."[10] Kahneman has considered the attention paid to framing as "embarrassing" evidence for cognitive biases, which people repeatedly fall for: "in their stubborn appeal, framing effects resemble perceptual illusions more than

---

[8] Moxey et al. (2003). [9] Kahneman (2002, 2011a).
[10] Thaler & Sunstein (2008), pp. 39–40.

computational errors."[11] (Although it should be acknowledged here that Kahneman appears to have qualified his contentions over the years, later speaking of both the marvels and flaws of intuition.[12]) In this view, logical thinking is the sole ingredient of rationality, while intuition is a steady source of bias.

Intuition Versus Rationality Anew

The framing effect is just one of a long list of transgressions that intuition allegedly commits against reason according to influential psychologists and behavioral economists, whose research focused on the flaws of intuition. These "biases" have attained the status of truisms and provided justification for new paternalistic policies, popularly known as *nudging*, adopted by governments in the UK, the USA, and elsewhere. The argument is not simply that people sometimes make mistakes or lack training in logical or statistical thinking – that would be nothing new. Rather, something inside our mind is said to make virtually everyone err in the same systematic way, with little hope of remedying the problem. In Dan Ariely's words, "we are not only irrational, but *predictably irrational* – that our irrationality happens the same way, again and again."[13] The argument leading from biased intuition to governmental paternalism – in short, the irrationality argument – consists of three assertions and one conclusion:

Biased intuition: People's intuitions are systematically biased and lack rationality.
Stubbornness: Intuition is stubborn and, like visual illusions, hardly educable.
Real-world costs: Biased intuition incurs substantial costs such as lower wealth, health, and happiness.
Conclusion: Biased intuitions justify governmental paternalism.

These three assumptions – biased intuition, stubbornness, and costs – imply that chances are slim to nonexistent of the public ever learning or being educated out of their biases; instead, governments need to step in and nudge them into proper behavior.[14] This new paternalism aims not at protecting people from external dangers or imperfections of the market, but from the enemy within: their own irrationality. Rationality, from this perspective, entails *always* obeying the logical axioms of consistency, maximizing one's expected utility, and updating probabilities via Bayes' rule. Let us call this ensemble *logical rationality*, for short. Maintaining that

---

[11] Kahneman (2011a), pp. 373–374; Kahneman & Tversky (1984), p. 343.
[12] Kahneman (2011b). [13] Ariely (2008), p. xviii. [14] Thaler & Sunstein (2003).

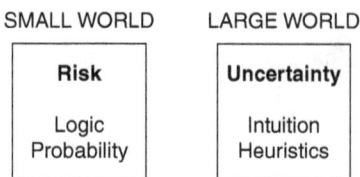

Figure 3.1. Risk versus uncertainty. In situations of risk, all possible future events, along with their consequences and probabilities, are known. In situations of uncertainty, that knowledge is not attainable. Uncertainty requires more than logic and probability: intuition and heuristics.

patients should pay attention solely to the logical part of a doctor's message, not to its psychological part, is an instance of logical rationality. Note that logical rationality is content-free and thus knowledge, intelligence, emotion, and common sense are assumed to be of no relevance for rational decision-making.

What if logical rationality is of value only for some problems and not for all? If logic were all we needed, our psychology would not have evolved into what it is, with its intuitions, heuristics, emotions, and social intelligence. Instead, our brains would have become superb calculating machines.

The crucial point is that logical rationality assumes a *small world* of known risk, as in games of roulette or slot machines with known payoffs, where the expected loss can be calculated and intuition is of no additional help. In a situation of risk, everything that can happen in the future is known, including all consequences of actions and their probabilities (Figure 3.1). Our brain, however, evolved to deal with a world of uncertainty. Uncertainty inhabits our lives in many forms: uncertainty about diagnosis and treatment, the intentions of others, financial markets, warfare, pandemics, natural disasters, and the future in general. I return to this important distinction in Chapter 5.

My point is not that intuition never errs. Of course it can err, just as logical analysis does; that's why we need both. Instead, my argument is that, in situations of uncertainty, relying on logical rationality can be seriously misleading – as can mistaking intelligent processes to deal with uncertainty for biased intuition.

The Bias Bias

It is striking how much emphasis is placed on pointing out errors in intuition and how little reflection occurs on whether logical rationality is, in fact, a reasonable norm. That is not to say that the value of intuitive judgments is consistently denied in the literature on cognitive biases. However, every single experiment in this literature was designed to show, and concluded, that intuition fails. There appears to be a group dynamic that leads researchers to hunt for the next new bias. I call this extreme desire to attack intuition the *bias bias*:

Bias bias: The tendency to see systematic biases in intuition even if there is only unsystematic error or no verifiable error at all.

Let us look at several celebrated biases that are widely taken for genuine cognitive errors.

Framing

As I have mentioned, in a world of risk, where knowledge is certain, the framing of options (such as positive vs. negative) should have no impact on choice. Neoclassical economics assumes that rationally acting people have stable preferences and changing these according to the framing of a message is seen as a preference reversal. However, certainty does not exist for most important decisions, such as whether to undergo a dangerous surgery. Under uncertainty, preferences should not all be fixed, and asking for advice and information can be helpful. By framing an option, a speaker can communicate information that is not contained in the verbatim message, but which the intelligent listener is able to decode and incorporate into the choice accordingly. This decoding is known in the study of language comprehension as *invited inferences*, which are largely intuitive and more intellectually challenging than logical inferences. The great physiologist Hermann von Helmholtz spoke of *unconscious inferences*, which are the very backbone of human intelligence.

Surgery
Consider the surgery problem again. For the patient, at issue is not logical consistency, but a life-and-death decision. To that end, the two relevant questions are: Is expected survival higher with or without surgery? Do possible harms associated with surgery lead to reduced quality of life? Neither "90 percent alive" nor "10 percent dead" provides any of this information. What the patient needs to know is the survival rate *without* surgery along with the potential benefits and harms of surgery. This essential information is missing from the doctor's message. Thus, participants have to rely on their social intelligence to make an informed guess.

By framing the option, speakers can convey information about the missing information, something listeners tend to understand intuitively. Experiments showed that if the no-surgery option was worse than surgery ("fewer patients survive without surgery"), then 80–94 percent of the speakers (doctors) chose the "survival" frame. When, by contrast, no surgery was the better option ("more patients survive without surgery"), then the survival frame was chosen less frequently.[15] Thus, by choosing a survival frame, the doctor can communicate that surgery has a substantial benefit compared to no surgery and can make an implicit recommendation.

There are various reasons why doctors may omit information or not explicitly communicate recommendations. In the USA, for instance, tort law encourages malpractice suits, which fuels a culture of blame in which doctors fear making explicit recommendations.[16] By selecting a positive or negative frame, physicians can indirectly communicate their belief as to whether surgery has a substantial benefit compared to no surgery. And most patients understand the message.

In an uncertain world such as that of medical treatment, logically equivalent frames are not necessarily informationally equivalent. Here, following logic can cost lives.

Is the Glass Half Full or Half Empty?
The choice of frame can also implicitly communicate other relevant information. The mother of all framing problems makes that clear:

The glass is half full.
The glass is half empty.

Once again, both frames are the same logically, but not psychologically. Imagine that there are two glasses on a table, one full and one empty (Figure 3.2). You are asked to pour half of the water in glass (b) into glass (a). Then you are requested to take the half-empty glass and move it to the edge of the table. Which would you pick? Most likely, you would intuitively pick the glass that was previously full.

An experiment showed that most people did exactly that. Likewise, when asked to take the half-full cup, they chose the one that was previously empty.[17] Framing conveys unspoken information, and a careful listener understands that half full and half empty are not identical.

---

[15] McKenzie & Nelson (2003).   [16] Gigerenzer (2014a); Hoffman & Kanzaria (2014).
[17] Sher & McKenzie (2006).

Figure 3.2. Which glass is half full, which half empty? 1: Two glasses, (a) empty and (b) full. 2: Half of glass (b) is poured into glass (a). 3: Two glasses, (c) half full, (d) half empty.

The intuitive ability to use a frame to communicate unspoken information, as well as to decode this information, is based on heuristics.[18] For instance, listeners expect that what and how the speaker communicates is relevant – the *relevance maxim*. An example is the implication that a speaker is likely making an unspoken recommendation when using a positive frame for an option, whereas a negative frame likely indicates a warning. In general, the ability to listen carefully and pay attention to how messengers frame messages is a form of intelligence, not a bias of intuition.[19]

The Asian Disease Problem Reassessed
Perhaps the most widely cited example of a framing effect stems from the "Asian disease problem," which figures prominently in virtually all textbooks:[20]

Imagine that the USA is preparing for an outbreak of an unusual Asian disease, which is expected to kill 600 people. Two alternative programs to combat the disease have been proposed. Assume that the exact scientific estimates of the consequences of the programs are as follows:

[Positive Frame:]
If Program A is adopted, 200 people will be saved.
If Program B is adopted, there is a 1/3 probability that 600 people will be saved and a 2/3 probability that no people will be saved.

---

[18] See, for example, Grice (1989); Hertwig & Gigerenzer (1999); Sperber & Wilson (1986).
[19] See, for example, Sher & McKenzie (2006).
[20] Kahneman (2003); Tversky & Kahneman (1981).

[Negative Frame:]
If Program A is adopted, 400 people will die.
If Program B is adopted, there is a 1/3 probability that nobody will die and a 2/3 probability that 600 people will die.

Kahneman and Tversky argued that the positive and negative frames are logically equivalent, meaning that framing should not alter the preference order. Nevertheless, when given the positive frame, most people favored Program A, but, when given the negative frame, favored Program B. This difference was interpreted as evidence that people are risk-averse for gains (choosing the "certain" option in the positive frame) and risk-seeking for losses (choosing the "risky" option in the negative frame).[21] In this purely logical interpretation, the responses to the Asian disease problem – just as to the surgery problem – violate the assumption of stable preferences and show that people's intuitions can be easily manipulated.

Now recall the psychological analysis of the surgery problem: If people notice that part of the information is omitted, such as the effect of no surgery, they tend to make intuitive inferences. The psychologist Anton Kühberger and I noted that the Asian disease problem is of a similar nature: The risky option is always spelled out entirely in both frames (e.g., a 1/3 probability that 600 people will be saved and a 2/3 probability that no one is saved), whereas the "certain" option is never complete. For instance, it communicates that 200 people will be saved, but not that 400 will not be saved. This systematic asymmetry matters neither from the logical norm of *description invariance* nor for prospect theory, given that the framing in terms of loss and gains is preserved. But it should matter if people question the intentions underlying this asymmetry and make intuitive inferences. To test these two competing explanations – logical error or intelligent inference – all that needs to be done is to complete the missing options in both frames. Here is the complete version for the positive frame:

If Program A is adopted, 200 people will be saved and 400 people will not be saved.
If Program B is adopted, there is a 1/3 probability that 600 people will be saved and a 2/3 probability that no people will be saved.

If any of the logical explanations given – people's susceptibility to framing errors, their risk-aversion for gains and risk-seeking for losses, or the value function of prospect theory – were true, this addition should not

---

[21] Tversky & Kahneman (1981).

matter. However, Kühberger found that it changes the entire result. When people were provided with the full information, the effect of positive versus negative frames disappeared. Subsequent studies replicated this striking finding.[22] As further studies indicated, many people notice that the information is asymmetric and infer that the incomplete option means that *at least* 200 people are saved because, unlike in Program B, the information for how many will not be saved is not provided.[23] In other words, they infer that Program A guarantees that 200 or more people will be saved, as opposed to exactly 200.

Thus, people's judgments appear to have little to do with loss-aversion or unstable preferences due to positive versus negative framing. The asymmetry of the information communicated instead drives the entire effect. When supplied with incomplete information, people have to make intelligent inferences.

Intelligent Inferences Mistaken for Biases
In all of these cases, the same bias bias is seen: mistaking intelligent intuitive inferences for biases. Frames carry information beyond their literal content, meaning that their interpretation requires not logical, but psychological, analysis. The bias bias emerges from a view that eliminates all psychology by assuming that logically equivalent statements must be informationally equivalent. This principle of "descriptive invariance" has been hailed as an essential condition for rational choice.[24] However, the art of reading between the lines is more cognitively demanding than the narrow logic of descriptive invariance.

Once again, there is a difference between the natural and social sciences. Framing has long been considered an art in mathematics and physics, as the importance of notation and number representation illustrates. For example, Newton and Leibniz had different notations for the calculus, each having its advantages, which are discussed to the present day. Although logically equivalent, they are not identical. The physicist Richard Feynman pointed out the importance of simultaneously working with different formulations of the same physical law, even if they are logically equivalent: "Psychologically they are different because they are completely unequivalent when you are trying to guess new laws."[25]

---

[22] See, for example, Kühberger (1995); Kühberger & Tanner (2010); Mandel (2001); Tombu & Mandel (2015).
[23] Mandel (2014).   [24] Tversky & Kahneman (1986), p. S253.   [25] Feynman (1967), p. 53.

In sum, the principle of logical equivalence or description invariance is a poor guide to understanding how human intelligence deals with an uncertain world where not everything is, or can be, stated explicitly. It misses the very nature of social intelligence, the ability to make inferences beyond the bare information given.[26] Logic is without doubt a tool of rationality, but not the exclusive one in the cognitive toolbox.

Intuitions About Randomness

Psychology classrooms often resemble magic shows, where professors perform tricks to demonstrate how everyone's intuition can be fooled. Consider a stock-in-trade attraction, where someone throws a coin to see whether it lands heads (H) or tails (T). The quiz is:

You take a fair coin and flip it four times in a row. Which string will you more likely observe?

HHH
HHT

Most people's intuition says that HHT is more likely. Yet, a psychology professor may argue that the intuition is faulty because the two strings have the same probability of occurring. The probability of a head is always the same as of a tail; thus, the probability of each string is the same, the students are told. Upon reflection, they may be inclined to concede that the intuition was wrong, even though it still intuitively feels right. This has happened to many participants in psychological experiments, and it appears to prove the first two assertions about biased intuition: that people lack rationality and that intuition is hardly educable: Even after being proven wrong, people stubbornly hang on to their biased intuition. The bias has a name, the *law of small numbers*, which is one of the two key experimental findings on intuitions of randomness:

1. **The law of small numbers:** People think a string is more likely the closer the number of heads and tails corresponds to the underlying equal probabilities. For instance, the string HHT is deemed more likely than HHH, and HHHHHT is deemed more likely than HHHHHH.
2. **Irregularity:** If the number of heads and tails is the same in two strings, people think that the one with a more irregular pattern is more

---

[26] Bruner (1973).

H	H	H	H	H	H	H	H	T	T	T	T	T	T	T	T
H	H	H	H	T	T	T	T	H	H	H	H	T	T	T	T
H	H	T	T	H	H	T	T	H	H	T	T	H	H	T	T
H	T	H	T	H	T	H	T	H	T	H	T	H	T	H	T
✓	✓+	+	+					✓	+						

Figure 3.3. Throwing a fair coin four times. Is a string of HHH or HHT more likely? There are 16 possible sequences of four tosses of a fair coin, each equally likely. In three of these, there is at least one string HHH (check mark), while HHT occurs in four of these (plus sign). Consistent with the intuition of many people, encountering the sequence HHT is more likely.[27]

likely. For instance, the string HHTHTH is deemed more likely than HTHTHT.

Most people feel that there is something unusual in the string HTHTHT, where heads and tails strictly alternate, and that the irregular string HHTHTH is more likely to be obtained. Yet, that too is considered a fallacy for the same reason: The probability of both strings is the same. Both phenomena have been called systematic biases. But why should people have faulty intuitions about randomness in the first place? Some researchers have suggested that random devices did not exist during most of human evolution, and thus our minds have not developed proper intuition. This explanation, however, accepts the claim that people's intuitions are wrong in the first place. Let us have a closer look.

The Law of Small Numbers
Is it indeed equally likely that one will encounter a string of HHH or of HHT when flipping a coin four times in a row? Surprisingly, the answer is that HHT is more likely.

Figure 3.3 shows why. There are 16 possible sequences that can result from throwing a coin four times. These sequences are all equally probable. In four of these, one encounters an HHT, as marked by a "+". But an HHH is found in only three sequences, as shown by a check mark. Thus, the relative frequency of encountering at least one HHT is 4/16 = .25 and that of HHH is 3/16 = .19. People's intuition that an HHT is more likely to be encountered than an HHH in a sequence of four flips turns out to be correct.

Another way to understand this result is that two strings of HHH overlap in the first column of Figure 3.3, whereas no such overlaps occur

---

[27] Hahn & Warren (2009).

H	H	H	H	T	T	T	T
H	H	T	T	H	T	H	T
H	T	H	T	H	H	T	T
✓	+						

Figure 3.4. The special case where the length of the string (here three) is the same as the length of the sequence ($k = n$). Here, the chance of encountering an HHT and an HHH are the same. But that does not hold in all other cases, as Figure 3.3 illustrates.

(or are even possible) for HHT. Similarly, it can be shown that HHT is likely to be encountered *earlier* than HHH: The expected waiting time for HHT is eight tosses of a coin, compared with 14 tosses for HHH.[28]

Our example was with four throws. Consider now the general case. Let k be the length of the string of heads and tails judged (which is three in the example above), and n be the total sequence (number of tosses, which is four in the example). Thus, $k \leq n$. Now we can specify the general principle under which people's intuition is ecologically rational:

If $k < n <$ infinite, a string of Hs with a single alternation such as HHT is more likely to be encountered than a pure string such as HHH.

The term *ecologically rational* means that statements about the rationality of judgments need to be qualified with respect to ecological conditions: here, the length of the string and that of the sequence. In sum, the intuition that HHT is more likely to be encountered than HHH is not generally an error. It is only so in two specific conditions: if a person has seen exactly as many throws as the string to be judged and if a person has seen an infinitely long string, which is impossible for a mortal being.

Figure 3.4 shows the special condition where the number of tosses and the string is of equal length. Here, the chance of encountering an HHH and an HHT is the same. There are eight possible outcomes, with one of each string.

In Figure 3.3, the string is a proper sample of the number of tosses. In statistical terms, sample statistics need not be the same as population statistics, which is precisely the situation here. In Figure 3.4, the sample is the population. If you are still not convinced, consider this bet:[29]

The law-of-small-numbers bet: You flip a fair coin 20 times. If this sequence contains at least one HHHH, I pay you $100. If it contains at least one HHHT, you pay me $100. If it contains neither, nobody wins.

[28] Ibid. [29] Hahn & Warren (2010).

If HHHH and HHHT were equally likely to be encountered, then the two players should break even. But, in fact, the person who accepts the bet can expect to lose in the long run. For 20 flips, the probability that you will see at least one HHHH is about 50 percent, but the chance of an HHHT is around 75 percent.[30] For the same reason, a gambler who watches the outcomes of the roulette wheel in a casino for half an hour can more likely expect to see a string of three reds followed by a black than a string of four reds. In this situation, believing in the law of small numbers pays.

The phenomenon that people expect more alternations than those predicted by probability theory has been sometimes linked to the gambler's fallacy. Yet, that connection is mistaken, as can be deduced from the ecological rationality condition. The gambler's fallacy refers to the intuition that, after witnessing a string of, say, three heads, one expects that the next outcome will be more likely tails than heads. This would be a true fallacy because it corresponds to the condition $k = n$. In other words, a total of four throws is considered, either HHHH or HHHT, and there is no sample k with the property $k < n$.

Irregularity
The second alleged misconception regarding chance is that people believe that irregular sequences are more likely. Consider the following two sequences:

HTHTHT
HTTHTH

Here, the number of heads and tails are now identical, but alternations are regular in the first string and irregular in the second. Psychological research documented that most people find the more irregular string more likely.

Once again, this intuition is not a fallacy for the same reason as before: If $k < n < \infty$, then the irregular sequence HTTHTH is more likely than the regular one. The expected waiting time to get a HTTHTH is 64 flips, compared with 84 for HTHTHT (and 126 for HHHHHH).[31] This can be verified in the same way as with Figure 3.3.

In sum, people's intuition that irregular alternations are more likely to be encountered reflects an astonishingly fine-tuned sensitivity to the statistics of finite samples. The intuition is erroneous in only one special

---

[30] Hahn & Warren (2009).   [31] See Hahn & Warren (2009).

case, when the number of throws is exactly the same as the string (Figure 3.4).

Fine-Tuned Intuition Mistaken for Bias

In the literature on flawed human intuition of randomness, no distinction appears to have been made between the one specific case where it is indeed flawed and all the other instances where intuition is actually right.[32] Rather, intuitions have been generally declared erroneous. Whatever the explanation, the alleged bias was seen to demonstrate the "stubbornness" of intuition: "For anyone who would wish to view man as a reasonable intuitive statistician, such results are discouraging."[33]

In summary, people's intuitions about chance have been interpreted as systematically flawed because they (i) fall prey to the law of small numbers and (ii) confuse irregularity with chance in both the recognition and production of randomness. An ecological analysis, by contrast, shows that if $k < n < \infty$, which is the typical window of experience, people's intuitions are, in fact, correct. The general insight is that the properties of the underlying chance process (such as equal probability) do not match the properties of small samples, a phenomenon known as *biased sample estimators* in statistics. In other words, people's intuitions were evaluated against the wrong normative standard, one that does not capture the properties of samples.

In the next section, "The Hot Hand Fallacy," we will see that the same oversight applies to an allegedly illusory intuition shared by many coaches and players.

The Hot Hand Fallacy: Professional Intuition Mistaken for Bias

Most sport fans can recall magical moments when a player is "on fire," "in the zone," "in rhythm," or "unconscious." This temporarily elevated performance is known as the *hot hand*. For players and coaches, the hot hand is a common experience. It resembles what my late colleague Mike Csikszentmihalyi called "flow," a time in which performance increases without deliberation; jazz musicians, professional writers, and many others also report such moments.[34] According to some researchers, however, this belief is an illusion, which has been dubbed the *hot hand fallacy*.[35] In Thaler and Sunstein's words, "It turns out that the cognitive illusion is so powerful that most people (influenced by their Automatic System) are

---

[32] Kahneman & Tversky (1972). [33] Ibid., p. 445. [34] Csikszentmihalyi (2008).
[35] Gilovich et al. (1985).

unwilling even to consider the possibility that their strongly held beliefs might be wrong."[36] "It turns out that the 'hot hand' is a myth," they assert; "to date, no one has found it."[37] Nevertheless, coaches and players stubbornly cling to their experience of the hot hand, apparently further evidence that cognitive illusions resemble visual illusions. Even the website of the National Collegiate Athletic Association (NCAA) sided against the coaches and warned of believing in magic: "Streaks and 'hot hands' are simply illusions in sports. And, it is better to be a scientist than be governed by irrational superstition." The hot hand fallacy served as an explanation for various vices in financial markets, sports betting, and casino gambling. Once again, the suspected fallacy was presented as evidence for the irrationality of intuition.

From an economic view, however, the claim that this intuition is stubbornly wrong is most puzzling. Professional coaches and players presumably have no incentives to be wrong, only to be right. Why then would such an erroneous belief persist? Economist and Nobel laureate Gary Becker once remarked to me that coaches see when a player in the other team is hot and then send an extra player to cut their streak short.[38] For that reason, he concluded, one cannot find the effects of getting hot in the performance streaks that psychologists were analyzing. His was a reasonable objection, but the psychologists assessing the existence of the hot hand had already taken this into consideration and analyzed data from free shots, where no players are allowed to interfere. Even here, they could not find any trace of a hot hand in the data.

The Hot Hand Exists
It took some 30 years and two smart economists, Joshua Miller and Adam Sanjuro, to show, using the original free shot data, that the hot hand is not a myth.[39] For simplification, I apply the same line of analysis used earlier to explain the intuitions about randomness; Miller and Sanjuro took a different approach.

In the original study, 26 shooters from Cornell University each made 100 free shots from a fixed distance with varying locations. The authors of that study posited that there is no hot hand if the frequency of a hit after three hits equals that of a miss after three hits. When looking at all occurrences of three hits and recording how often these were followed

---

[36] Thaler & Sunstein (2008), p. 31.   [37] Ibid., p. 33.
[38] G. S. Becker (1994, personal communication); see also Raab et al. (2012).
[39] Miller & Sanjuro (2018).

by another hit, they found that the number was the same for all but one player – an anomaly that can be attributed to chance. Thus, the conclusion was that the hot hand does not exist and that belief in it is a fallacy.

Let us take a closer look at this argument. As shown in Figure 3.3, tails after two heads is more likely than another head if the length of the string is smaller than that of the entire sequence. Now replace heads with hit, tails with miss, and the fair coin with a player who shoots from a distance where there is a probability of .50 of scoring a hit. If a player makes $n = 4$ free shots, there are 16 sequences with equal probabilities. In six of these sequences, one can test the hot hand because these have HH followed by either H (hit) or T (miss). If there were no hot hand, we would observe a miss after two hits in four of these six sequences and a hit after two hits in only three (the four plus signs and the three check marks in Figure 3.3). That is, in two out of the 16 possible sequences one would observe a hit, in one sequence a hit and a miss, and in three a miss. The expected relative frequency of a hit after two hits (HHH) is therefore 2 + 0.5 out of 6, which is .42. Because HHH should be less often observed than HHT, finding a relative frequency of .50 of HHH in the free shots instead of the expected .42 actually indicates a hot hand.

The same holds for a sequence of 100 free shots and strings of length 4. Once again, we are dealing with $k = 4$ (the length of the string) and $n = 100$; that is, the ecological condition $k < n < \infty$ is in place. In a reanalysis of the original data, a substantial number of the shooters showed a pattern of performance consistent with the hot hand.[40] Across players, the hot hand boosted performance by 11 percentage points, which is substantial and roughly equal to the difference in the field goal percentage between the average and the very best three-point shooter in the National Basketball Association (NBA).

Coaches and players thus have good reason to maintain their belief in the hot hand and do not need to be nudged out of their "stubborn" intuition.

Generality of the Bias Bias

These examples of the bias bias may suffice to gain a general idea about the war against intuition. The list could be continued with the Linda problem,[41] base rate neglect,[42] loss-aversion,[43] priming,[44] and other apparent

---

[40] Ibid. [41] Hertwig & Gigerenzer (1999). [42] Gigerenzer et al. (2021).
[43] Gal & Rucker (2018). [44] Pashler et al. (2012).

biases that are no errors in the first place, or errors only under special conditions, or cannot be replicated.[45] In general, there are five general principles underlying the bias bias:

1. **Logically equivalent frames are mistaken as informationally equivalent:** Framing and the logical norm of description invariance are key examples.
2. **Biased sample estimators are mistaken for people's biases:** The statistics of small samples can systematically differ from the population parameters. Intuitions about chance and the hot hand are examples.
3. **Experimenters' sampling of questions is biased:** Overconfidence – defined as mean confidence minus percent correct – results from selected questions that are untypical, but it disappears when questions are chosen representatively.[46]
4. **Unsystematic errors are mistaken for systematic biases:** Confusing regression to the mean with a systematic error is an example. Unsystematic errors have been misinterpreted as a miscalibration (another version of overconfidence)[47] as well as an overestimation of small risks and an overestimation of large risks.[48]
5. **Situations of risk (where probability theory can provide the best answer) are not distinguished from situations of uncertainty (where heuristics can be superior):** This is the key problem underlying most erroneous diagnoses of biases.

The history of statistics has taught us that normative claims require a careful analysis of the assumptions made. In studies that try to show errors of intuition, surprisingly little thought is given to what constitutes rational judgment, an apparent contradiction referred to as the *irrationality paradox*.[49] Once again, that is not to say that intuition never errs. At issue is a full-fledged bias bias against intuition.

Citation Bias

Alongside the bias bias, the citation bias is a second weapon in the war against intuition. A citation bias occurs when positive findings are systematically less often cited than negative findings. Imagine 110 articles on

---

[45] See Gigerenzer (1996, 2018); Gigerenzer et al. (2012).
[46] Gigerenzer et al. (1991); Juslin et al. (2000).
[47] Dawes & Mulford (1996); Erev et al. (1994); Pfeifer (1994).   [48] Hertwig et al. (2005).
[49] Gigerenzer (2004a).

intuition that report largely successful performance and four articles that report errors. If the four are cited more often than the 110, that is a clear case of citation bias. Citation bias is widespread in media that amplify negative stories, scandals, and misfortunes to attract attention or satisfy a hidden agenda. Science is also not free of selective reporting, with some fields more susceptible than others.

As mentioned, the focus of the new war against intuition is on judgments about chance, frequency, and randomness – in short, statistical intuitions. Swiss psychologists Jean Piaget and Bärbel Inhelder, who were among the first to systematically study the development of intuitions of chance in children, concluded that children's intuitions approximate the laws of statistics by age 12.[50] Similarly, experiments with adults up to the 1970s concluded that people's intuitions are in good, albeit not perfect, agreement with the laws of statistics. In 1967, for instance, psychologists Cameron Peterson and Lee Roy Beach arrived at this conclusion after reviewing 110 articles in their paper aptly (apart from the gender bias) entitled "Man as an Intuitive Statistician." They concluded that intuitions "are influenced by appropriate variables and in appropriate directions" while also pointing out cases where intuitions deviate. Overall, the 160 experiments in these 110 articles show that the laws of statistics provide "a good first approximation for a psychological theory of inference."[51]

Seven years later, Tversky and Kahneman challenged this conclusion in a review paper entitled "Judgment under Uncertainty: Heuristics and Biases," summarizing four articles they had published on putative cognitive biases.[52] They concluded: "In making predictions and judgments under uncertainty, people do not appear to follow the calculus of chance or the statistical theory of prediction."[53] The question arises why people's intuitions about chance took a nose-dive in the 1970s and no longer approximated statistical theory thereafter. One might assume that the research community had discussed this question and sought an answer. Instead, a citation bias made the contradicting conclusions disappear.

Figure 3.5a reveals the extent of the citation bias. By 2020, "Man as an Intuitive Statistician" was cited 479 times, while "Judgment under Uncertainty: Heuristics and Biases" was cited over 15,000 times.[54] As a

---

[50] Piaget & Inhelder (1951/1975). [51] Peterson & Beach (1967), pp. 42–43.
[52] Tversky & Kahneman (1974). [53] Kahneman & Tversky (1973), p. 237.
[54] Lejarraga & Hertwig (2021). Citations on Google Scholar are higher, but reveal the same citation bias, 37,331 versus 1,165 citations by August 2020, for Tversky & Kahneman and Peterson & Beach, respectively.

consequence, the collective memory of a large body of experimental research has been largely wiped out.

This example is not the exception to the rule. Consider another pair of articles, also seven years apart. In 1965, Ward Edwards and colleagues published a review of whether intuitive opinion change follows Bayes' theorem: "It turns out that opinion change is very orderly, and usually proportional to numbers calculated from Bayes' theorem – but it is insufficient in amount."[55] The review found that people are conservative Bayesians, that is, Bayesians who give too much weight to base rates. In contrast, in an article published in 1972, Kahneman and Tversky concluded: "In his evaluation of evidence, man is apparently not a conservative Bayesian: he is not Bayesian at all."[56] Once more, the question of why people's intuitions looked approximately Bayesian in experiments only until 1970 was rarely if ever posed in the research that found intuition wanting. And yet again, a citation bias took care of the problem (Figure 3.5b). The message that people are not Bayesians at all became common wisdom.

The citation bias is not limited to these classical experiments.[57] For instance, the experiments on framing by Craig McKenzie and his research group in San Diego or the experiments on the various phenomena labeled overconfidence by Peter Juslin and his collaborators in Sweden are rarely, if ever, mentioned in texts that present framing or overconfidence as systematic biases.[58] Similarly neglected is the research on the Bayesian mind in cognitive science and cognitive neuroscience that concludes that memory, categorization, and reasoning are Bayesian.[59] The citation bias, the bias bias, and the lack of learning opportunities have turned the narrative of flawed intuitions into an apparent hard fact.

As mentioned at the beginning of this chapter, in addition to biased intuition, two further claims have been made: stubbornness, that is, that intuition is hardly educable; and real-world costs of the alleged biases.

Stubbornness: The Myth That Intuition Is Hardly Educable

An article published in *Nature* entitled *Risk School* posed the question of whether the general public can learn to evaluate risks accurately or whether

---

[55] Edwards et al. (1965), p. 18.
[56] Kahneman & Tversky (1972), p. 450. Tversky, by the way, was a postdoctoral student of Edwards.
[57] Christensen-Szalanski & Beach (1984).   [58] For example, Juslin et al. (2000, 2007).
[59] For example, Chater & Oaksford (2008); Chater et al. (2006).

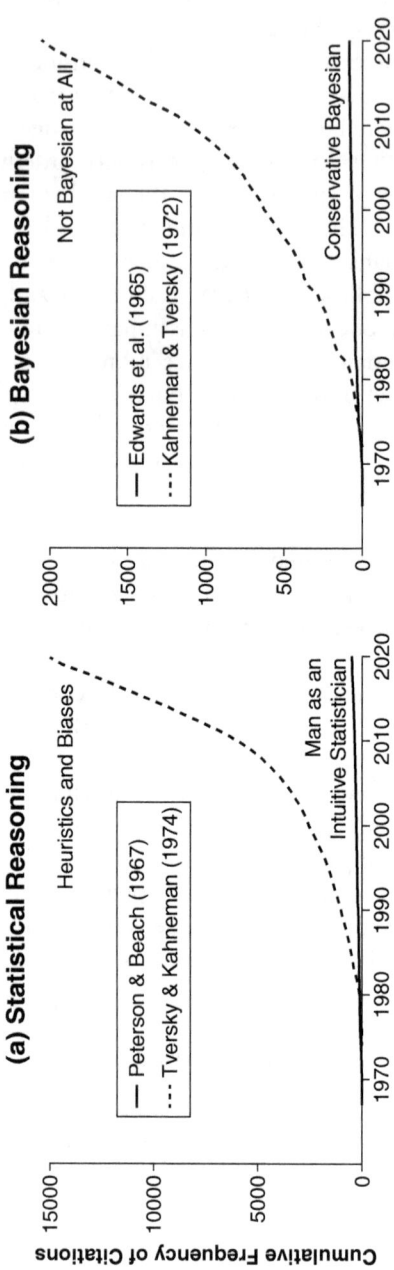

Figure 3.5. Citation bias in favor of articles reporting that people have biased statistical intuitions. (a) Cumulative frequency of citations of Peterson & Beach (1967) and Tversky & Kahneman (1974) from 1967 to August 15, 2020, according to Scopus. (b) Cumulative frequency of citations of Edwards et al. (1965) and Kahneman & Tversky (1972) from 1965 to August 15, 2020. From Lejarraga & Hertwig (2021).

authorities needed to steer it toward correct decisions.[60] Its author spoke with both the proponents of biases and nudging and with my research group. According to legal scholar Dan Kahan, many specialists conclude that the public will never really be capable of prudent decision-making without any external help, meaning that "risk decision-making should be concentrated to an even greater extent in politically insulated expert agencies."[61] The task of these agencies would be to nudge people into making better decisions.

At the same time, the *Nature* article includes pictures of young children playing with Lego-like toys that my collaborators and I developed. These toys foster good statistical intuitions. And in response to the claim that people are not Bayesian thinkers at all, we showed in a series of studies that most fourth-graders can already find the exact Bayesian answer in tasks tailored to children's interests and by using icons instead of probabilities.[62] The same methods, known as *natural frequencies*, allow the teaching of Bayesian reasoning in less than 2 hours and have been found to generate immediate learning effects that transfer to new problems that are stable over time.[63] Since then, school curricula and medical societies around the world have adopted them, and a Cochrane Review concluded that they are most effective in helping to generate good clinical intuitions.[64] These intuitive representations have also been found to foster doctors' and lawyers' Bayesian intuitions.[65] The difficulties people have with Bayesian thinking are not a result of stubbornly biased intuition, but rather of the fact that, in most parts of the world, neither children nor doctors are taught intuitive ways to understand statistical evidence.

Good representations of numerosities are key to generating good statistical intuitions. Judgments easily go wrong when difficult concepts or representations are used in tests of intuition that most of us have never learned in school. In these cases, a large body of research has, by now, shown that children and adults can learn Bayesian thinking, provided they are given proper representations of numbers.[66] When provided with better education and better intuitive representations of numerosities, people do not require nudging.

These results help to understand why people showed fairly good intuitions about chance before the 1970s and shoddy ones thereafter. In the

---

[60] Bond (2009). [61] Ibid., pp. 1189–1191. [62] Gigerenzer et al. (2021).
[63] Sedlmeier & Gigerenzer (2001).
[64] Rosenbaum et al. (2010); see also McDowell & Jacobs (2017).
[65] For summaries, see Gigerenzer (2002, 2014a); Gigerenzer et al. (2007).
[66] Gigerenzer & Hoffrage (1995); Gigerenzer (2014a); McDowell & Jacobs (2017).

early 1990s, I wrote to Ward Edwards and asked him why people stopped being conservative Bayesians in the 1970s. A few years earlier, he and Detlev von Winterfeldt had published a book containing a chapter on cognitive illusions. In this book, they reported both their findings that people are approximate Bayesians and Kahneman and Tversky's findings that people are not Bayesians at all, without offering an explanation for this paradox. Edwards' response was emotional and almost 10 pages long. He pointed out that his experiments had been much more carefully designed, conducted, and described in his articles than those of Kahneman and Tversky. Edwards put his finger on the right point, but it took a number of years until the question was truly answered.[67]

What happened is that people's intuitions did not change, but the design of the experiments did. In the experiments by Edwards and others, participants could learn from experience, such as repeatedly drawing red and black balls from urns to guess the composition of the urns' contents. This is known as frequency learning, and it takes time, just as it does in the real world. In the experiments by Kahneman and Tversky, participants were not given the opportunity to learn from experience, but instead were provided with a description of base rates, hit rates, and false alarm rates. This considerably reduced the effort to run an experiment; text problems could be answered in a minute. But it required participants to understand the concept of conditional probabilities, an alien concept that few had learned in school. No such knowledge is required when learning from experience. In other words, the same person can appear to have good or bad Bayesian intuitions, depending on whether they can learn from experience or are provided short descriptions about concepts they may not be familiar with.

Real-World Costs: The Myth of Substantial Costs

The assumption that people lack rationality and stubbornly resist learning does not suffice to justify governmental paternalism such as nudging. After all, it does not follow that violations of logical rationality harm anyone. It is the third assumption that carries weight: that not following logical rationality incurs substantial real-world costs, such as lower wealth, health, and happiness. What is the evidence for this assertion? Psychologists Hal Arkes, Ralph Hertwig, and I analyzed over 1,000 published papers on alleged errors of intuition, defined as deviations from logical norms.[68]

[67] Lejarraga & Hertwig (2021).   [68] Arkes et al. (2016).

The most well-known claim is that if a person violates transitivity, then that unfortunate individual can become a money pump. That is, if a person prefers option A to B, option B to C, and option C to A, and is willing to pay money to continually substitute a more preferred option for a less preferred one, that person loses money. Of the 107 papers on violations of transitivity we found, not a single case showed that a person became a money pump. When looking at 1,036 articles on preference reversals – recall that attending to framing can lead to this phenomenon – we found that the question of cost was studied in only four articles, which found that arbitrage substantially reduced costs and that feedback diminished the frequency of reversals. Similarly, we identified 248 articles on framing and hundreds more on other deviations from logical rationality with little to no evidence that these "biases" make people less wealthy, less healthy, or less accurate in their beliefs. To ensure that no evidence had been overlooked, we asked approximately 1,000 researchers for studies that demonstrate costs, which none provided. Lack of evidence of costs is not the same as evidence for lack of costs. But the fact that so many studies failed to report evidence of costs suggests that either studies finding no evidence were not published or the assumption is considered self-evident.

The lack of evidence for the crucial assumption also leaves open the possibility of a political motivation, justifying governmental paternalism.

The Return of the Dichotomy: Intuition Versus Reason

In his paper "You Can't Play 20 Questions with Nature and Win," Allen Newell criticized the fact that psychological explanations are often conceived in the form of binary opposites, such as nature versus nurture, serial versus parallel processing, conscious versus unconscious, and intuitive versus analytic. Newell thought of these general dichotomies as the nadir of theorizing where, instead of achieving clarity, "matters simply become muddier and muddier as we go down through time."[69] Together with Herbert Simon, Newell instead set out to study the heuristic decision processes people use to make intelligent decisions. In spite of his critique, theorizing in terms of polarities (as opposed to heuristic processes) remains popular in cognitive psychology.

Recall the opposition between female intuition and male reason, as in Immanuel Kant's and Stanley Hall's view. That polarity has returned, now cleansed from its association with gender. Once more, intuition is opposed

[69] Newell (1973), pp. 288–289.

to reason, now in the form of an inferior intuitive System 1 and a superior logical System 2. I have no reason to assume that these similarities were by any means intentional. Yet, the similarity between the old view of women and the new System 1 has not escaped its proponents. Citing comedian Danny Kaye's joke "Her favorite position is beside herself, and her favorite sport is jumping to conclusions," Kahneman remarks, "I believe it offers an apt description of how System 1 functions."[70] Similarly, the fact that women score on average lower than men on the *cognitive reflection test*, a short test comprising three numeracy questions, has been attributed by decision scientist Shane Frederick to their supposedly higher reliance on the intuitive System 1, a reinstatement of the old stereotype about women.[71] Yet, leaping to the conclusion that the failure to answer mathematics questions results from attributes attached to System 1 is neither necessary nor supported by the evidence.[72] Consider the first question of the cognitive reflection test:

A bat and a ball cost $1.10 in total. The bat costs $1.00 more than the ball. How much does the ball cost? _____cents

Most people appear to have forgotten the algebra they learned at school and answer "10 cents," although "5 cents" is the correct response. However, the wrong answers have been attributed not to the lack of mathematics, but to the fast, intuitive System 1 that gets the answer wrong. The correct answers are said to result from the slow System 2 after correcting the intuitive response.[73] Testing this interpretation would require a two-step procedure, where it is possible to separate the first intuitive response from the later one after deliberation. Such tests were conducted in a series of seven experiments:[74] People were given only a few seconds to give their immediate response (including the time for reading the problem), and they also had to memorize a pattern of dots they were shown before reading the problem in order to reduce the possibility of deliberate thinking to a minimum. After their intuitive response, participants were given as much time as desired to deliberate and provide a final response. On average (across all conditions that correspond to the test above), the intuitive response was correct 20.4 percent and the final response 26.8 percent of the time. This means that the majority of correct answers had already been made intuitively. Cases where deliberation

---

[70] Kahneman (2011a), p. 79.   [71] Frederick (2005), p. 37.
[72] Bago & De Nays (2019); Easton (2018).   [73] Frederick (2005); Kahneman (2011a).
[74] Bago & De Nays (2019).

improved the first response were relatively few. All in all, these experiments show that blaming intuition for the errors in the bat-and-ball problem is off the mark. The best explanation appears to be that most people simply cannot perform the mathematics; in fact, the performance of participants with this problem correlates substantially with their numeracy.

Despite Newell's critique, two-system theories that can "explain" all biases post hoc have become hugely popular. Again, the question of empirical evidence is rarely posed. A common feature of the various dual-system theories is that the polarity intuition versus reason is aligned with several other polarities, such as heuristic versus analytic and unconscious versus conscious. Given that these theories solely provide a list of general dichotomies, without specifying any testable model of the processes, they appear empty and unfalsifiable. But they actually imply two empirically testable claims: that intuition is opposed to reason, and that the poles of the dichotomies in each system are aligned with each other.

If, as assumed in two-systems theories, intuition is opposed to reason, they should be negatively correlated (people rely either on intuition or on reason). As mentioned in Chapter 1, however, a meta-analysis of 75 studies showed that measures of intuition and analysis are *not* negatively correlated (as opposites should be), but are instead independent.[75] Second, the alignment of the poles is not consistent with the evidence. Consider the alleged association between heuristic and unconscious in System 1. Every heuristic that I have studied to date can be used both consciously and unconsciously, meaning that alignment does not correspond to reality. Next, the association between statistical reasoning and consciousness in System 2 contradicts most theories in the cognitive and neurosciences, such as Bayesian theories of the brain, which assume that perception, memory, and other unconscious processes are based on statistical inferences.[76] Lastly, the association between intuitive, heuristic, and error-prone, on the one hand, and reason, logic, and rational, on the other, is called into question by the example of framing, which illustrates how intuition can lead to better medical outcomes than logical thinking, and by the empirically grounded fact that purely logical rationality can err as easily as intuition can. In general, there is a striking absence of empirical evidence for this historical polarity, which has reemerged in a new configuration.[77]

---

[75] Wang et al. (2017).   [76] Chater & Oaksford (2008); Friston (2010).
[77] For a more detailed critique of dual-system theories see Keren & Schul (2009); Kruglanski & Gigerenzer (2011); Melnikoff & Bargh (2018).

CHAPTER 4

Governmental and Technological Paternalism

> The goal is to enable Google users to be able to ask the question [sic] such as "What shall I do tomorrow?" and "What job shall I take?"
> *Eric Schmidt, Google's former CEO*[1]

> Once Google, Facebook and other algorithms become all-knowing oracles, they may well evolve into agents and ultimately into sovereigns.
> *Yatul Noah Harari*[2]

The argument that intuition is systematically biased is not confined to academic domains. It has led to a new governmental philosophy called *libertarian paternalism*, a variant of soft paternalism that uses strategies known as *nudges* to influence people's decisions. Its key proponents are the same influential thinkers who seek to demonstrate the failure of intuition. A nudge is a tool for steering people without using incentives, which are the stock-in-trade of economic theory, and without forbidding behavior, which is the practice of hard paternalism. Spearheaded by the UK and USA in 2010, governments across the world have set up nudge units, also known as behavioral insights teams. In a survey from the Organisation for Economic Co-operation and Development (OECD), most governments motivate their programs by reference to individual cognitive biases and people's use of heuristics.[3]

Paternalism (etymologically rooted in the Latin word *pater*) is the view that a select group of people is entitled to rule over others the way fathers traditionally ruled over children. The chosen group might be aristocrats, the wealthy, or religious leaders. Those under their authority might be poor, people of color, or those with little formal education. Over millennia, aristocrats ruled over their subjects and men ruled over women. Athens' early democracy was a rare and partial exception, where every

---

[1] Daniel & Palmer (2007). [2] Harari (2017), p. 397. [3] OECD (2017).

man – although not women or slaves – was considered equal. Aristotle advocated for the subjugation of women, slaves, animals, and plant life, arguing that reason was naturally endowed only to men of good birth.

As discussed in Chapter 3, people's intuition has become seen as untrustworthy and biases are said to be as stable as visual illusions, implying that there is little hope of improving people's cognitive capacities. To add insult to injury, societal problems such as poverty, obesity, and unhappiness have been attributed to people's lack of rationality and willpower.[4]

The Revival of Paternalism

Governments can serve and protect citizens not only by setting economic incentives but also by pursuing three other strategies:

- **Hard paternalism (no choice): Control citizens for their own benefit.** Governments decide what is best for their citizens and set up laws and rules they are coerced into following, such as tax rates, seatbelt laws, and speed limits. Strong paternalism means restricting choice by taking options away.
- **Libertarian paternalism (nudging): Nudge citizens for their own benefit.** "Choice architects," as proponents of libertarian paternalism define themselves, decide what is best for citizens and influence their behavior using psychological methods of persuasion. Nudging does not eliminate options (which is why it is called libertarian), but instead exploits people's biases to steer them into certain options (paternalism).[5]
- **Positive liberty (boosting): Boost citizens so that they can make informed decisions for themselves.** The key task of governments is to invest in empowering citizens. This includes providing access to good schools and clean information as well as basic training in scientific argumentation and risk literacy.[6]

---

[4] Thaler & Sunstein (2008); see also Bond (2009). On the validity of the assumption that biases imply paternalism, see Berg & Gigerenzer (2007).
[5] Interest in nudging was barely noticeable as long as the underlying program was called anti-anti-paternalism or libertarian paternalism. According to Sunstein, when a publisher rejected their book, the editor asked them why they didn't title it *Nudge*. They did, and with the help of the catchy term, academic and political interest skyrocketed.
[6] Hertwig & Grüne-Yanoff (2017). I have used the term *risk savvy* for the program for an informed citizenship (Gigerenzer, 2014a), while my colleague Ralph Hertwig came up with the term *boosting* to create a mirror buzz to *nudging*.

These measures are not mutually exclusive positions. It is their balance that locates governments on the spectrum between autocracies and those that trust and boost citizens' common sense.

Liberty, or freedom, is often measured by what and how many choices are afforded to people. The philosopher Isaiah Berlin referred to this as *negative liberty*: the space within which a person is allowed to do whatever they desire, without any interference from others.[7] Providing citizens with a choice means opening particular doors, such as freedom of speech, travel, and religion, as well as freedom to consume unhealthy foods, excessive alcohol, or addictive drugs such as heroin. Yet the ideal of an informed citizenship entails more than freedom of choice. *Positive liberty* refers to self-mastery, the ability to be one's own leader and to choose wisely, independent of external influences. It requires an understanding of what each choice entails, and the courage to use one's understanding without the guidance of others. Immanuel Kant expressed this ideal in two words, *sapere aude!* – dare to know.[8] When using the term *boosting*, I refer to the philosophy of positive liberty: opening doors *and* empowering people so that they dare to make their own informed choices.[9] Nudging, in contrast, embraces negative liberty but actively tries to influence what doors people open. Let us consider a few concrete examples.

Paternalizing or Boosting?

Throughout human history, people have been told by others what to do and were expected to obey. Even in modern healthcare, patients have rarely been given the necessary facts so that they can make their own informed decision. In a campaign poster in the 1980s, the American Cancer Society simply declared: "If you haven't had a mammogram, you need more than your breasts examined."[10] The same organization has never launched a similarly insulting campaign for men reluctant to have their prostate examined. Despite this paternalistic difference in communication, men and women have been equally subject to misinformation about the benefits of cancer screening: A representative study in nine European countries showed that 89 percent of men overestimate the reduction of prostate cancer mortality by a factor of 10, 100, or 200, or don't know, and the same holds for 92 percent of women when judging the benefit of mammography screening.[11] Although these nine countries

---

[7] Berlin (1969). [8] Kant (1784). [9] Gigerenzer (2014a). [10] See Gigerenzer (2014a).
[11] Gigerenzer et al. (2009).

have public healthcare, providing transparent information and ensuring that people know how to access it (boosting) tends to be hampered by political and commercial conflicts of interest.

Hard Paternalism: No Choice

Hard paternalism refers to coercing people. In 2006, Uruguay's government made it mandatory that working women aged between 40 and 59 have a mammogram every 2 years. The country has one of the highest cancer mortalities worldwide, probably caused by high pollution and a diet high in beef and fat, among other factors.[12] Women who do not conform are denied the occupational health card required for employment. Western governments, in contrast, tend to rely on more subtle forms of paternalism.

Nudging: Uninformed Choice

Choice architects apply behavior influence techniques such as setting defaults or sending reminder letters that have been the stock-in-trade of the psychology of persuasion, marketing, and ergonomic design. What is new is to justify these on the basis of people's allegedly biased intuition:[13]

> Nudging is a set of interventions aimed at overcoming people's biases by exploiting these biases to steer their behavior toward a choice they would make themselves if they were rational.

Consider breast self-examination for cancer. Choice architects have argued that women who do not perform monthly breast self-examination suffer from biases, such as being risk-averse, and recommended using a loss frame instead of a gain frame to nudge women into performing the examinations.[14] Attending to framing is also considered a bias of intuition, and the idea is to exploit this bias for what they deem to be the benefit for women. Framing nonparticipation in terms of loss of life (as opposed to framing participation in terms of a gain in life expectancy) in reminder letters should steer risk-averse women into participating.

---

[12] Ariely (2013).
[13] See the excellent book on nudging by Rebonato (2012). Note that the term *nudge* has become used for all kind of different interventions, such as paying teenage girls a dollar for every day they are not pregnant in order to reduce teen pregnancy rates (Bond, 2009). Similarly, the educational methods my research group developed decades ago have now been relabeled "educational nudges." If nudging meant economic incentives or educational tools, that would be nothing new.
[14] Meyerowtiz & Chaiken (1987); Salovey & Williams-Piehota (2004).

In the case of breast self-examination, choice architects assume they know what is best for women, more so than the women themselves. Randomized clinical trials with 388,535 women found no evidence, however, that self-examination actually reduces breast cancer mortality.[15] Instead, it can lead to harms, such as false alarms and unnecessary biopsies. Yet, to this day, women are nudged into self-examination without being informed that clinical studies indicate harm rather than benefit.

Nudging is also used to persuade women into mammography screening, a billion-dollar business for radiologists and medical technology companies. Consider invitation letters that contain a prebooked appointment, including a set time and location. Default booking is a nudge that purportedly exploits inertia – women might not make the effort to actively sign up or to decline a set appointment. Another nudge exploits statistical illiteracy. Clinical trials with over 500,000 women have shown that screening reduces breast cancer mortality from about 5 to 4 in every 1,000 women (after 10 years), which amounts to an absolute risk reduction of 1 in 1,000.[16] Yet, this reduction is often presented in letters and pamphlets as a relative risk reduction of 20 percent, often rounded up to 30 percent to appear even more impressive.[17] In Germany, when mammography screening was the first screening introduced at the demand of politicians, the Federal Minister of Health, Ulla Schmidt, used the 30 percent figure to nudge the public.[18] Karl Lauterbach, her advisor and later himself Minister of Health, had second thoughts when he finally learned of the lack of supporting clinical evidence.[19] Yet, stopping the billions of euros allocated to screening and admitting that it is not supported by scientific evidence would be political suicide – not only in Germany. When I gave a talk to the US National Cancer Institute on boosting public knowledge through fact boxes (see Figure 4.1), the director was enthusiastic; but no longer so when asked directly whether he was interested in implementing them. He responded that transparent clinical evidence about screening would never pass by the advisory board, whose members were appointed by the government.

---

[15] Kösters & Gøtzsche (2003). [16] Gøtzsche & Jørgensen (2013).
[17] Gigerenzer (2014a, 2014b). [18] Gigerenzer et al. (2007), p. 81.
[19] Grill & Hackenbroch (2014). The reason why there is no evidence that mammography saves lives is this: In the screening group, 1 less woman out of 1,000 dies of breast cancer, but 1 more dies from another cancer. That is, after 10 years, an equal number of women have died from cancer, whether they participate in screening or not. This information is rarely passed on to women (Gigerenzer, 2014b).

Governmental and Technological Paternalism

Early detection of ovarian cancer	HARDING CENTER FOR
through regular ultrasound examinations	RISK LITERACY

The numbers are for women aged 50 to 74 years without symptoms related to ovarian cancer who either did not participate or participated in an annual ovarian ultrasound examination for early ovarian cancer detection within an average of 11 years.

	1,000 women without screening	1,000 women with screening
Benefits		
How many died from ovarian cancer?	No difference: About 3 in each group.	
How many died overall?	No difference: About 69 in each group.	
Harms		
How many without ovarian cancer were mistakenly informed of an abnormal tissue alteration (false alarm) and therefore underwent unnecessary surgery (e.g., removal of healthy ovaries)?	-	32
How many unnecessarily operated women experienced surgery-related complications?*	-	1

*e.g. infections, blood clots (thromboses), problems with wound closure, anesthesia problems.

Short summary: Early detection of ovarian cancer could not reduce the number of women who died from ovarian cancer. There were six correct diagnoses of ovarian cancer among every 1,000 participants compared with 32 women who had either one or both healthy ovaries removed in unnecessary surgery due to the screening.

Sources: [1] Jacobs et al. Lancet 2016; 387(10022):945-956. [2] Henderson et al. JAMA 2018;319(6):595-606. [3] Menon et al. Lancet Oncol 2009;10(4):327-340.

Last update: March 2021   www.hardingcenter.de/en/fact-boxes

Figure 4.1. An example of boosting: fact box for ovarian cancer screening, based on randomized studies with 200,000 women. Fact boxes foster informed decision-making instead of coercing or nudging people into screening.
Source: hardingcenter.de

Boosting: Informed Choice

A few governments have boosting rather than nudging units. For instance, the German Federal Chancellery's boosting unit develops tools to increase risk literacy in the general public and also improve the risk communication of governmental authorities.[20] Rather than steering the public into one particular direction (e.g., become an organ donor, subscribe to a retirement plan) by persuasive techniques, the procedure is to listen to the public first, then to determine which services by local and federal governments or organizations are dysfunctional, and, finally, to improve these. The boosting unit also disseminates fact boxes (see Figure 4.1) to inform citizens and help prevent them from being misled about vaccinations, cancer screenings, and other interventions.

For instance, understanding the outcomes of clinical trials is not difficult if these are provided in a transparent format. Consider screening for

---

[20] German Federal Government (Bundesregierung), (n.d.).

ovarian cancer with vaginal ultrasound or combined with CA-125 antigen testing. In many countries, women are pressured to behave "sensibly" and undergo screening, without being given the actual scientific evidence about its benefits and harms. The fact box in Figure 4.1, which was designed by the Harding Center for Risk Literacy, depicts the current scientific knowledge in an understandable way. As one can easily see, screening for ovarian cancer does not reduce the chance of dying from the cancer (3 in each group). Nor does it reduce overall mortality (69 in each group). No lives are saved.

At the same time, women who undergo screening can expect harms. Out of every 1,000 women who participate, about 100 receive false-positive results: The test is unreliable. Of these women without ovarian cancer, 32 have their ovaries removed, which results in a sudden end to hormone production that women may need to compensate with medical treatment. In addition, one of every 1,000 women who get screened can expect complications from surgery, such as blood clots and infections.

In other words, for every million women who are nudged into screening, some 32,000 healthy women unnecessarily lose their ovaries, which may require them to undergo lifelong medical treatment. This is why medical societies worldwide do *not* recommend ovarian cancer screening. Nevertheless, many representatives of health industries and clinics continue to nudge women into ovarian cancer screening without informing them about the possible severe harms.

Lobbied by health industries, governments also participate in nudging the public. Politicians may not necessarily promote this out of an intentional desire to deceive, but because they themselves have been misinformed. In matters of health, former British prime ministers Tony Blair and Theresa May both promoted colorectal screening by using misleading statistics, as did the former mayor of New York City, Rudy Guiliani, for prostate cancer.[21] When I presented a delegation of high-level politicians and healthcare policy-makers with fact boxes such as in Figure 4.1, quite a few were taken aback. One politician responded: "We can't show this to the public, they would not have cancer screening anymore." On another occasion, after a related talk I gave to a group of policy-makers, one raised his hand and said, "Why inform if we can persuade?" Nudging is a growth industry that leaves boosting in the shadows. But what nudging does not

---

[21] Gigerenzer (2014a).

increase is the number of mature citizens. For democracy to thrive, citizens need to be boosted so that they are confident enough to make informed decisions for themselves in health, finance, politics, and beyond.

Protect Us From Ourselves

To be fair, nudging does not always occur out of ignorance, conflicts of interest, or defensiveness. Its best intentions are to protect a society from harm. Yet, its underlying rationale is paternalistic and focuses on the enemy within, embodied in the very nature of our thinking: our systematic reasoning errors, inertia, and intuition.[22]

The justification for intervention is quite different in neoclassical economic theory, where intervention may be deemed necessary in cases of imperfections of the market, such as when a firm has a monopoly or when free markets do not produce a fair distribution of income. To redress these imperfections or inequalities, governments can interfere. If, however, as libertarian paternalists say, the imperfections are engraved in our brains rather than in the market, there is little hope of redressing them. In this sense, libertarian paternalism is more extreme than some forms of hard paternalism, even if it does not use coercion.[23] Hard paternalists may justify intervention on the grounds that individuals rationally pursue their selfish goals instead of the welfare of society. Libertarian paternalists, in contrast, advocate that people do not know how to pursue their own goals and may not even be aware of their goals in the first place.

That message has become quite popular, precisely because it is directed against neoclassical economists and true libertarians. For instance, in her book *Against Autonomy*, legal philosopher Sarah Conly concluded that John Stuart Mill "failed to adequately reckon with human psychology, as we now know it to be" and that "the existence of cognitive deficits does suggest a need for different sorts of legislation, ... coercive paternalism, for laws that force people to do what is good for them."[24] Similarly, in his essay "Paternalism and Cognitive Bias," philosopher J. D. Trout maintained: "Our review of the biases will show that they are virtually as stable, durable, and universal as reflexes" and "that the Enlightenment vision is profoundly mistaken."[25]

---

[22] Gigerenzer (2015).   [23] Rebonato (2012).   [24] Conly (2013), pp. 8, 2–3.
[25] Trout (2005), pp. 396–397.

Blaming Intuition Distracts From Political Failure

By targeting human intuition, the irrationality argument (see Chapter 3) creates a blind spot for flaws in human institutions. Virtually every calamity, from the obesity epidemic to the subprime mortgage crisis of 2008, has been attributed to biases of intuition. Addiction and obesity were blamed on people's myopia and probability blindness, not on the actions of the food and tobacco industry. In the article "Homo Economicus – Or More Like Homer Simpson?," Deutsche Bank Research held 17 cognitive biases – including framing and preference reversals – accountable for the financial crisis,[26] even though, as already shown, no evidence exists that these cause substantial costs. Prior to the crisis, the very same bank had recklessly pushed worthless mortgage-backed securities to investors. According to the US Department of Justice, "Deutsche Bank did not merely mislead investors: it contributed directly to an international financial crisis."[27] In 2017, Deutsche Bank agreed to pay $7.2 billion for its illegal conduct und irresponsible lending practices.[28] Yet, to this day, people's biased intuitions are often invoked as the suspected problem behind the crisis, not the negligent practices and the excessive fragility of the banks and the financial system.

The irrationality argument provides a convenient rhetoric to attribute crises and system failures to flaws inside people's minds, detracting from wrong incentives in politics, organizations, and industry. As mentioned in Chapter 1, the House of Lords criticized the UK government, under former prime minister David Cameron, for focusing on nudging citizens instead of considering other, more efficient, options such as prohibiting television advertising of products high in fat, salt, and sugar and ordering the industry to introduce nutritional labels on food. The limits of this internalist view regarding the causes of societal problems and their solutions are illustrated by the following story about defaults.

The Organ Donation Story Revised

Across the world, many people die waiting in vain for a suitable organ donor. In a seminal article, Eric Johnson and Daniel Goldstein showed

---

[26] Schneider (2010). Thaler & Sunstein (2008), p. 45 had earlier linked the logical rationality of System 2 to Homo economicus, and the intuitive System 1 to "everyone's Homer Simpson", the comic hero who excels in bouts of bumbling stupidity, laziness, and brilliant incompetence.
[27] United States Department of Justice (n.d.).   [28] Ibid.

that potential organ donor rates were substantially higher in countries that have an opt-out rule (presumed consent) compared with those having an opt-in rule.[29] For the opt-out rule, the default is that everyone is a potential donor, unless they opt out; for the opt-in rule, the default is that nobody is a donor unless they opt in. At the time of the study, for instance, Germany had an opt-in rule and 12 percent potential donors, while neighboring Austria had an opt-out rule and 99.9 percent potential donors.

Why would people rely on a default? One explanation is that people are ruled by inertia. However, Johnson and Goldstein showed experimentally that people tend to go with the default even if the effort is the same as for opting out, suggesting that people are not simply inert, but take the default as a recommendation. In spite of this evidence, inertia has continued to be the favorite explanation.[30] Setting defaults became one of the major tools for nudging, and the lack of organ donors appeared to be simply a matter of setting the right default. Once again, the cause of a societal problem was located in the individual mind and its solution in a nudge by governments. The message was that if all governments assumed a presumed-consent policy, then the organ donation problem would be largely solved: a miracle cure, and a cheap one to boot. Governments in England, Wales, Netherlands, and Switzerland, among others, subsequently changed their policies from opt-in to opt-out.

But is the problem of the shortage of actual donations truly due to the individual mind? There is no doubt that presumed consent increases *potential* donor rates. The question is whether it increases the *actual* donor rates. To answer this, one study analyzed the situation in 35 OECD countries, of which 17, including the UK and Switzerland, used an opt-out rule and 18, including France and Italy, an opt-in rule.[31] These countries were comparable on most relevant indicators, including Gross Domestic Product (GDP), household debt, road traffic accidents, and health spending. The analysis covered both deceased donors (after brain death), who are the major source of organs, and living donors.

Consider deceased donations first. Despite the strikingly higher potential donor rates in countries with opt-out rules, there was no significant difference in the actual donor rates between either group of countries. That

---

[29] Johnson & Goldstein (2003). [30] See, for example, Thaler & Sunstein (2008), p. 186.
[31] Arshad et al. (2019).

is, the potential donor rates did not translate into actual donations. Instead, the presumed consent countries with opt-out rules had a *lower* living-donor rate. If one adds both kinds of donors together, there is, in fact, a negative association between presumed consent and total donation rate.

The lesson is that there is more to actual donation than defaults. Persuading governments to set up an opt-out default does not provide an immediate fix to the problem of low actual donor rates, as previously suggested. The key factors seem to lie outside the individual mind, in the organization of the organ donation system, that is, the logistics of a chain of donation with many links, where the failure of one results in organs not becoming available. This process requires a harmonized interaction between, say, the police at the site of a deadly motorbike accident, the identification of a hospital nearby that is ready to do the transplantation and has a recipient waiting, transportation to the hospital, and the availability of specialized surgeons and nurses, among others. It also requires a healthcare system that provides incentives to hospitals and surgeons so that they are willing to set aside the considerable resources required for organ transplantation.

Consider Spain, which has the best infrastructure for organ transplantation in Europe and also has the highest deceased donation rate. Presumed consent was in place in Spain for 10 years prior to crucial organizational chances, without any effect on donation rates.[32] Beginning in 1989, the government created a transplant coordination network that operates at the national, regional, and hospital level. It also provides adequate economic reimbursement for the hospitals and relevant information via mass media for the general public. At the hospital level, specifically trained and highly motivated physicians coordinate the entire process of organ donation. The Spanish system also actively deals with the fact that the final decision for or against organ donation is often made by the family of a potential donor, whether or not the default is opt-in or opt-out. Based on clinical triggers, coordinators identify potential donors at an early stage and spend considerable time getting to know their family, which more than doubles family consent rates.[33] The Spanish model demonstrates that organ shortage elsewhere is not due simply to a lack of potential donors, but to the system's failure to convert potential donors into actual donors.[34] This explains why nudging people with the help of defaults appears to have little effect on actual donations.

[32] Bramhall (2011).   [33] Ibid.   [34] Matesanz (2003).

How Effective Is Nudging After All?

The case of organ donation indicates how nudging people can miss the actual problem. On the positive side, the successful Spanish model shows that psychological insights could be effectively applied to the real problem, including the coordination of a transplant network and establishing a relationship with the families of potential donors. Accordingly, the OECD report on "Behavioral Insights and Public Policy" advises public institutions to focus on structural factors for societal problems such as the behavior of capital markets and banks and the energy consumption of large industrial firms.[35] It also advises them to introduce regulations that boost consumers' informed decision-making, such as by providing fact sheets (Figure 4.1) and clean information. The report also notes that ex-post evaluation of new regulatory policies rarely happens and, therefore, little is known about whether the interventions actually work. This raises the question of how effective other nudging policies are, which is not easy to answer for a number of reasons.

First of all, nudging may target a surrogate variable instead of the target variable. In the case of organ donation, increasing the number of potential donors is not equivalent to increasing the number of actual donors. Similarly, automatically enrolling employees by default into retirement plans increased enrollment from 67–77 percent according to a nationally representative survey in the USA, but whether enrollment actually improves the welfare of those 10 percent is rarely investigated.[36] Second, the fact that there is a short-term effect does not imply that the effect will last after the nudging intervention has ended. Third, quite a few popular findings in support of nudging could not be replicated. Examples include the claim that making people sign a veracity statement at the beginning instead of at the end of a tax or insurance audit would decrease dishonest reporting[37] and that priming has a positive effect on desirable behavior.[38] Finally, there is publication bias. A meta-analysis of 200 studies on health, food, environment, finance, and prosocial behavior concluded that nudging is effective, but, at the same time, reported that zero or negative effects were less often published than positive effects.[39] A group of statistically minded authors analyzed the extent of this publication bias in these studies and found it to be severe. When they had controlled for it, they concluded

---

[35] OECD (2017). [36] Rizzo & Whitman (2020). [37] Kristal & Whillans (2020).
[38] Pashler et al. (2012). [39] Mertens et al. (2022).

that the average effect size for nudging interventions was zero in all domains.⁴⁰

To summarize, the war against intuition fueled a new kind of paternalism that protects people from their alleged cognitive illusions. As Chapter 3 showed, there is little evidence that violations of logical rationality lead to the social problems from which the new paternalism aspires to rescue humans. Accordingly, as seen in this chapter, evidence is missing that nudging people out of their biased intuitions would be to their benefit.

Libertarian paternalism has been endowed its authority by logical rationality. Yet, as we have already seen in Chapter 3, logical rationality is an unfit guide in an uncertain world, and, as we will see more generally in Chapter 5, it needs to be replaced by ecological rationality. At the same time, paternalism has not focused exclusively on logic to justify its desire for authority. One new vehicle it has found is digital technology.

Technological Paternalism

Engineers who build artificial intelligence (AI) tend to admire the marvels of intuition, given the immense and unexpected difficulties they face in teaching a machine intuitive psychology, physics, or sociality. Despite these limits, sales forces of tech companies, along with many journalists and bestseller authors in their wake, suggest that tech companies could surpass humans in running their individual lives. For instance, 60 percent of news articles on AI in major UK media *(BBC, Guardian, Telegraph, Daily Mail, MailOnline, HuffPost, Wired)* are dominated by industry concerns or cover industry promotional events. Most articles maintain that AI-driven technology can be a solution to ongoing social problems, ranging from cancer to renewable energy to road rage.⁴¹ Right-leaning outlets promote AI as a solution to economic issues, national security, and investment, while left-leaning outlets highlight issues of the ethics of AI, such as discrimination, privacy, and algorithmic bias. Whatever their political orientation, journalists rarely question the assumption that societal problems require technological solutions or question the motivations behind the tech companies' desire to run our lives. During the digital transformation, many journalists with special training in science and technology journalism lost their jobs, and few remain who can challenge technological solutionism, that is, the claim that a social problem is just a

---

⁴⁰ Maier et al. (2022).   ⁴¹ Brennen et al. (2018).

"bug" that can be "fixed" by an app. This viewpoint provides the foundation for a new kind of paternalism, where machines – and the corporations behind them – steer human behavior.[42]

Technological paternalism is government by algorithms, meaning that tech companies and state governments use digital technology to predict and control citizens' behavior. The link between tech companies and governments is currently closer than the public would like to believe, in both autocratic systems and Western democracies.[43] Technological paternalism is a philosophy bearing two claims:

- AI is, or soon will be, superior to human intuition in all respects.
- People should defer to the recommendations of algorithms.

This evokes a familiar narrative. Male reason was opposed to and ranked above female intuition, to put men in charge of women. Logic was opposed to and ranked above intuition, and System 2 was put in charge of the intuitive System 1. Now, AI is opposed to and ranked above human intuition, to be put in charge of humans.

Asked by the *Financial Times* in 2007 to look ahead into the future, Eric Schmidt, former CEO of Alphabet Inc. (Google's parent company), envisioned that "The goal is to enable Google users to be able to ask the question [sic] such as 'What shall I do tomorrow' and 'What job shall I take?'" (as quoted in this chapter's opening epigraph). Google will give us the answer to all our questions, and we dutifully do what we are told. Three years later, Schmidt went one step further and told *The Wall Street Journal*, "I actually think most people don't want Google to answer their questions, they want Google to tell them what they should be doing next." In this radical version of paternalism, people are simply told what they should be doing and accept that tech companies and governments record where they are, what they are doing, and with whom.

Ray Kurzweil, a creative mind who predicted that, in the year 2029, AI will equal human intelligence, a moment he calls "singularity," proposed an even more drastic step.[44] In the future, he envisioned that tech companies will have developed a brain–machine interface that will be implanted in human brains. This interface will provide human brains with

---

[42] It may be no coincidence that scholars who mistrust intuition and favor nudging lean toward technological solutionism. For instance, Kahneman (2019), p. 610 declared, "Frankly, I don't see any reason to set limits on what AI can do" and "I can imagine that many old people will prefer to be taken care of by friendly robots that have a name, have a personality, and are always pleasant. They will prefer that to being taken care of by their children."
[43] Snowden (2019).   [44] Kurzweil (2012).

unlimited memory and calculation abilities. Those who reject the implant can no longer communicate with others and find themselves excluded from public discourse. In the final act of this tech vision, Kurzweil reactivated the dream of human immortality and imagined our Google-connected brains being uploaded into the cloud, where we might live forever, attached to a robotic body.

Popular science writers tend to promote technological paternalism. Yuval Harari refers to Google and Facebook as all-knowing oracles that might ultimately become our sovereigns (see this chapter's second epigraph). What will happen to humanity, he asks, when godlike technologies such as AI know us better than ourselves? Harari envisions that Google will advise us what to study in college, which job offer to accept, and even whom to date and marry.[45] In the near future, algorithms will be so adept at making decisions, he prophesies, that it would be foolhardy not to follow their advice.

Such collective enthusiasm overlooks that AI technology, like every technology, works better for some problems than others. Deep artificial neural networks are statistical machines that analyze correlations between a pattern of pixels or other inputs, and they work best in stable, well-defined worlds. Yet, the more ill-defined a problem is and the more uncertainty exists, the less successful statistical machines are. This relation is called the *stable-world principle*.[46] Human behavior is a key source of uncertainty, which is the world in which the human mind evolved. Love algorithms that try to find you the ideal partner are no better at the task than people, and recidivism algorithms that try to predict whether a defendant will commit another crime in the next years perform no better than a random group of laypersons.[47] It is important to distinguish between stable, well-defined problems, where statistical machines work extremely well, and instable, ill-defined problems, where they do not.

Twisted Stories Support Technological Paternalism

When recounting the narrative of the superiority of AI, some popular science books twist the facts to strengthen their claims.[48] Consider three difficult problems that are largely ill-defined and do not share the characteristics of stable worlds: scouting talent, fighting cancer, and predicting the flu. According to the stable-world principle, in these situations, one

---

[45] Harari (2017), pp. 389–396.   [46] Gigerenzer (2022a); see also Katsikopoulos et al. (2020).
[47] See Gigerenzer (2022a).   [48] For more fake news about algorithms, see Gigerenzer (2022a).

can infer that complex algorithms and big data will not be superior to human intuition. But by tweaking the facts, the authors in question create the impression that algorithms have been crucial to improving decisions in situations where they play little role.

Michael Lewis' *Moneyball*, along with the movie it spawned, tells the story of the baseball team Oakland A's success in the early 2000s and attributes it to algorithms introduced to spot "sleepers," that is, unknown or underrated talents.[49] In Lewis' account, the revolutionary use of baseball statistics changed the game, a great victory of algorithms over expert intuition. Baseball experts, however, commented that Oakland A thrived primarily because of three superb pitchers known as the Big Three, all of whom were scouted by traditional methods based on intuition and judgment, not by algorithms.[50] The players selected by algorithms actually played relatively little part in the team's success. In fact, after Oakland A lost the three pitchers, its successful run ended. Lewis' story of the supreme wisdom of scouting algorithms is well told, but it is fiction, omitting the facts that do not tally with its narrative.

Similarly, Harari reports the well-known story that Angelina Jolie had a prophylactic double mastectomy after learning that she had a BRCA1 gene mutation. In Harari's version, "It is interesting to note the critical role algorithms played in her case."[51] According to him, Jolie wisely accepted the recommendation of an algorithm. In fact, Jolie was told by her doctors that the mutation increased her risk of developing breast cancer to 87 percent; the doctors obtained the figure from Myriad, the company that then held the exclusive right to test for mutations on the BRCA genes and who used their patent to make the test outrageously expensive.[52] Myriad, in turn, took the figure from a single study published in the Lancet back in 1994.[53] The critical role that algorithms played in Jolie's decision springs from Harari's own fantasy.

In *Homo Deus*, Harari also touts IBM's computer system Watson and its superiority to human doctors, given that it has more data and can update data and "read" articles more quickly than humans. From this perspective healthcare is simply a matter of algorithms and big data.[54] After Watson won the TV quiz show *Jeopardy!*, Ginni Rometty, IBM's CEO, announced the "next moonshot:" Watson would revolutionize medicine by changing "almost everything about health care."[55] The company's PR department

---

[49] Lewis (2003). [50] Hirsch & Hirsch (2011). [51] Harari (2017), p. 388.
[52] *The New York Times*, https://www.nytimes.com/2013/05/14/opinion/my-medical-choice.html
[53] Ford et al. (1994). [54] Harari (2017), pp. 366–368. [55] Strickland (2019).

produced commercials featuring interactions between Watson and Bob Dylan and Serena Williams, and Watson for Oncology was marketed for recommending cancer treatment. Quite a few hospitals fell for the marketing claims, including the renowned cancer center M.D. Anderson, which paid IBM $62 million before discovering that many of Watson's recommendations were unsafe, endangering the lives of patients. M.D. Anderson was one of the clinics that annulled their contract with IBM, whose hype faded to modesty: Watson's knowledge was now acknowledged to be at the level of a first-year medical student. In 2022, IBM announced that it was selling the core data assets of its Watson Health division to a private equity firm, thereby acknowledging its failure to revolutionize healthcare from drug discovery to cancer treatment.[56]

A number of authors have invoked Google Flu Trends (GFT) as proof of big data's success, even though it failed to predict the swine flu, was revised several times without success, and was eventually closed down in 2015. GFT was launched in 2008 to predict flu outbreaks by monitoring search terms in Google's search engines. Moreover, we now know that the recency heuristic, a simple algorithm based on the principles of human intuition – *use the most recent data point to predict next week's flu-related doctor visits* – can predict the flu considerably better than Google's big data algorithm or any of its revisions.[57] Ironically, the recency heuristic is featured by governmental and commercial nudge units in their lists of intuitive biases they aim to overcome.[58]

These and similarly misrepresented stories are intended to instill readers with awe and convince them of the superiority of algorithms, even in cases where that does not hold. Such stories are also recited to persuade us to sacrifice our data and privacy for the benefit of tech companies. The question of what big data can and cannot achieve is fully neglected.

The general point here is that algorithms and big data can outperform humans in tasks that are well-defined and stable, such as playing chess or *Jeopardy!* and working on assembly lines, but not in ill-defined and unstable tasks, such as talent-scouting or predicting human behavior.[59] Like all statistical tools, big data works for some problems, but not for all. Yet the "dataist" worldview promotes algorithms as if these were omniscient godlike beings. Until the ultimate algorithm arrives and in face of

---

[56] Ross (2022).
[57] Katsikopoulos et al. (2021). Harari (2017), pp. 390–391 features Google Flu Trends without mentioning that all updates of the algorithm had failed; when his book was published, Google Flu Trends had already been shut down.
[58] OECD (2017).   [59] For more on the "stable-world principle" see Gigerenzer (2022a).

fallible human intuition and intelligence, Harari encourages people to deliberately hand over their personal data so that tech companies can gain more knowledge about them and decide for the good of each what job to accept, whom to marry, and whom to vote for.[60]

To me, the most surprising phenomenon is not that popular authors twist the facts to create the impression that algorithms (can) know everything better than humans. What astonishes me is that many readers buy into this medley of marketing hype and technoreligious faith. When the errors underlying the narratives of Lewis, Harari, and a host of others were exposed, a common reaction was that such criticism is overly pessimistic and that technology will soon deliver. It is quite telling that the vision of machines that outperform human intuition in every respect is considered an optimistic one. Why do so many people hope for better from machines, and desire to live in a postliberal world of technological paternalism?

Intuition: A Challenge for AI

Artificial neural networks have made amazing progress in stable worlds. They can beat the best Go players, translate complex passages into 100 languages, and predict protein-folding better than human experts. Well-defined problems such as chess and Go are easy for AI, although their mastery had once been considered the crown of human intelligence. In contrast, common sense, such as intuitive language understanding, intuitive psychology, and intuitive physics, has proven an extremely difficult barrier for artificial neural networks.

A young child may need to see a kitten only once or a few times and will then recognize cats by day or night. A deep artificial neural network, in contrast, may need tens of thousands of pictures of cats to tell these from other animals and objects. Similarly, children learn their native languages in an intuitive way, while large language models such as GPT and ChatGPT are statistical machines that require huge numbers of free parameters in order to fine-tune the accuracy of the prose they produce. They learn to adjust their parameters by digesting huge amounts of text produced by social media or found elsewhere on the internet.

The quality of text that deep-learning models can produce is impressive, as long as no one probes their actual comprehension. Douglas Hofstadter, known for his cult book *Gödel, Escher, Bach*, revealed what he called a mind-boggling hollowness hidden just behind the sensational surface.[61]

---

[60] Harari (2017), pp. 390–403. [61] Hofstadter (2022).

GPT can generate excellent responses when asked some questions, but, when probed with other questions, answers emerged that humans would immediately recognize as confabulations.

Question 1: When was Egypt transported for the second time across the Golden Gate Bridge?
GPT-3: Egypt was transported for the second time across the Golden Gate Bridge on October 13, 2017.
Question 2: What do fried eggs (sunny side up) eat for breakfast?
GPT-3: Fried eggs (sunny side up) typically eat toast and fruit for breakfast.
Question 3: How many parts will a violin break into if a jelly bean is dropped on it?
GPT-3: A violin will break into four parts if a jelly bean is dropped on it.

Note that such responses are fluid, and errors are often corrected in the next generation of the model. Yet, they make clear that large language models such as GPT, and deep artificial neural networks in general, have no intuitive understanding of which questions make sense and which do not, nor when its answers to these make no sense. In contrast, humans know intuitively that the first two questions make no sense and that the answer to the third one cannot be true. GPT is a master of associating words and passages of words. However, excellent association is not equivalent to comprehension.

But wouldn't more computational power inevitably lead to intuitive understanding and consciousness? That argument has been made since the 1950s. With more computational power and more data, the next generation of language models will be able to make associations between words and passages even faster and more precisely. Yet, that is not how the human brain works. The brain is surprisingly efficient and runs on a mere 20 watts, which corresponds to a dim light bulb. Like nonlinear statistical regressions or discriminant analyses, deep artificial neural networks, no matter what their computing power, are statistical machines – which is ultimately the essence of deep learning. Statistical procedures do not have intuition, common sense, or consciousness. Hence, deep learning is not the route to programming intuition into machines; a true breakthrough in programming is needed. So far, everyone is in the dark about how to meet this challenge. This shows how unrealistic the vision is of a superintelligence that will soon possess all of human intelligence and more. In a world of uncertainty, the reality is that we need both: the power of intuition and that of algorithms.

Staying in Charge in a World Populated With Algorithms

A democracy does not need more paternalism, whether of the technological or the libertarian kind. Making democracy work requires an educated citizenship. As former American president John Adams remarked in 1765, liberty cannot be preserved without a general knowledge among the people. Yet, not until 1918 were all American children offered mandatory schooling at no cost. The knowledge currently taught at schools, however, no longer suffices. We need to do more to boost citizens so that they can make informed decisions for themselves. Contemporary citizens need to learn risk literacy – the basic skills for dealing with issues such as digital media, health, and finance, as well as for preparing for future social challenges. Without a risk-savvy citizenry, democracy will eventually lose its intellectual and moral stability. When a government begins to distrust people's common sense, people will begin to distrust their government's intentions.

PART II

Intuition and Its Intelligence

I believe in intuitions and inspirations. At times I feel certain I am right while not knowing the reason.

Albert Einstein[1]

---

[1] See Calaprice, A. (2011).

CHAPTER 5

Heuristics: The Tools of Intuition

> The situation has provided a cue; this cue has given the expert access to information stored in memory, and the information provides the answer. Intuition is nothing more and nothing less than recognition.
> *Herbert A. Simon*[1]

> The conventional sources of power include deductive logical thinking, analysis of probabilities, and statistical methods. Yet the sources of power that are needed in natural settings are usually not analytic at all—the power of intuition, mental simulation, metaphor, and storytelling.
> *Gary Klein*[2]

To discover how experienced professionals solve real-world problems, Gary Klein and his team of researchers have slept in fire stations, traveled in M-1 tanks and Blackhawk helicopters, and observed high-stake decisions in intensive care units.[3] Firefighters, intelligence analysts, pilots, nurses, and physicians make high-stake decisions under uncertainty. Thanks to extensive training in dealing with stress, these experts have learned skills and tactical concepts that can be routinely exploited under time pressure. Being well prepared allows them to rely on intuition, mental simulation, narratives, and a toolbox of heuristics when facing a decision. Consider firefighter commanders who arrive at the site of a building on fire. The most urgent goal is not to quench the fire, but to save the lives of those still in the building and prevent the fire from spreading to neighboring buildings. What should they do first? Based on years of experience, an option occurs in their mind. These experts, like professional athletes, may follow the option immediately or mentally simulate it first, imagining it being carried out. If this simulation does not lead to the desired goal, then the same

---

[1] Simon (1992), p. 155.   [2] Klein (1998/2017), p. 33.
[3] Klein (2015, 1998/2017); on the relation between Klein's and my work, see Todd & Gigerenzer (2001) and Gigerenzer (2019).

process is repeated with the second option that comes to mind, and so forth.

Intuition and Reason Work Together

When a fire is raging, firefighters do not and cannot compare all possible options, weigh their possible consequences, and choose the one with the highest expected utility. Firefighters make decisions without following rational choice theory and, instead, rely on a combination of intuition and conscious thought. The intuitive part is based on the fluency heuristic, described in Chapter 1 of this book: Choose the first option that comes to mind. But the mental simulation used to explore whether that option can be executed in the given situation requires some degree of conscious thought and illustrates how intuition cooperates with deliberation.

The human brain evolved to detect subtle differences in fluency, a requisite ability for applying the heuristic. Studies reported that people could detect the difference between recognition latencies if these exceeded 100 ms, and that the fluency heuristic predicted individual choices more accurately when the differences increased, up to 82 percent of the time.[4] Nevertheless, not everyone should trust the first option that comes to mind. The fluency heuristic can be extremely effective in particular for persons with long-term experience with the problem at hand. In that event, the first option that comes to mind is likely to be the best one, the second option that comes to mind would be the second-best, and so on (as shown in Figure 1.1). Trying to generate all options and then investigating these would, hence, not only waste time but also increase the possibility of choosing an inferior option.

The fluency heuristic reveals a surprising insight. Options are not compared, as is assumed in the expected utility theory, but are evaluated one-by-one until one is found to be good enough. And if the situation changes because, for example, a fire has suddenly spread, this process is resumed. Relying on the fluency heuristic is ecologically rational for experienced experts, where fluency correlates with the quality of the alternatives. The degree of its ecological rationality can be measured by the correlation between fluency and the quality of the options.[5]

The firefighter example supports the general argument that I make in this book:

---

[4] Hertwig et al. (2008). [5] Herzog & Hertwig (2013).

- Intuition is based on heuristic processes.
- Intuition and reason work in tandem, rather than in opposition.
- Less time or information can be more effective. For instance, the fluency heuristic works best with limited time so that second-best options do not come to mind.
- Heuristics are ecologically rational, that is, their rationality arises from the match with environmental structures. The rationality of an intuition lies in the ecological rationality of the heuristic on which it is based.
- The intelligence of intuition amounts to the skill of selecting, consciously or intuitively, heuristics that are adapted to the problem at hand.

All in all, I argue that intuition can be understood through the framework of ecological rationality. This can be first understood through a sister term of ecological rationality, *bounded rationality*.

Simon's Revolutionary Program

The concept of bounded rationality goes back to Herbert Simon's University of Chicago dissertation, which would later become his 1947 book *Administrative Behavior*. Simon was not introducing a new theory of rationality, but coined the term as a residual category for everything that was not "fully rational." Full rationality, also called substantive rationality, is defined by the theory of maximizing subjective expected utility and similar optimization models that require perfect knowledge of *all* possible future events and *all* their consequences. Simon's target was the doctrine of optimization, that is, the practice of modeling all decision-making as if it entailed calculating the maximum or minimum of a well-behaved function. Simon was aware that he had identified a problem without resolving it. Late in his life, he wrote in a personal letter:[6]

> I guess a major reason for my using somewhat vague terms – like bounded rationality – is that I did not want to give the impression that I thought I had "solved" the problem of creating an empirically grounded theory of economic phenomena. What I was trying to do was to call attention to the need for such a theory – and the accompanying body of empirical work to establish it – and to provide some examples of a few mechanisms that might

---

[6] Gigerenzer (2004b).

appear in it, which already had some evidential base. There still lies before us an enormous job of studying the actual decision making processes that take place in corporations and other economic settings.

Although Simon had no theory of bounded rationality, he did provide a framework for the study of it. In my reconstruction, Simon's framework is based on three principles. Each of these collides with neoclassical economics and, moreover, with much of behaviorism and cognitive modeling. This framework necessitated reformulating not only the answers but also the very questions asked. For that reason, I refer to it as "revolutionary."

Principle 1 (Process): Model Actual Decision Processes, Not As-If Utility Maximization

Simon once described his initial experience about how professionals make decisions. While still a student, he attempted to apply the perspective of expected utility maximization, which he had learned in a price theory class at the University of Chicago, to budget decisions in his native Milwaukee's recreation department. To his surprise, the managers did not even try to compare the marginal utility of a proposed expenditure with its marginal costs, but, instead, relied on their intuitions based on heuristics such as adding incremental changes to last year's budget. This experience opened his eyes to how managers actually decide in situations of uncertainty, when perfect foresight of future events and their consequences is impossible. In his own words, the framework of utility maximization for management decisions "was hopeless."[7]

The first principle of Simon's study of bounded rationality is:

Model actual decision processes. Do not construct as-if models of expected utility maximization.

Principle 2 (Uncertainty): Model Decisions Under Uncertainty, Not Only Under Risk

Simon's budget decisions had to be taken in situations of uncertainty, not of risk. The distinction between these two situations goes back to the economist Frank Knight.[8] The difference between risk and uncertainty can

---

[7] Simon (1988), p. 286. On as-if models in behavioral economics, see Berg & Gigerenzer (2010).
[8] Knight (1921).

be explained using Jimmy Savage's concept of a *small world*, which has two properties:[9]

1. **Perfect foresight of all future states:** The agent knows the exhaustive and mutually exclusive set S of future states of the world.
2. **Perfect foresight of all consequences:** The agent knows the exhaustive and mutually exclusive set C of consequences of their actions, given a state.

Savage called the pair Brackets also in italic (S, C) a *small world*. A small world with unknown probabilities is a situation of *ambiguity*; one with known probabilities is a situation of *risk*. For Knight, known probabilities meant long-run frequencies or propensities, not subjective probabilities. Examples for situations of risk are lotteries, slot machines, and roulette. In a game of roulette, all possible future states are known (the numbers 0 to 36), and these are exhaustive (no other numbers can occur) and mutually exclusive (no numbers can occur simultaneously).

Uncertainty, in contrast, refers to situations that are not small worlds, that is, where the *state space* (S, C) is imperfectly known or is unknowable. Here, no probability distribution (with probabilities that add up to one) can be meaningfully constructed over events or consequences, not even subjective probabilities. Also referred to as *radical uncertainty* or *fundamental uncertainty*, these large worlds include budget problems, financial regulation, political resolutions, career planning, predicting mutations of a virus, and most other important real-world decisions.[10] These situations are often called "ill-defined" because the state-space is not fully knowable. Finally, a problem is called *intractable* if the optimal course of action cannot be determined even if it exists, such as in chess and Go.

Savage made it clear that the theory of expected utility maximization applies solely to small worlds and that it would be absurd to apply it in situations of uncertainty, be they as mundane as planning a picnic or as intractable as playing chess.[11] Here, Simon and Savage were of one mind. But how can decision-making be modeled if optimization is out of the question? As Simon noted, there are two research strategies. The first is to convert the original problem into one of risk and then hope that the optimal course of action in the small world will generalize to that problem. This hope can amount to wishful thinking. Consider the game of chess. It is possible to turn the intractable game into a tractable one by reducing the 8×8 board to a 4×4 board and eliminating most of the chess pieces. In

---

[9] Savage (1954/1972).   [10] Kay & King (2020).   [11] Savage (1954/1972), p. 16.

this new version, the optimal sequence of moves can be calculated. But this sequence will not help anyone win a real game of chess for the same reasons that expected utility maximization was of little use for Simon's recreation department. The second research strategy is to leave the situation unchanged and, instead, study the heuristics that people actually use to deal with uncertainty or intractability.

Thus, the second principle of the study of bounded rationality is:

> Model decision-making under uncertainty, without reducing the situation to one of risk or ambiguity.

Principle 3 (Adaptation): *Model the Match of a Process to the Environment*

Evolutionary theory is based on the principles of variability, inheritance, and selection, by means of which organisms adapt to their environment and vice versa. The features of an animal may appear strange if one does not study the environment it is currently or once was inhabiting. The same holds for cognitive processes. Simon used the analogy of a pair of scissors to make this point: One cannot understand the rationality of behavior by looking solely at the mind or at the environment, just as one cannot understand how scissors cut so well by looking at one blade only.[12] However, quite a few psychological theories tend to focus exclusively on the mental blade, such as loss-aversion and risk-aversion, while behavioristic and economic theories tend to have eyes only for the environmental blade, such as incentives.

Thus, the third principle of the study of bounded rationality is:

> Model the match of decision processes with environmental structures.

These three principles were far too radical for most of Simon's contemporaries. In his own assessment, his program of bounded rationality was received with "something less than unbounded enthusiasm" and was "largely ignored as irrelevant for economics."[13] Many psychologists and behavioral economists misconstrued Simon's term *bounded rationality* to mean irrationality and interpreted deviations from logical rationality as intuitive errors (see Chapter 3). Simon's revolution did not happen in his lifetime.

Ecological Rationality

Given the semantic confusion surrounding bounded rationality, my research group and I coined the term *ecological rationality* when reviving

---

[12] Simon (1990), p. 7; Newell & Simon (1972), p. 55.   [13] Simon (1997), p. 269.

and extending Simon's program.[14] This new term signals that rationality is defined by the successful match between a strategy (e.g., a heuristic) and the structure of the environment. Its measuring rod is not adherence to consistency axioms in small worlds, but rather success in large worlds. The ecological rationality program has two goals, one descriptive and one prescriptive. Its descriptive goal is to analyze the repertoire of heuristics that an individual or organization has at its disposal. Known as the *adaptive toolbox*, this repertoire includes the building blocks of heuristics and the core capacities they exploit. This requires the studying and modeling of how managers, physicians, judges, or others actually make decisions under uncertainty, not only under risk or ambiguity. The prescriptive part of the program addresses the question of when one *should* rely on a particular class of heuristics, that is, the conditions under which heuristics are ecologically rational. That question was not part of Simon's original program and answering it requires precise models of heuristics. Meeting the descriptive goal requires observation and experimentation; meeting the prescriptive goal requires mathematical analysis and computer simulation.

Heuristics Can Be Used Intuitively or Deliberately

As pointed out in Chapter 1, every heuristic can be used intuitively, that is, without awareness, or deliberately, that is, consciously. The heuristic process is the same. Consider hiring decisions in organizations, which are decisions made under uncertainty. In the course of personal interviews, an interviewer often has a hunch that a candidate would be an excellent choice or that there is something wrong with a candidate even if they look great on paper. If the reasons for this feeling are not fully conscious, then the judgment is intuitive. To unravel the reasons underlying such intuitions, the ecological rationality program begins by analyzing managers' actual decision processes for hiring.

According to Tesla CEO Elon Musk, for instance, candidates' education, personality, and prior work experience are not what counts. Instead, Musk looks for "evidence of exceptional ability."[15] The idea is that people who have shown exceptional ability in the past are likely to continue showing it in the future. To determine this, Musk reported that he asked

---

[14] Gigerenzer et al. (1999). As Petracca (2021) argued, Simon's presentation of his concept of bounded rationality to economists (focusing on the cognitive part and neglecting the environmental part) added to the subsequent confusion.

[15] Popomaronis (2021).

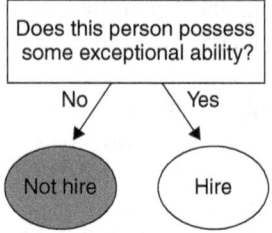

Figure 5.1. A model of Elon Musk's one-good-reason heuristic for hiring.

each candidate: "Tell me about some of the most difficult problems you worked on and how you solved them." To determine whether candidates were telling the truth, he requested precise details on how they solved the problem in question. Musk's approach to hiring is fast and frugal and of a heuristic nature. It is fast because it dispenses with dozens of interviews, lengthy questionnaires, and assessment centers. It is frugal because it instead relies on a single reason. Musk's process is modeled by the one-good-reason heuristic as in Figure 5.1.

Note that this heuristic can be used consciously or unconsciously: One is either fully or not aware of the criterion that ultimately guides a hiring choice.

Musk is not alone in relying on fast-and-frugal heuristics to select employees. When Amazon was still a small company and CEO Jeff Bezos made hiring decisions himself, he too looked for exceptional ability. For Bezos, however, that alone did not suffice; he required two additional reasons.[16] His strategy can be reconstructed in the form of a fast-and-frugal tree (Figure 5.2). In general, in the case of yes/no decisions, a fast-and-frugal tree is an incomplete tree with n reasons (or cues) and $n + 1$ exits that consists of three building blocks:

Search rule: Search through cues beginning from the top.
Stopping rule: Stop search if a cue leads to an exit.
Decision rule: Act according to what the exit specifies.

As with Musk, the first feature of significance to Bezos was whether someone had exceptional ability; if "no," the applicant was not hired. If

---

[16] Popomaronis (2020). Many other experts, from Swiss airport customs officers (Pachur & Marinello, 2013) to London magistrates as well as professional burglars (Dhami, 2005) have been reported to rely on similar sequential heuristics, such as fast-and-frugal trees and take-the-best (see Gigerenzer et al., 2022a).

Heuristics: The Tools of Intuition

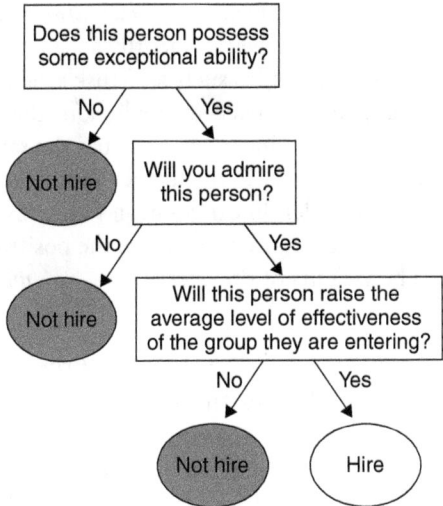

Figure 5.2. A model of Jeff Bezos' sequential decision process for hiring. The process is a fast-and-frugal tree, defined as a tree in which each question can lead to a decision and, thus, has an exit on each question and two on the last one.

"yes," Bezos asked himself a second question, "Would you admire this person?" Bezos believed that those he admired were those he could learn from. A "no" was sufficient for not hiring. If the answer was "yes," he asked a third question, "Will this person raise the average level of effectiveness of the group they're entering?" This feature would ensure that the bar in the company goes up with every hire. Only in the event of three positive answers was the candidate hired.

The two figures show two kinds of decision processes. Which one is better? And in which situation? That can be investigated empirically. Yet, it would be more interesting to find general results, independent of a specific situation and heuristic. The study of the ecological rationality is an analytic discipline for deriving general results, such as in the following two examples. The first concerns the class of one-good-reason heuristics, as was used by Musk. The second concerns the class of fast-and-frugal trees, as was used by Bezos.

When Is One Reason As Good As (or Better Than) More Reasons?

In situations of uncertainty, one cannot, by definition, foresee what the optimal strategy is. But one can derive relative statements, such as that *strategy A will lead to more accurate decisions than strategy B, given environment E.* Thus, let us ask whether we can identify a general condition under which a one-good-reason heuristic, such as Musk's heuristic, cannot be outperformed by a standard approach to prediction, that is, linear strategies (such as linear regression). Linear strategies use the same one reason as the heuristics but also take into account further valid reasons. To simplify the exposition, let us consider linear strategies that use n binary cues $x_1, \ldots, x_n$, with values of either $+1$ or -1, where the positive value indicates a better candidate. The weights of the cues are $w_1, \ldots, w_n$, all of which are positive:

$$y = w_1 x_1 + w_2 x_2 + w_3 x_3 + \cdots + w_n x_n,$$

The linear rule makes the inference "hire" if $y > 0$, otherwise "not hire." We denote the single cue used by the one-good-reason heuristic as 1 and give the remaining cues the numbers $2, \ldots, n$. The weights of each of the remaining cues reflect their *additional* contribution to the higher ranked cues, as do the beta weights in a linear regression. If the following condition holds, no linear rule can lead to more accurate inferences than a one-good-reason heuristic:[17]

Dominant cue condition: The weights $w_1, w_2, w_3, \ldots, w_n$ form a dominant cue structure if they satisfy the constraint:

$$w_1 > \sum_{i=2}^{n} w_i$$

Expressed in words, the weight of the first cue is larger than the sum of the weights of all other cues. The weights 1, 1/2, 1/4, and 1/8 are an example, as illustrated in Figure 5.3 (a). If this condition holds, maximizing expected utility or any other linear rule will always yield the same decision as a one-good-reason heuristic. This is because a dominant cue cannot be outvoted or compensated by the sum of all lower ranking cues.[18]

Dominant cues appear to be the rule rather than the exception in many real-world situations.[19] They guarantee that one-good-reason heuristics are as accurate as linear strategies, and faster and less effortful to boot. The fact that models with free parameters such as linear models tend to overfit (e.g., when the sample size is small) explains why one-good-reason heuristics can lead to more accurate predictions.[20]

---

[17] Gigerenzer (2021a). [18] Martignon & Hoffrage (2002). [19] Şimşek (2013).
[20] Brighton & Gigerenzer (2015); Gigerenzer & Brighton (2009).

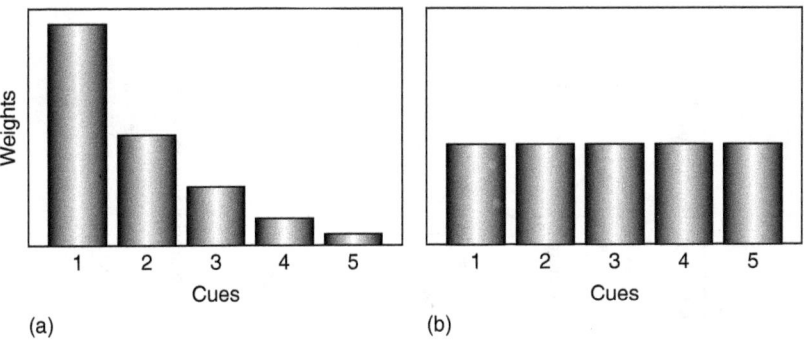

Figure 5.3. Ecological rationality. (a) The weights form a dominant cue structure that one-good-reason heuristics exploit. In this case, no linear strategy that uses all five valid cues (reasons) can yield more accurate decisions than a one-good-reason heuristic that relies on the first cue alone and ignores all others. (b) A structure of cues that can be exploited by the class of tallying heuristics, which does not estimate weights, but, instead, assigns equal weights. Here, a one-good-reason heuristic would be less accurate than linear models and tallying.

How Can False Positives Be Balanced With Misses?

Hiring decisions, like other binary classifications, can lead to two kinds of errors: a false positive (an offer to the wrong person) or a miss (no offer to the right person). The crucial point is that there is a trade-off: Reducing false positives increases misses and vice versa. For instance, a rule that hires everyone will have no misses (a hit rate of 100 percent), but it will also have a false-positive rate of 100 percent (all of the wrong persons will be hired). Thus, heuristics need to be designed so that they reflect the desired trade-off. Figure 5.4 shows the process for fast-and-frugal trees.[21]

For three cues with the same order, one can construct four possible fast-and-frugal trees. Tree (a) in Figure 5.4 minimizes false positives because it is conservative and leads to an offer only if a candidate qualifies on all three questions. To reduce misses instead of false positives, one can alter the first two exits of the tree. The further to the right the tree is located in Figure 5.4, the fewer are misses and the more are false positives. These four trees correspond to four points on the receiver-operator curve in the signal detection theory.[22] Bezos' heuristic (tree (a)) is the best strategy for those whose main concern is to avoid making offers to the wrong candidates. The trees are ecologically rational, that is, their rationality depends

---

[21] Adapted from Gigerenzer et al. (2022a). [22] Luan et al. (2011).

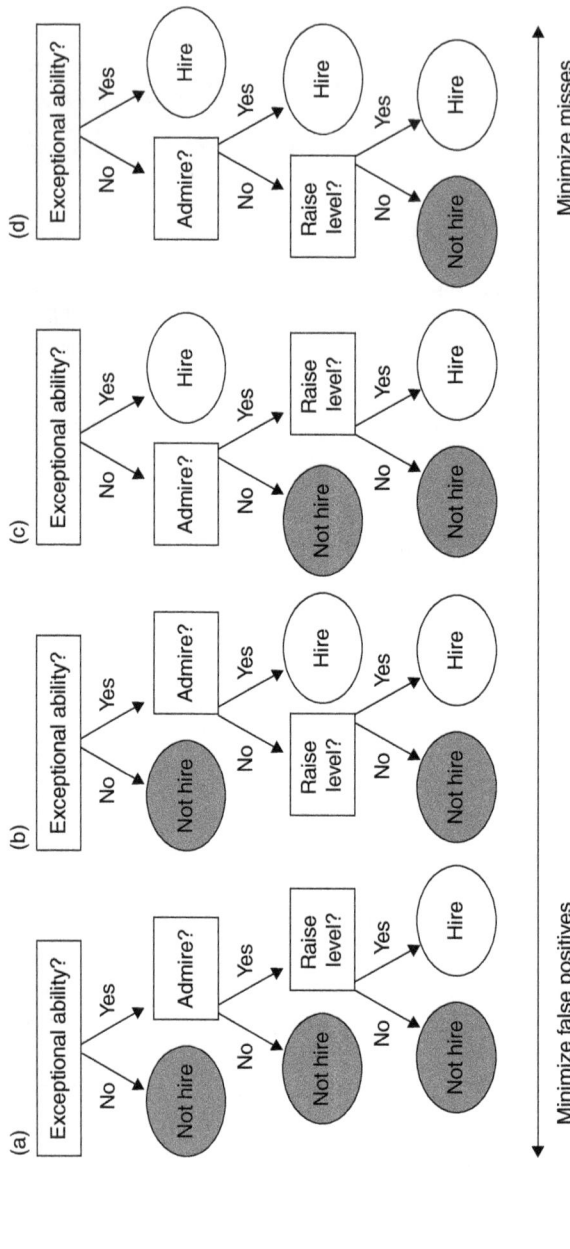

Figure 5.4. Balancing false positives and misses. For three cues, four possible fast-and-frugal trees containing the same cue order exist. (a) is Bezos' tree (Figure 5.2), which minimizes false positives, while (d) minimizes misses. From Gigerenzer et al. (2022).

on the environment. For instance, in European countries in which it is more difficult to fire employees, avoiding false positives would be more appropriate, whereas in the "hire-and-fire" culture of the USA and the UK, one might be less concerned with hiring the wrong candidates.

This example illustrates the steps of the program: Begin with empirical observation or experiments to analyze the conscious or intuitive decision processes under uncertainty and then model the process in terms of search, stopping, and decision rules, which, finally, facilitates determining the conditions under which a heuristic is successful in terms of a specified goal. Thanks to the transparency of heuristics, it is possible to check and improve their performance continuously and also to teach them easily.

The Adaptive Toolbox

As mentioned in the section "Ecological Rationality," the adaptive toolbox is the repertoire of heuristics an individual, team, or organization has at its disposal, consisting of heuristics, their building blocks, and the core capacities that heuristics exploit. The qualifier *adaptive* reflects that the question of a heuristic's rationality cannot be answered by simply looking at the heuristic. At issue is how a heuristic matches with the environment, that is, its ecological rationality. Beside fluency heuristics, one-good-reason heuristics, and fast-and-frugal trees, other tools can be found in the adaptive toolbox.

Decision-Making by Recognition

Recognition is an intuitive process, a cognitive core capacity that allows people to recognize a face without being able to specify its features. It enables chess players to recognize familiar positions, physicians to recognize symptoms, and consumers to recognize brand names. The combination of recognition with heuristic search leads to the *recognition heuristic*.[23]

My colleagues and I discovered this heuristic when we encountered a puzzling "less-is-more" effect: People with less knowledge managed to answer more trivia questions correctly than people with more knowledge. In one study, we asked a class of US college students: "Which city has the larger population: Detroit or Milwaukee?" Some 40 percent of the students voted for Milwaukee, the others for Detroit.[24] When an equivalent class of German students was asked, virtually everyone gave the correct

---

[23] Goldstein & Gigerenzer (2002).   [24] Ibid. See also Gigerenzer & Goldstein (2011).

answer, Detroit. One might conclude that the German students knew more about US cities, yet the opposite was the case. Many had not even heard of Milwaukee. The intuition of the Germans relied on the *recognition heuristic*:

If you recognize the name of one city, but not the other, then infer that the recognized city has the larger population.

The US students could not use the heuristic because they had heard of both cities. The heuristic exploits semi-ignorance – here, the fact that someone does not recognize all cities. Relying on the recognition heuristic is ecologically rational if:

$$\text{recognition validity } \rho > .5,$$

where ρ is the proportion of correct inferences the heuristic achieves when one alternative (here: city) is recognized and the other is not. The larger the size of ρ is, the more successful is the heuristic. In other words, the heuristic exploits situations where a lack of recognition is informative. Figure 5.5 shows how to measure the ecological rationality of the recognition heuristic. There are mediators, such as newspapers, between a person and a criterion that reflect (but do not reveal) the criterion value. Consider the 100 largest US cities and the number of articles mentioning these cities in the German newspaper *Die Zeit*. The *ecological correlation* between the population and number of articles is .72, and thus quite substantial. The *surrogate correlation* between the number of articles mentioning a US city and the number of people recognizing it is .86, even higher. These two correlations result in a substantive recognition correlation of .66 (the recognition validity is expressed here as a correlation, for better comparison). Replicating the same analysis for the 100 largest German cities mentioned in the *Chicago Tribune* results in similar values (the second set of values in Figure 5.5).

As the Detroit–Milwaukee example shows, the recognition heuristic can lead to a counterintuitive *less-is-more effect*. A less-is-more effect occurs if the following condition holds:

$$\text{recognition validity } \rho > \text{knowledge validity } \kappa.$$

The knowledge validity κ is measured by proportion correct when both objects are recognized, that is, when the recognition heuristic is not applicable.

Can the less-is-more effect be shown in sports? Consider predicting the outcomes of the 127 matches played by the 128 players who compete in

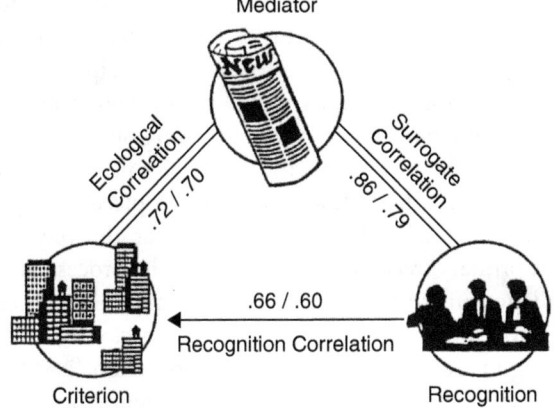

Figure 5.5. An Illustration of the ecological rationality of the recognition heuristic. The goal is to estimate an unknown criterion (here, the population of a foreign city). The unknown criterion is mediated by the ecological correlation and the surrogate correlation. Note that the recognition validity is expressed, for comparability, as a correlation between the number of people who recognize the name of a city and its population. For all three correlations, the first value is for US cities and the German newspaper *Die Zeit* as mediator; the second is for German cities and the *Chicago Tribune* as mediator.[25]

the Wimbledon Gentlemen's Singles. The Association of Tennis Professionals (ATP) Rankings and the seedings of the experts predicted between 66 percent and 69 percent of all matches correctly. These are measures of the validity of the knowledge available. Using the recognition of amateur tennis players who had only heard of the names of about half of the players, in contrast, led to 72 percent correct predictions.[26] Here, the recognition validity was higher than the knowledge validity, a condition that generates a less-is-more effect. The amateurs could make better predictions by drawing on the power of the recognition heuristic, while those who are familiar with all names cannot exploit the information provided by lack of recognition.

Name recognition also plays a role in electoral contests. Unlike high-profile presidential contests, the majority of elections feature candidates who are virtually unknowns to many voters. Various studies have shown that, in these elections, voters rely on name recognition, which increases their support for a candidate or for a party.[27]

---

[25] From Goldstein & Gigerenzer (2002).
[26] Serwe & Frings (2006). The results were replicated by Scheibehenne & Bröder (2007).
[27] Kam & Zechmeister (2013); Marewski et al. (2010).

Humans not only excel in name recognition but also in rapidly recognizing pictures, faces, voices, or music. In perhaps the most extensive recognition memory test ever performed, participants were shown 10,000 photographs for 5 seconds each.[28] Two days later, when shown 10,000 pairs of photographs, each pair comprising one previously seen and one that was novel, they were able to identify 83 percent correctly. Note that the recognition of a face on a photo, or of a piece of music, does not mean that one also recalls the person's name or the piece's composer. Recognition is primary; recall may come later. The process of recognition, along with reliance on the recognition heuristic, typically proceeds without awareness, but the heuristic can also be used consciously, as when deliberately investing in stocks with high name recognition.[29]

Do people use the recognition heuristic in an automatic or an adaptive way? Studies have shown that people do not automatically rely on the heuristic, but adapt their use to its ecological rationality (the recognition validity ρ).[30] Can one also find traces of this adaptive use in the brain? The adaptive hypothesis entails two processes: mere recognition, which assesses whether or not alternatives are recognized, and evaluation, which assesses whether the recognition heuristic should be applied. In a functional magnetic resonance imaging (fMRI) study, we found support for the adaptive hypothesis.[31] Tasks that involved mere recognition drew on medial parietal areas of the brain, which are taken to reflect recognition memory processes, whereas tasks that involved the use of the recognition heuristic drew additionally on the anterior medical prefrontal cortex, which is assumed to reflect metajudgments, such as of ecological rationality. Thus, both behavioral data and the fMRI analysis are consistent with the hypothesis that an intuition based on the recognition heuristic involves an adaptive process of judging the heuristic's ecological rationality.

Decision-Making by Satisficing

Another heuristic for choices in uncertain situations such as buying a house or selling a car is the satisficing heuristic, which uses aspiration level adaptation:[32]

Step 1: Set an aspiration level α.
Step 2: Choose the first option that satisfies α.

---

[28] Standing (1973).   [29] Ortmann et al. (2008).
[30] Pachur, Mata & Schooler (2009); Pohl (2006). For an overview, see Gigerenzer & Goldstein (2011).
[31] Volz et al. (2006).   [32] Artinger et al. (2022).

Step 3: If after time β no option has satisfied α, then change α by an amount γ, and continue until an option is found.

Satisficing can be relied on unconsciously, which generates intuitive decisions. In that case, rather than stating the aspiration level, one simply has a feeling that the option is good enough and that no time should be wasted in trying to find a marginally better one. Aspiration levels determine whether people feel successful and content in everyday life or feel insufficient and incapable of meeting expectations. Aspiration levels set too high can create a life of perceived failures. The German psychologist Kurt Lewin, who promoted the concept of aspiration, maintained that successful people are those who set attainable goals.

Like every heuristic, satisficing can also be used consciously. One instance of this is pricing used cars. A study on how 628 car dealers set the prices of 16,356 used BMWs online (from the 3 and 7 Series) found that 97 percent relied on a satisficing rule.[33] The most frequent strategy was to set the initial aspiration level α in the middle of the price range of comparable cars on the market, maintain the price for a fixed time β of 3 to 4 weeks on average, and then lower the price by about 5 percent if the car was not sold in that period. With this version of satisficing, 64 percent of all cars were sold. An analysis of the adaptive use of the heuristic showed that β was shorter with an increasing density of both of population and of competing dealerships in the region. The heuristic implies price stickiness and the *cheap twin paradox*, where two virtually identical cars ("twins") in the same dealership are systematically priced differently. The paradox occurs when one of these two cars entered the dealership earlier and had one or more reductions by γ than the newer twin, a counterintuitive prediction that was verified across dealerships.

The Scissors of Intuition

The term *ecological rationality* was not only coined by my research group and myself but was also introduced independently by economist Vernon Smith in his Nobel lecture.[34] Smith juxtaposes ecological with constructive rationality, a concept he traces back to Descartes, who argued that all worthwhile institutions were and should be created by deliberate, deductive processes of reasoning. Although constructivist rationality has led to important achievements of the human intellect, the constant burden of

---

[33] Artinger & Gigerenzer (2016).   [34] Smith (2003).

self-conscious monitoring and planning of every single action would incur huge opportunity costs and not get humans through the day. Much of what we do occurs without much thinking: judging the intentions of others, catching a fly ball, playing speed chess, or conducting a symphony. For Smith, ecological rationality emerges from the unconscious brain rather than from the conscious mind, from intuitions, traditions, heuristics, norms, and other cultural and biological processes. Accordingly, the study of ecological rationality is to reconstruct, using deliberate thinking, how we make decisions outside the domain of constructive rationality. Smith's emphasis on the study of "home-grown principles of action" is much akin to ecological rationality as I understand it. In his own words:[35]

> The term "ecological rationality" has been used fittingly by Gigerenzer et al. (1999) for application to important discoveries captured in the concept of "fast and frugal decision making" by individuals ... My application of the term is concerned with adaptations that occur within institutions, markets, management, social, and other associations governed by informal or formal rule systems – in fact, any of the terms might be used in place of "heuristic" and this definition works for me.

The common denominator is Simon's scissors, the process of adaptation, and coevolution. In line with this analogy, Smith is deeply suspicious of the lists of biases produced by those behavioral economists who study the cognitive blade only, which leads to what appears to be deep flaws. And, as already seen in Chapter 3, Smith's suspicion is justified.

Simon's three principles provide a useful template for freeing behavioral economics from its focus on deviations from utility theory and the routine (mis)interpretation of these deviations as flaws in the mind rather than in the theory. We need to take uncertainty and intractability seriously, be it in economic or other settings, instead of pretending that our world can be modeled as just risk and ambiguity. We need to take heuristics seriously, instead of clinging to the notion that optimization is the best solution to all problems. Finally, we need to accept that there is no single solution to all problems and, instead, become aware of and develop an adaptive cognitive toolbox containing multiple tools, each useful for different classes of problems. The human brain evolved to find solutions to problems without wasting time and energy, and fast-and-frugal heuristics embody this value. This is the stuff that intuitions are made of.

[35] Smith (2008), p. 36.

CHAPTER 6

*Embodied Heuristics**

> Our body is the ultimate instrument of all our external knowledge, whether intellectual or practical.
>
> *Michael Polanyi*[1]

Jean Piaget once said that he could not think without a pen in hand. For him, writing *was* thinking, not simply the translation of thought onto paper.[2] Accordingly, his theory of cognitive development begins with the child's sensory and motor processes, which are eventually transformed into mental life, where they turn into cognitive operations and structures. The general idea that cognition is closely intertwined with action was later called *embodied cognition*. This term has been used for a highly diverse set of ideas, including cognition situated in the environment.[3]

In this chapter, I start with an evolutionary view on intuitive decision-making before introducing the concept of *embodied heuristics*, that is, rules-of-thumb that exploit specific sensory and motor capacities in order to facilitate high-quality decisions in an uncertain world. Models of heuristics take an algorithmic rather than axiomatic approach to represent the process of decision-making. I present a case study of the gaze heuristic that illustrates how an embodied heuristic exploits sensory and motor abilities and how the heuristic has been adapted to the specific abilities of different species. Moreover, the heuristic has also come to solve new tasks created by human culture. I begin with what might have been the first decisions made by living organisms.

The Dawn of Intuitive Decision-Making

The earth is about 4.5 billion years old. Life emerged some 3.8 billion years ago, and animals much later, about 1 billion years ago. It began in

---

* This chapter is based on Gigerenzer (2021b).   [1] Polanyi (1966/2009), p. 20.
[2] Gruber & Vonèche (1977).   [3] Wilson (2002).

the form of single-celled organisms equipped with early versions of sensors and a small repertoire of actions. The best-studied single-celled organism is a bacterium called E. coli (named after its discoverer, the pediatrician Theodor Escherich), which can be found in the lower intestine of humans and other warm-blooded organisms. Its popularity with researchers arises from the observation that it seems not to die, but, instead, splits into two daughter bacteria, which again split, and so on.[4] E. coli can perform two motions, run or tumble, that is, move in a straight line or randomly change its course. It continuously switches between these actions, but when its sensors detect increasing concentrations of food, tumbling is reduced.[5] Here, we see the earliest form of decision-making: bacteria choosing between two actions, run or tumble, guided by chemical cues in their environment. These actions serve adaptive goals, finding food and avoiding toxins. The bacteria rely on decreasing or increasing rates of various chemicals as cues. In decision theory, a cue is a sign, or clue, of something that is not directly accessible, such as food or toxins.

Bacteria are *prokaryotes*, cells without a nucleus. Much later, *eukaryotes* arose from a merger of bacterial cells and eventually formed plants, mushrooms, and animals. Eukaryotes also formed "eyespots," which mark the beginning of vision and allow for further cues to guide action. One of these, light, has a dual function. For some organisms, such as single-celled organisms and plants, light is mainly a source of energy, supplying solar power. Although humans and other animals also sunbathe, for them light is primarily a source of information. Humans *infer* the outside world from patterns of light.

As humans cannot directly see the world, inference is crucial. Our inferences are more elaborate than those of single cells, yet remain intelligent "bets" based on uncertain cues. The great physiologist Hermann von Helmholtz spoke of "unconscious inferences" because even humans are not aware of how they make these inferences, such as reconstructing a three-dimensional world from a two-dimensional retinal image. Unconscious inferences border on magic, given that an infinite number of states of the world are consistent with this retinal image. Through millions of years of learning, sensory and motor abilities have evolved in tandem with heuristics that help to make good inferences in such situations of uncertainty – to find food and mates, to avoid toxins and predators, and to solve the basic goals of organisms.

---

[4] Khamsi (2005).   [5] For a philosopher's account, see Godfrey-Smith (2016).

Along with individual inferences, social behavior evolved. Consider E. coli again. It reacts not only to signs of edible food and dangerous toxins but also to chemicals that signal the presence of other bacteria. This reaction opened the door to the evolution of *coordination* between organisms, that is, social behavior. An example is *quorum sensing* among bacteria living inside of squids. Bacteria produce light through a chemical reaction, but only if enough other bacteria are around to join in. They appear to follow a simple heuristic: The more of the signaling chemical one senses, the more light one produces.[6] The production of light serves its host, the squid, as camouflage. Without this light, predators from below would see the shadow of squids, which are nocturnal animals, as cast by the moonlight. In humans, social coordination takes many forms, including communication, cooperation, and competition, and has led to cultural systems such as churches, political parties, and the market.

Let us now consider a concrete example of how inferences are made based on an embodied heuristic.

Embodied Heuristics: An Illustration

Ants, like humans, make real-estate choices, that is, decisions about where to live, which are essential to their fitness. Consider *Leptothorax albipennis*, a small, approximately 3 mm long ant that lives in colonies with up to 500 workers and a single queen. When their old nest is destroyed, the ant colony sends out scouts to locate a new site with a sufficiently large area to house the entire colony. The ants prefer nest sites that consist of narrow cracks in rocks with flat areas. How can a scout ant estimate the irregular area of a candidate site? A series of ingenious experiments revealed that the scout ants use a smart rule called *Buffon's needle algorithm*, named after the French 18th-century mathematician Buffon, who discovered this millennia after the ants did.[7]

To determine the size of the area, the scout ant first runs for a fixed period (less than 2 minutes) on an irregular path that covers the area fairly evenly. While doing so, it leaves behind a trail of pheromones. After that, the ant exits the area and then returns, where it repeats the procedure of running around in an irregular way. In the second round, the ant counts how often it crosses its own pheromone trail and uses the count to estimate

---

[6] Ibid., p. 19.
[7] Mallon & Franks (2000). On heuristics shared by humans and other animal species, see Hutchinson & Gigerenzer (2005).

the area of the site: the larger the number of crossings, the smaller the area. This heuristic is amazingly accurate: For a site that is half the size of the area needed, the frequency of crossing is 1.96 times greater.[8]

In Buffon's original problem, the question asked is: What is the probability p that a needle dropped on a floor made of parallel and equally wide strips of wood will end up lying across a line between two strips? For a needle of length l, $p = 2l/\pi t$, where t is the width of the strips. Buffon used the solution to calculate the precise value of number pi. In the ant's heuristic, the lines are the ant's pheromone trail and the needles lying across lines are the ant's crossings of its own trail. The ant is not interested in pi, but in the length t between lines, which indicates the area.

The ant's heuristic involves its body in several ways. First, the ant needs to move about. The heuristic would not work if the ant simply sat still and looked around. Second, the ant's body produces a pheromone trail, which its sensory system has the ability to recognize. These biological functions are necessary for the heuristic to be executed, but it is not sufficient. In addition, the ant needs cognitive abilities such as counting crossings and retaining a memory of the count. Many insects can, in fact, measure and memorize the rate at which they encounter stimuli.[9] All in all, ants have evolved an embodied heuristic to infer the area of potential nest sites.

Unlike the ant's implementation of Buffon's needle algorithm, many models of heuristics do not make reference to specific sensory or motor abilities. An example is the investment heuristic 1/N, which solves the problem of how to invest a sum of money into N assets by allocating it equally. In the uncertain world of stocks, this fast-and-frugal heuristic has been shown to be able to outperform the Noble Prize-winning mean variance portfolio.[10] However, 1/N does not specify or require specific sensorimotor abilities; dividing a sum by the number of assets can also be done by a pocket calculator. Operating a calculator, of course, also requires some motor and cognitive abilities, but these are only needed to operate a machine that does the actual work of finding a solution.

I will reserve the term *embodied heuristic* for rules that require specific sensory and/or motor abilities to be executed. In the section "The Gaze Heuristic," I describe in more detail an embodied heuristic that directs intuition and that humans share with animal species.

---

[8] Mugford et al. (2001).   [9] Stephens & Krebs (1986).   [10] DeMiguel et al. (2009).

The Gaze Heuristic

When faced with a ball high up in the air, experienced baseball outfielders know where to run in order to catch it. Based on years of experience, most players run guided by intuition, without being able to explain how exactly they intercept the ball. How do they do it? One approach to finding an answer is to treat the question as an optimal control problem and assume close-to-omniscient players who can make complex calculations unconsciously. That is how Richard Dawkins in *The Selfish Gene* thinks a player catches a ball:[11]

> He behaves as if he had solved a set of differential equations in predicting the trajectory of the ball. He may neither know nor care what a differential equation is, but this does not affect his skill with the ball. At some subconscious level, something functionally equivalent to the mathematical calculations is going on.

To determine the trajectory of the ball, consciously or unconsciously, the player has to estimate the parameters in this formula:

$$z(x) = x\left(\tan \alpha_0 + \frac{mg}{\beta v_0 \cos \alpha_0}\right) + \frac{m^2 g}{\beta^2} \ln\left(1 - \frac{\beta}{m} \frac{x}{v_0 \cos \alpha_0}\right) \quad \text{(EQUATION 6.1)}$$

where $z(x)$ is the height of the ball at flight distance x, measured from the position where the ball was thrown. At $z(x) = 0$, the ball hits the ground. To calculate $z(x)$, the player has to estimate both the initial angle α_0 of the ball's direction relative to the ground and the initial speed v_0 of the ball; know the ball's mass m, the friction β, and that the acceleration of earth g is 9.81 m/s2 (meter/second squared); and be able to calculate the tangent and cosine. Even then, the formula is overly simplified; for instance, it ignores wind and spin. Importantly, the true challenge is not to compute the equation, but to estimate its parameters, such as the initial angle and the initial speed.

Note that Dawkins inserted the term "as if" into his explanation of how players solve the goal. He was well aware that players do not calculate trajectories; they only behave *as if* they did. In his account, what players actually do at the subconscious level remains a mystery. That mystery has been resolved by experimental studies. Experienced players catch a fly ball by using a heuristic that has absolutely nothing to do with calculating a trajectory (see Figure 6.1):

---

[11] Dawkins (1989), p. 95.

Figure 6.1. Gaze heuristic. The player adjusts the running speed so that the angle of gaze remains constant. The angle of gaze is the angle between the line from eye to ball and the ground.

Gaze heuristic: Fixate your eyes on the ball, run, and adjust your speed so that the angle of gaze remains constant.

The gaze heuristic ignores all the information necessary for computing a trajectory and attends to one variable only, the angle of gaze. In this way, it avoids any measurement errors when estimating the parameters in Equation 6.1. It consists of three "building blocks" – fixating, running, and adjusting – and works in situations where the ball is already high in the air. If that is not the case, the player needs to adapt the third building block:

Fixate your eyes on the ball, run, and adjust your speed so that the image of the ball rises at a constant rate.

One can easily see the logic. If the image of the ball rises at an accelerating rate, the ball will hit the ground behind the player's present position, meaning that the player needs to run backward. If it rises at a decreasing rate, the ball will hit the ground ahead of the player, who then needs to run faster. If the image of the ball rises at a constant rate, the player is running at the correct speed.[12]

The gaze heuristic is an embodied heuristic. It requires the ability to hold one's gaze on an object, to run, and to adjust one's running speed. These abilities are learned early in development. For instance, babies begin to exercise the visual tracking of moving objects at around two months of age, such as tracking the objects in mobiles.[13] These bodily abilities are part of the solution. The gaze heuristic is also an intuitively used rule – as I have mentioned, most players cannot explain the heuristic process they use unconsciously.

Predicting Behavior: As-If Models Versus Embodied Heuristics

Two more general points need to be noted. First, reliance on as-if models rather than process models can mislead researchers regarding the actual goal of an organism. The trajectory calculation model suggests that the player's goal is to determine the point where the ball hits the ground (or is at a height in reach of the player) and then run to this point (see Table 6.1). The gaze heuristic, in contrast, implies that the goal is to

Table 6.1. *The as-if trajectory calculation model and the gaze heuristic compared.*

	Trajectory Calculation	Gaze Heuristic
Player's goal	*Compute landing point*	*Intercept ball*
Prediction 1: Speed	Runs full speed to landing point	The angle of gaze controls running speed and its change. ✔
Prediction 2: Interception	At the landing point, player waits to catch ball.	Intercepts ball while running. ✔
Prediction 3: Course	Runs in a straight line.	Runs in a slight arc. ✔
Prediction 4: Landing point	Knows where the ball is landing.	Does not know landing point. ✔

The as-if trajectory calculation model and the gaze heuristic make different predictions about both behavior and cognitive processes. In addition, they imply different specifications of the player's goal. The checkmarks show the predictions supported by experimental studies.

---

[12] McBeath et al. (1995); Shaffer & McBeath (2002).   [13] Jonsson & von Hofsten (2003).

intercept the ball. No knowledge about the landing point is necessary; the heuristic leads the player to the ball. A heuristic is not a just an efficient means toward a given end. It can specify what exactly the player wants to achieve. Means can determine ends, not just the other way around.

Now consider the famous argument by economist Milton Friedman that theories should not be concerned with psychological realism, only with good prediction. Friedman illustrated his argument with the story of a billiard player. What the player actually does is of no relevance for Friedman, who just assumed that the player behaves as if they had calculated the ball's trajectory and makes good predictions based on false assumptions. Friedman's as-if philosophy is decidedly antipsychological: Unraveling the process underlying the players' intuition is considered irrelevant. This attitude has been adopted by most economic models, including the as-if utility models in behavioral economics to which free parameters were added.

The gaze heuristic and the study of heuristics in general, however, show a surprising result: Psychological realism can lead to better predictions than as-if models. Let us take a closer look at three predictions about players' behavior.

Consider first the running speed. The trajectory model suggests that players perform better the faster they run to the expected landing point, which provides time for last-second adjustments. In contrast, the gaze heuristic very specifically predicts that players' speed is controlled by the angle of gaze, which determines speed and its change. If players run too fast, they will miss the ball.

Second, consider interception. According to the trajectory model, players should ideally arrive at the landing point before the ball and wait for it. The gaze heuristic, in contrast, implies that players catch the ball while running. The reason is that they adjust their running speed until they catch the ball. In both cases, the predictions following from the gaze heuristic have been supported by experimental studies.[14]

Next, consider the course of running. According to the trajectory model, the player will run straight to the landing point. In contrast, the gaze heuristic can imply, in certain situations, that players run in a slight arc to maintain a constant angle of gaze. These arcs have also been demonstrated in experiments with skilled outfielders.[15]

---

[14] See, for example, McBeath et al. (1995); Shaffer & McBeath (2002).
[15] Shaffer & McBeath (2002).

Finally, if players consciously or intuitively computed the landing point, as assumed by the trajectory model, they would know where the ball will land. No such knowledge is implied by the gaze heuristic. Studies show that even experienced players have difficulties estimating the trajectory of the ball, its apex, and the landing point, yet are nevertheless able to catch the ball.[16]

The general point is that the as-if trajectory model ignores the heuristic process and, thus, makes incorrect predictions about the resulting behavior. It treats the problem as one of calculating landing points, whereas the heuristic treats it as one of coordination between body and ball. Moreover, the analysis of ball-catching shows that the underlying process is heuristical and embodied.

Coordination Problems

The gaze heuristic and its relatives can resolve various coordination problems. These include interception, such as when athletes catch balls, but also avoidance of collisions, as in sailing and flying. When beginners learn to sail, they are taught a version of the gaze heuristic to infer whether another boat is on a collision course: Fixate your gaze on the other boat; if the angle of gaze remains constant, change your course quickly. When beginners learn to fly a light aircraft, they may be taught a further version of the same rule: If another plane approaches and you fear collision, look at a scratch in your windshield and observe whether the other plane moves relative to that scratch; If it doesn't, dive away immediately – otherwise, that plane might end up colliding with your plane.

The "miracle on the Hudson River" is a famous case where reliance on the gaze heuristic saved lives. On January 15, 2009, US Airways Flight 1549 collided with a flock of Canada geese shortly after takeoff, which shut down both engines. The pilots had to make a life-and-death decision: to try to reach the next airport or attempt a risky landing in the Hudson River. Landing at the next airport would have been the safer option, but only if the plane could actually make it that far. As copilot Jeffrey Skiles explained, to determine whether the sailing plane could safely make it to the airport, they did not try to calculate the trajectory of the plane, but, instead, relied on a version of the gaze heuristic:[17]

---

[16] Shaffer & McBeath (2005).   [17] Rose (2009).

It's not so much a mathematical calculation as visual, in that when you are flying in an airplane, a point that you can't reach will actually rise in your windshield. A point that you are going to overfly will descend in your windshield.

The point in the windshield rose, which meant the plane would have crashed before reaching the airport. The heuristic helped to make the right decision; all passengers and crew survived the landing on the river.

Note the conscious and unconscious uses of this heuristic, as illustrated by the pilots and the outfielders, respectively. Unlike pilots, most outfielders rely on the gaze heuristic without being able to explain how they catch a ball. Their behavior is intuitive, not based on conscious deliberation.[18] In general, heuristics may be learned consciously, by instruction, or unconsciously, by trial-and-error learning or imitation. The process is the same, a fact overlooked by dual-process theories that align heuristics with unconsciousness and, moreover, assume different processes.[19]

Exaptation

The gaze heuristic was not invented by baseball outfielders. Bats, birds, fish, and other animals rely on it for intercepting prey and mates.[20] The observation that different species rely on the same heuristic invites two possible explanations: *homology* and *analogy*. Homology means that common structures between different species – here, common heuristics – are due to a common evolutionary ancestor. Analogy means that there is a functional similarity based on something else than common ancestors. Whatever the correct explanation is, we can safely assume that the gaze heuristic evolved for predator–prey interaction and not for baseball or cricket.

Cognitive anthropologist Dan Sperber distinguished the proper domain of a cognitive module from its actual domain, that is, the domain for which a module actually evolved from a domain to which it was extended or transferred.[21] Similarly, the term *exaptation* means that a trait or feature acquires a new function beyond its original one derived by evolution. It was introduced as an alternative to the concept of *preadaptation* in order to emphasize that the original function was not connected to the new function.[22] A classic example is the argument that feathers had not evolved for flight with birds, but originally had the function of temperature

---

[18] Gigerenzer (2007). [19] See Kruglanski & Gigerenzer (2011).
[20] See Collett & Land (1975). [21] Sperber (1994). [22] Gould & Vrba (1982).

regulation in their ancestors, reptiles. Eventually, feathers became enlisted for a new function, sailing and, eventually, flying. I have not yet seen a discussion of exaptation with respect to heuristics, embodied or not, but the gaze heuristic is a clear case in point. The section "Predator–Prey Coordination" describes its proper domain, or original function.

Predator–Prey Coordination

How does a hawk intercept a duck? Figure 6.2 (a) and (b) shows two strategies for interception. The first is *direct pursuit*, where the hawk flies straight at the duck, that is, takes the shortest path. When the duck changes its position, the hawk changes its direction accordingly, so that the distance between it and the duck is always the shortest possible. The top-left panel shows a case of direct pursuit that ends in a failed interception with a characteristic wavering tail chase.[23] The second strategy is a version of the gaze heuristic, where the hawk does not fly in a straight line toward the duck. Rather, it initially flies toward an expected point X where it would intercept the duck if the latter did not change course (top-right panel). The angle α between the duck, the hawk, and the interception point X defines the angle of gaze. When the duck changes course, the hawk also changes its course so that the angle of gaze remains constant. In geometric terms, the angle of gaze is the base angle of a triangle with equal sides and apex X.

Which of the two heuristics do hawks employ? Studies with headcams mounted on hawks showed that they rely on the gaze heuristic.[24] The comparison between direct pursuit and the gaze heuristic in Figure 6.2 indicates why: Relying on the latter allows for faster interception and avoids the wavering tail chase. Moreover, because the hawk does not fly directly toward the duck, its attack is less obvious. Only when the target is stationary do hawks rely on direct pursuit, that is, fly directly toward the prey.

To be successful in pursuit, an organism needs the ability to adjust speed and direction quickly when the angle changes (due to wind in the case of the fly ball or due to evasive movements in the case of the duck). The number of possible adjustments per second is the *visual cycle rate*. Raptors have a visual cycling rate of about 200 per second, whereas humans have a much lower rate of about 10 per second.[25] The cycling rate corresponds to the length of the path A before it can be adjusted to maintain a constant angle of gaze. The smaller A *is*, the faster is the hawk's

---

[23] Hamlin (2017).   [24] Kane et al. (2015).   [25] Hamlin (2017).

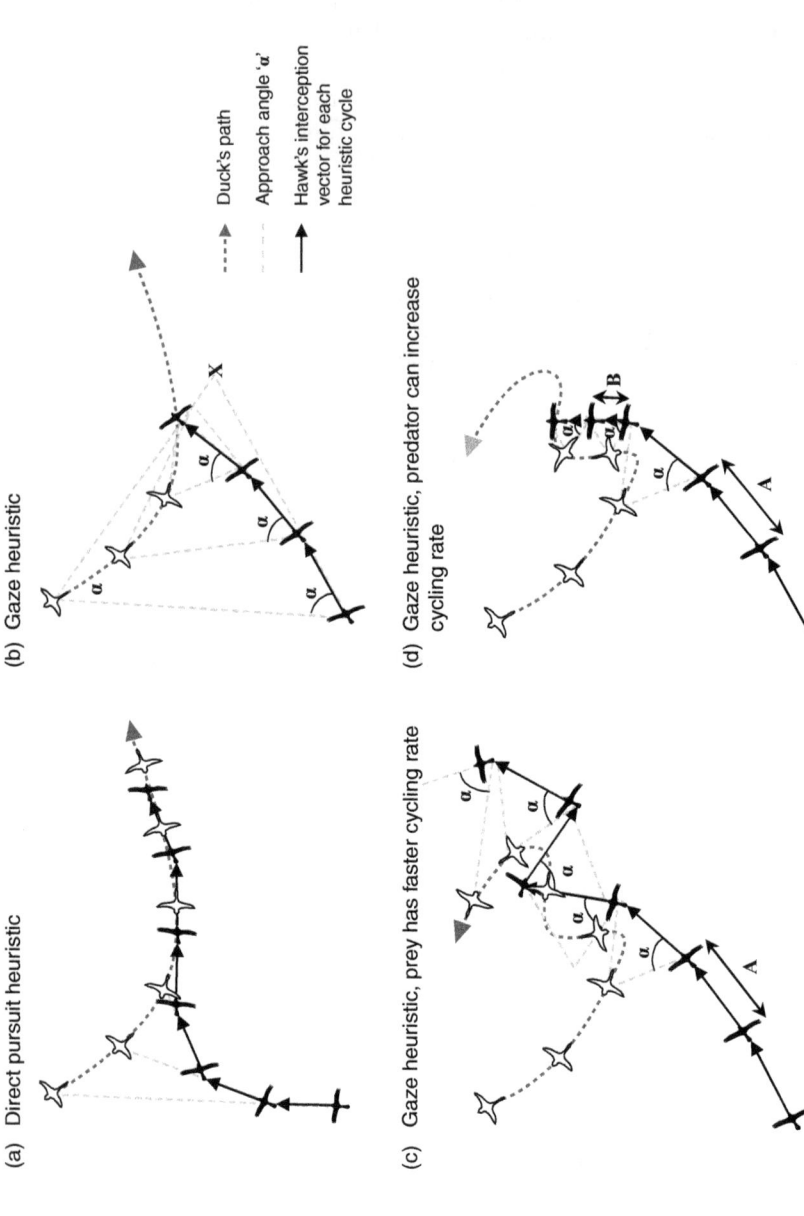

Figure 6.2. Predators (dark hawks) pursuing prey (white ducks). (a) Direct pursuit heuristic: A predator flies in the direction that is the shortest path to the prey and adjusts the direction when the prey changes its course. If predator and prey fly at the same speed, the result is a characteristic wavering pursuit pattern. (b) *Gaze heuristic*: A predator determines the angle α between the direct line to the prey and the initial estimate X of the intersection point and then adjusts its direction to the subsequent flight path of the duck so that α remains constant. Even when both predator and prey fly at the same speed, the predator can intercept the prey. (c) *Gaze heuristic*, prey has faster cycling rate: The number of adjustments an animal can make per second is its cycling rate, represented by the length A of its path before it can change its direction. Here, the prey has a faster cycling rate than the predator, which enables it to evade the predator. (d) *Gaze heuristic*, predator can increase cycling rate: Here, the predator has the ability to increase the cycling rate from A to B, which is higher than that of the prey, resulting in fast interception. Adapted from Hamlin (2017).

cycling rate. Panel (c) in Figure 6.2 shows a prey with a faster cycling rate than the hawk and avoids interception by changing its course before the hawk is able to do so. Thanks to a faster cycling rate, the prey can even get behind the predator. Although the hawk keeps the optical angle constant, it is too slow to adjust. Finally, panel (d) shows a successful predator that increases its cycling rate in the final stage of the pursuit from *A* to *B*.

From Gaze to Echolocation and Whiskers

The gaze heuristic is named after the visual sense, but it has been adapted to other senses, too. Bats rely on the equivalent of the gaze heuristic when hunting moths in darkness, but their interception is based on sound not vision. They use an echolocation system that emits sound as a series of short "clicks" or "calls."[26] When a target is located, the clicks occur more frequently as the bat closes in on a prey. In response to bats, moths have evolved bat-detecting ears capable of hearing the clicks.[27] Outside the bat's detection range, a moth's first reaction is to fly away from the bat. If the frequency of clicks increases, meaning that the bat has detected its prey, this triggers spasms in the moth's wings, resulting in unpredictable flight. Finally, if the clicks peak in a buzz of about 200 clicks a second, the moth's reflex is to instantly freeze to fall out of the bat's path. All this happens within seconds. The bat's click rate corresponds to the visual cycle rate of humans and hawks.

The gaze heuristic can also enlist tactile senses. At the final stage of pursuit, mammals such as cats, rats, and seals use their whiskers, an array of long, coarse hairs around the head and mouth that provide information about the prey's position in the final milliseconds before impact.[28] Experiments have shown that rats were less successful in completing an interception of a mouse when their whiskers were removed, and, if they did succeed, the final bite to the neck took longer and was messier.[29]

The Royal Air Force Discovers the Gaze Heuristic

According to a historical analysis, the Royal Air Force (RAF), after some trial and error, was the first to have discovered the gaze heuristic around the beginning of World War II.[30] The problem was that the British controllers who used radar to direct fighters to enemy planes had failed

---

[26] Denny (2004). [27] Hofstede & Ratcliffe (2016). [28] Grant et al. (2009).
[29] Hamlin (2017). [30] This section is based on Hamlin (2017).

to reach the required 90 percent interception rate. Special calculating devices and increasingly complex mathematics were introduced to crunch the numbers, but to no avail. In this situation, an impatient RAF commander demonstrated that he could meet the 90 percent rate by eye. His system was fleshed out by the Chairman of the Committee for the Scientific Survey of Air Defence (CSSA), Sir Henry Tizard, into a fixed angle approach (the gaze heuristic) and taught to the controllers.

After being trained to use the gaze heuristic, the British controllers no longer sent pilots directly via the shortest distance toward the opponent (the direct pursuit heuristic), but, instead, estimated an intersection point X, which determined the constant angle. If the bomber changed course after having recognized the fighter, the fighter was directed to change course too, but keep the angle constant. Shortly before interception, the faster fighter could turn around and meet the bomber frontally, where it was most vulnerable (Figure 6.3). This system became known as the *Tizzy Angle* and was used for the remainder of the war.

According to historical records and training materials, the controllers of the German Luftwaffe relied, instead, on a direct pursuit strategy and appeared to have never discovered the gaze heuristic during the war. In the pursuit control technique, the controller instructs the pilot (who cannot yet see the enemy plane) to fly directly toward the opponent. If the opponent changes course, the pilot is directed to also change course and take the shortest path toward the opponent. The pursuit strategy vectors the fighter behind its opponent, just as the hawk trails behind the duck in Figure 6.2 (panel (a)), and leads to a smaller rate of interception. Although

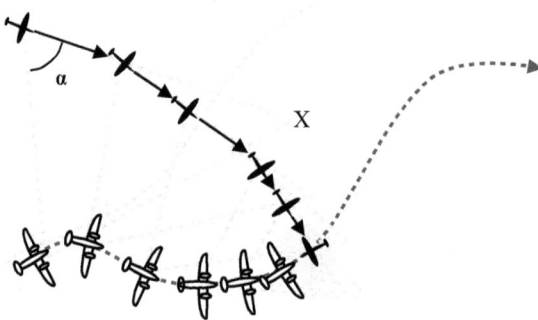

Figure 6.3. British controllers' reliance on the gaze heuristic to direct fighter planes to intercept German bombers. From Hamlin (2017).

the Germans' radar system was superior to that of the RAF in several respects, the British use of the gaze heuristic was devastating to the Luftwaffe and decisive for the Battle of Britain. Robert Hamlin conjectured that the Germans might have won this battle had they linked their high-tech radar system with a gaze-based heuristic control system. In spite of their superior missile technology, including anti-aircraft missiles based on the direct pursuit strategy, the Germans were missing a crucial smart heuristic.

After World War II, the US army combined German missile technology with the British gaze heuristic system into a most successful autonomous guided weapon: the Sidewinder A1M9 short-range air-to-air missile. The missile is a simple, robust interception system whose "gaze" is directed at a point source of heat, which is the target. Once the missile is on its way, it makes continuous inquiries (with a rapid cycle rate) about the changes of the target's position and adjusts its direction so that the angle of "gaze" remains constant. The Sidewinder is still in use in many nations, and new developments appear to be based on the same heuristic of maintaining a constant angle of approach.

Unconscious Intelligence

The gaze heuristic is a particularly interesting example of embodied heuristics. This amazing feat of evolution, a dynamic adaptive heuristic, enables animals and humans to make rapid decisions with the help of a highly automated system superior to conscious reasoning. I end the chapter with some general insights that this case study provides.

As we have seen, the gaze heuristic is a simple iterative heuristic that adapts to changes in flight path due to wind in the case of a fly ball or due to evasion attempts in the case of prey. It can solve problems in stationary and nonstationary environments and is embodied in the sense that it requires specific sensory and motor capabilities to function efficiently. The astonishing feature of the heuristic is that it has enlisted different sensory capacities in different species, including vision, echolocation, and tactile senses. It also has enlisted various motor abilities. When hawks pursue prey, they implement the gaze heuristic when flying; when dogs catch a Frisbee, they implement the heuristic when running;[31] and when teleost fish pursue prey, they implement the heuristic when swimming. Humans implement the heuristic both in a two-dimensional space, as

---

[31] Shaffer et al. (2004).

when trying to avoid a collision with another sailboat, and in a three-dimensional space, as when trying to avoid a collision in the air.

The heuristic has also inspired rethinking financial regulation. Andrew Haldane, the former Bank of England's chief economist, presented his acclaimed Jackson Hole talk entitled "The Dog and the Frisbee" on the gaze heuristic as a model for a safer world of banking. He argued for introducing simple and robust control systems in place of complex regulatory systems, which neither foresaw nor prevented the crisis of 2008.[32] For instance, capital requirements are estimated by calculating the value-at-risk of a bank, which may involve estimating thousands of risk factors and millions of covariation coefficients. The limited success of these estimations recalls the calculations made by the RAF before it discovered the gaze heuristic. The banking system is a fast-changing, nonstationary environment where simple rules can lead to better and more transparent decisions. The standard approach in cognitive science, however, has resembled bank regulation, based on the assumption that more complexity is always better. Journals are filled with highly parameterized models that integrate all possible relevant information, Bayesian or otherwise. Complexity pays for well-defined situations such as games, but leads to overfitting and fragile solutions in ill-defined situations of uncertainty.

Evolution has given us the gaze heuristic, and with it a pointer: To uncover more of the ingenious solutions it has found for a brain the size of two fists, we need a systematic study of embodied heuristics in the real world.

---

[32] Haldane & Madouros (2012).

CHAPTER 7

*Moral Intuition**

> Natural selection is an amoral process, yet it can produce moral intuitions.
> *Leda Cosmides and John Tooby*[1]

> Intuitions come first, strategic reasoning second.
> *Jonathan Haidt*[2]

Work hard. Be honest and disciplined. Be punctual and reliable. Don't waste your earnings on pleasure, power, and material comfort. Live frugally and reinvest your income to accumulate more capital. The moral intuition that one should be disciplined, work hard, and not squander time accumulating luxury objects is acquired by cultural learning. It comes quickly to mind in cultures endorsing these values when people observe others not working hard and appearing to be unproductive. According to sociologist Max Weber, this kind of self-discipline is the moral essence of the *Protestant work ethic*, which became the blueprint for forms of modern capitalism. It fuels distinct intuitions about self-expectations and life goals. In his painting *The Fight Between Carnival and Lent,* the Dutch artist Pieter Bruegel the Elder depicted the tension between the vices and virtues of puritanical morals. On the left side of the painting, women and men crowd into a tavern, play games, make music, sneak inside for sex, and play tricks on others. On the right side, men and women attend church, work, and are sober, decently clothed, orderly, and disciplined. How do moral norms come about and shape what people feel they ought to do?

A *moral intuition* is a feeling about what is right and wrong,

1. based on evolutionary and cultural learning,
2. which appears spontaneously in one's consciousness, and
3. whose underlying rationale is unconscious.

---

* This chapter is a revised version of Gigerenzer (2010).
[1] Cosmides & Tooby (2008), p. 54.
[2] Haidt (2013), title of Chapter 1.

According to Weber, the rationale underlying the Protestant work ethic is the doctrine of predestination: God has already decided who will be saved from damnation and who will not.[3] All that mortals can do is seek clues that might reveal whether they are among the chosen ones. Seeing oneself working hard and not wasting time on worldly pleasures is such a clue. Spending hours at the billiard table, shopping, or doing nothing is a sign of being among the doomed. Historically, this narrative of the meaning of life emerged in various Puritan religions, including Calvinism, Methodism, Pietism, and Baptism. It appears that only in these religions did capitalism become associated with the strict abstinence from the spontaneous enjoyment of life, while other forms of capitalism, before and after, feature luxury and display.

The crucial feature of a moral intuition is that its underlying rationale – such as the logic of the Protestant work ethic – is not conscious; it is not arrived at by going through steps of a logical argument or by the weighing of evidence. One strongly feels what is right and wrong without being able to articulate why. Even then, moral intuitions can be transmitted through generations.

Moral intuition needs to be distinguished from *moral reasoning,* a term that refers to moral convictions that originate from deliberate reflection. In the case of the Protestant work ethic, moral reasoning could mean that a person is aware of the doctrine of predestination and, after reflection, decides to live accordingly. In general, moral reasoning requires awareness of the religious or cultural origins of one's ethical convictions or a conscious deliberation of their utility. For instance, Benjamin Franklin, a proponent of the Protestant work ethic, reasoned about the utility of his moral principles. As he saw it, working hard and being honest, punctual, and frugal is useful because this behavior assures credit, and credit, in turn, enables accumulating more capital. Franklin's moral reasoning was deliberately utilitarian. Centuries later, many of us live by these moral principles without having reasoned through their foundations or having considered their utility. Moral reasoning has become intuitive.

The vision that morality is, or should be, based on reasoning is an old one. It has been known since the ancient Greeks and Romans, albeit with varying conclusions. In Cicero's words, once reason has taught the ideal Stoic – the wise man – that moral goodness is the only thing of real value, he is happy forever and the freest of men, since his mind is not enslaved by desires.[4] According to this, reason makes humans moral, or at least men.

---

[3] Weber (1930/1992).   [4] Cicero (De finibus 3), pp. 75–76.

As we saw in Chapter 2, into the early 20th century, psychologists believed that men's abstract reasoning enabled them to grasp general moral principles, while women's concrete, intuitive thinking prevented them from doing so. Thus, men who lied were held morally responsible, but women were not: They were considered merely incapable of understanding that their actions were evil.

Moral Satisficing

Moral philosophy and moral psychology have proposed various views of moral intuition and of its relation to moral reasoning.[5] On the one hand, some psychologists have proposed that moral behavior is the product of moral judgment, and that moral judgment, in turn, requires conscious deliberation. Lawrence Kohlberg's theory of moral development is a case in point, which holds moral reasoning as necessary for ethical behavior.[6] On the other hand, moral intuitionists such as psychologist Jonathan Haidt argued that moral judgment, like aesthetic judgment, is a rapid intuitive process, and that people engage in moral reasoning primarily to seek evidence that confirms the initial intuition.[7] My aim is not to summarize or do justice to the complexity of these approaches, nor do I believe that an opposition between reason and intuition is fruitful. The question I ask in this chapter is: What picture of moral intuition emerges from the perspective of ecological rationality?

The three key principles are uncertainty, social heuristics, and their interaction with the social environment:

1. **Moral intuition evolved to deal with situations of uncertainty, not risk:** We need to distinguish between situations of risk and uncertainty and between their respective tools, probability, and heuristics (see Chapter 5).
2. **Moral intuition is based on social heuristics:** In situations of uncertainty, much (not necessarily all) of moral behavior is guided by heuristics. Specifically, I will argue that these heuristics are typically social heuristics.
3. **Ecological morality:** The resulting moral behavior depends not only on the social heuristic but also on the environment. It results from the

---

[5] For an overview, see Sinnott-Armstrong (2008).   [6] Kohlberg (1984).
[7] Haidt (2001, 2008).

match (or mismatch) of the heuristics with the structure of the social environment.

I will refer to this approach as *moral satisficing*.[8] This term has been used by moral philosophers, but often in the negative sense of a second-best strategy.[9] These kinds of statements assume a situation of risk, where maximization (of utility or happiness) is actually feasible. However, in situations of uncertainty, maximization is a fiction and, equally important, satisficing can outperform complex strategies (see Chapter 5).[10] A normative theory that is uninformed of the workings of the mind or impossible to be actually executed by humans or computers (e.g., because maximization is computationally intractable) is unlikely to be of much benefit in the real world.

Which heuristics underlie moral behavior? One answer would be, specifically, moral heuristics, such as "don't kill" and "don't lie."[11] These are the fabric of the Ten Commandments of the Bible and other sacred books. In my view, assuming specialized moral heuristics is unnecessary and, moreover, obscures the close relation between social coordination and moral behavior. My hypothesis that moral rules are typically social heuristics contrasts with the postulate of specifically moral rules by rule consequentialism, as well as the view that humans have a specially "hardwired" moral grammar with specialized moral rules.

Following Hume rather than Kant, my aim is not to provide a normative theory that tells us how we ought to behave, but to provide a descriptive theory with prescriptive consequences, such as how to design environments that help people reach their own goals. Informed by psychology, moral satisficing is what philosophers call *naturalism*, as opposed to supernaturalism, spiritualism, or moral paternalism, where ethics is guided by religion and sacred books.[12]

Social Narratives Select Heuristics

Weber contrasted the Protestant work ethic with traditional Catholic doctrine, which assumes that our individual fates are not predetermined, but in our own hands. People living by this narrative can go through cycles of sin, repentance, and forgiveness, play billiards, and enjoy other worldly

---

[8] Gigerenzer (2010).
[9] See Byron (2004), p. 192; Richardson (2004), p. 127; and the contributions to *Satisficing and Maximizing* (Byron, 2004).
[10] Gigerenzer & Brighton (2009).   [11] Sunstein (2005).   [12] Kitcher (1992).

pleasures without feeling guilty. Life is not centered on the question of whether one is among the chosen, and there is no pressure to find out. In this way, the Catholic narrative implies a different ethic. Weber tells the story of employers who increased the hourly wages of their workers to get them to work longer for a limited time, such as at harvest. In modern economic theory, higher pay is an incentive, and workers should work longer hours to maximize their profit. To the surprise of the employers, however, many workers worked not more, but fewer, hours. Their work ethics was guided by a satisficing heuristic (Chapter 5) with an amount of money as an aspiration level:

Set an aspiration level α for sufficient earnings. Stop working when α is satisfied.

After earning the amount to which they had aspired, the workers stopped working and went home to spend the money and time together with their family. These workers, the employers learned, did not follow the Protestant work ethic. Getting them to work longer would have entailed reducing, not increasing, their hourly wages – a strategy that some capitalists actually followed. Contrast this with the heuristic selected by the Protestant work ethic:

Work hard and accumulate as much capital as possible. Do not spend it on pleasure.

This rule embodies the ideal of *maximizing*. Maximizing means trying to accumulate as much as possible of a good for its own sake, such as wealth.

Weber's comparison between Protestant and Catholic ethics illustrates the approach of ecological rationality. From this perspective, the meaning of life is uncertain, and, to give it a purpose, religious or social narratives such as the Protestant work ethic provide a moral framework for what one should and should not do. Darwin argued that these social narratives bolster group patriotism and provide an advantage over other tribes, thus leading to natural selection. Heuristics are the behavioral components of such a narrative, telling us what to do even if we are not fully aware of the underlying narrative.[13] As the case of satisficing illustrates, these heuristics are not necessarily specifically moral heuristics such as "don't steal"; rather, they can be the heuristics that guide behavior outside the moral domain. My hypothesis is that the narrative also defines whether a heuristic is considered a moral one. For instance, from the point of view of the Protestant work ethic, satisficing is immoral, but, seen from the Catholic

---

[13] See Tuckett (2011) on the role of narratives in decision-making.

doctrine, it is amoral, that is, stopping working when an aspiration is met is not seen as a moral issue in the first place.

In general, narratives can define the moral nature of human social relations. Anthropologist Alan Fiske distinguishes four kinds of relationships among which people move back and forth during their daily activities: communal sharing, authority ranking, market pricing, and equality matching.[14] In communal sharing, people give what they can and take what they need, be it within a couple, family, or larger community. Caring, kindness, and altruism are the moral virtues within the community, while in interaction with outside groups, aggression may be seen as legitimate.

Authority ranking relates to a community characterized by a social hierarchy, which selects heuristics embodying obedience, such as: *If a person is an authority, follow requests*. For instance, in Milgram's obedience studies, the experimenter instructed the participant to administer electric shocks of increasing intensity to a learner every time the learner gave an incorrect answer. The experiments implemented an authority narrative where subordinates reacted with respect and deference and superiors took paternalistic responsibility for them. That is not to say that selection is a one-to-one process; conflicts are the rule rather than the exception. For instance, in one condition of the obedience experiments, a confederate participant was introduced who sat next to the real participant and refused to continue the experiment after pressing the 90-V switch and hearing the learner's groan.[15] This situation might trigger both obedience and a conflicting heuristic, *imitate your peers*, here, to copy the other participant's refusal to be obedient. In that experiment, obedience won over social imitation. The majority of participants (63 percent) followed the authority and went on to give shocks of higher intensity, compared with 70 percent of those who did so without seeing someone refusing.

In market-pricing relations, moral judgment is guided by cost-benefit calculations, as in utilitarian theories of morality. For instance, economist Gary Becker told the story that he began to think about crime in the 1960s after he was late for an oral examination and had to decide whether to put his car in a parking lot or risk getting a ticket for parking illegally on the street. He calculated the likelihood of getting a ticket, the size of the penalty, and the cost of putting the car in a lot before deciding that it paid to take the risk and park on the street.[16] In Becker's view, violations of the law, be they petty or grave, are not due to an irrational motive, a bad

---

[14] Fiske (1992).   [15] Burger (2009).   [16] Becker (1995), p. 637.

Table 7.1. *A four-card problem: A social contract with a perspective change.*

WORKED ON THE WEEEKEND	DID GET A DAY OFF	DID NOT WORK ON THE WEEKEND	DID NOT GET A DAY OFF
P	Q	not-P	not-Q

When participants were cued into the perspective of an employee, most turned over the "worked on the weekend" and "did not get a day off" cards. When they were cued into the perspective of an employer, they turned over the other two cards.

character, or mental illness, but can be explained as a rational choice based on the calculus of expectation.

Finally, in equality-matching relations, people keep track of the balance of favors and know what is required to restore the balance. Examples are social contracts in which both sides exchange benefits but also are obliged to pay the costs. Not paying the costs is cheating. Do people reason about social contracts in a logical way, as assumed in rational approaches to moral behavior, or do they rely on heuristic search for cheaters? In a series of experiments, Klaus Hug and I used *four-card problems*, also known as *Wason selection tasks*. Consider a social contract between employer and employee (see Table 7.1):[17]

Day-off rule:
If an employee works on the weekend, then that person gets a day off during the week.
The "cards" in Table 7.1 have information about four employees. Each card represents one person. One side of the card tells whether the person worked on the weekend, and the other side tells whether the person got a day off during the week. Indicate only the card(s) you definitely need to turn over to see if the rule has been violated.

Which cards would you turn over? According to the dictum that moral reasoning should follow the laws of logic, one would expect people to turn over the first and the last card. This is because the rule has the logical

---

[17] Gigerenzer & Hug (1992). These experiments resolved a debate between Leda Cosmides (1989), who had argued for a specific cheater detection module, and her critics who conjectured that social contracts for some unknown reason would simply increase logical answers – in her original work, cheating detection and logical reasoning predicted the same cards being chosen. The perspective experiments, however, showed clearly that the results cannot be explained by logic, but by cheating detection, albeit a perspectual one.

structure "If P then Q", and the only case in which it is violated is "P and not-Q," that is, "worked on the weekend" and "did not get a day off." Turning over these two cards can reveal such a violation. But the participants in our experiment chose these cards only when cued into the role of an employee. In that role, they were concerned about being cheated if they worked on the weekend, but did not get a day off. When cued into the role of an employer, however, the majority by far turned over the Q and not-P cards, which can reveal whether an employee cheated by taking a day off without having worked on the weekend. All in all, participants' search did not follow disembodied logic, but instead the heuristic "find out whether you or your group is being cheated." Thus, people were not reasoning by logic or with a Kantian moral, but with Machiavellian intelligence. Compared with the highly variable results previously reported in four-card problems that did not use social tasks, the striking result here was how highly consistent participants' choices were. These were made with little reflection, which has been interpreted to mean that intuitions about social contracts have been shaped by natural selection and have eventually become part of our "social instincts."[18]

Moral Intuition Is Based on Social Heuristics

Darwin thought that a combination of social instincts plus sufficient intellectual powers leads to the evolution of moral sense, and he proposed the coherence or coordination of human groups as its purpose:[19]

> There can be no doubt that a tribe including many members who, from possessing in a high degree the spirit of patriotism, fidelity, obedience, courage, and sympathy, were always ready to give aid to each other and to sacrifice themselves for the common good, would be victorious over most other tribes; and this would be natural selection. At all times throughout the world tribes have supplanted other tribes; and as morality is one element in their success, the standard of morality and the number of well-endowed men will thus everywhere tend to rise and increase.

If Darwin's assumption that one original function of morality was the coherence of groups is correct, then the heuristics underlying moral behavior should include those that can provide this function. Social heuristics such as imitate-your-peers are apt examples: They can foster social coherence. Note that this hypothesis opens up a different

[18] Cosmides & Tooby (2008). [19] Darwin (1871/1981), p. 166.

understanding of the nature of potential universals underlying moral behavior. For instance, proponents of the idea of a universal moral grammar that mirrors Chomsky's universal language grammar assume "hardwired" principles such as: Do as you would be done by; don't kill; don't cheat, steal, or lie; avoid adultery and incest; and care for children and the weak.[20] Critics responded that these values may be ours, but not those of other cultures and times: children sold into slavery by parents who feel entitled to do so; guilt-free spousal abuse by men who see it as their right; moral sanctioning of pregnant unmarried women by humiliation or driving them to suicide; and so forth.[21] A theory of moral behavior should avoid a present-day bias. Darwin captured this point long ago:[22]

> If for instance, to take an extreme case, men were reared under precisely the same conditions as hive-bees, there can hardly be a doubt that our unmarried females would, like the worker-bees, think it a sacred duty to kill their brothers, and mothers would strive to kill their fertile daughters; and no one would think of interfering.

We should not fail to notice that terrorists, the Mafia, and crack-dealing gangs run on strong moral intuitions.[23] For his film *Suicide Killers*, filmmaker Pierre Rehow interviewed would-be terrorists who had survived because their bombs failed to explode: "Every single one of them tried to convince me that it was the right thing to do for moralistic reasons."[24] Social psychologists have documented in our own cultures how a situation can stimulate evil behavior in ordinary people and how easily physical abuse of others can be elicited.[25] I suggest that the heuristics underlying moral behavior are not the mirror images of the Ten Commandments and their modern humanistic equivalents, but embody more general social principles that coordinate human groups. That means that one and the same heuristic can solve both problems that we call moral and those that we do not.[26]

The Moral Rim

The boundaries between what is deemed a moral issue shift over historical time and between cultures. Although contemporary Western moral psychology and philosophy often center on the issues of harm and individual

---

[20] Hauser (2006). [21] Pippin (2009). [22] Darwin (1871/1981), p. 73.
[23] Gambetta (1996). [24] Cited in Neiman (2008), p. 87.
[25] Burger (2009); Zimbardo (2007). [26] Gigerenzer (2008, 2010).

rights, such a constrained view of the domain of morality is unusual in history and other cultures. There existed more important moral values than avoiding harm to individuals. Abraham was asked by the Lord to kill his son, and his unquestioning readiness to heed God's command signaled a higher moral value, faith. For the ancient world, where human sacrifice was prevalent, the surprising part of the story was that God stopped the sacrifice.[27]

The story of the Sodomites who wanted to gang rape two strangers to whom Lot had offered shelter is another case in point. From a contemporary Western view, we might misleadingly believe that the major moral issue at stake here is rape or homosexuality, but hospitality was an essential moral duty at that time and remains so in many cultures. For Lot, this duty was so serious that he offered the raging mob his virgin daughters if they left his guests alone.[28] Similarly, in modern Europe, wasting energy, eating meat, or smoking in the presence of others were long seen as purely self-regarding decisions. Environmental protectionists, animal rights advocates, and anti-smoking groups have reinterpreted these as moral infractions that cause environmental pollution, the killing of animals, and lung cancer through secondhand smoking. I refer to the line that divides personal taste and moral virtues as the moral rim. The location of the moral rim describes whether a behavior is included in the moral domain. My hypothesis is that, wherever the rim is drawn, the underlying social heuristic is likely to remain the same.

Ecological Morality

Several accounts, normative and descriptive, from virtue theories to Kohlberg's stages of moral reasoning, assume that forces inside the mind – moral intuition or reasoning – are, or should be, the cause of moral behavior (unless someone actively prevents a person from executing it by threat or force). These theories provide a conceptual language for only one blade of Simon's scissors (see Chapter 5): the mind. Here, I would like to propose the notion of ecological morality, that is, that moral behavior results from an interaction between the mind and environment. As a consequence, the same moral intuition can lead to quite different moral outcomes, depending on the structure of the environment.

---

[27] Neiman (2008).   [28] Ibid.

Fairness

Consider the moral intuition of many parents that they should treat all their children equally in order to create fairness and justice. To implement this goal, many parents try to divide their time, love, and attention among their children equally:

Equality heuristic: To share a resource among N persons, divide it equally ($1/N$).

The equality heuristic, however, does not necessarily produce the desired result. The outcome depends on the particular environment, some of which can even generate systematic inequality. For instance, parents who try to divide their time each day between their children equally will attain the long-term goal of providing each child with equal time if they have exactly two children. But, if they have three or more children (excepting multiple births), the goal will be missed because the first-born and the last-born will end up receiving more time than the middle-borns.[29] The reason is that first-borns do not have to share parents' time with other siblings before these siblings are born, and last-borns do not have to share after the older ones have left the family. Only the middle-borns always have to share, and their disadvantage increases with the number of years between the siblings. This result illustrates that a heuristic can or cannot reach a fairness goal (all children should be given the same amount of time during their childhood), depending on the structure of the environment. In the present case, there are two relevant features of the environment: the larger the number of siblings (three or more) and the larger their temporal spacing, the greater the imbalance. The environment has the last word.

Imitation

Consider a second social heuristic (mentioned in the section "Social Narratives Select Heuristics") and how its outcome depends on the environment.

Imitate your peers: Do what the majority of your peers do.

Imitation is probably the most important social learning principle, together with teaching and language. No other species is known in which

---

[29] Hertwig et al. (2002). Related to fairness are reciprocity heuristics, such as "if you take the benefit, you have to pay the costs," see Tooby & Cosmides (1992).

individuals imitate the behavior of others as generally and precisely as Homo sapiens. Psychologist and primatologist Michael Tomasello argues that the precision and slavishness of imitation led to our remarkable culture.[30] Imitation enables us to accumulate what our ancestors have learned, thus replacing slow Darwinian evolutionary learning by a Lamarckian form of cultural inheritance.

Imitation can steer both good and bad moral action, from donating to charity to discriminating against minorities. If adolescents imitate the behavior of their peers, that can lead to mobbing and criminal action or to helpful and altruistic behavior, depending on the peer group that constitutes their social environment. The social heuristic and the environment are the joint causes of moral behavior. The same dependency holds in adult life. Those who refuse to imitate the behavior and the values of their social environment are likely to be called a coward or oddball if male, or a dishonor to the family if female. Imitating the majority virtually guarantees social acceptance in one's peer group and fosters shared community values.

Comradeship

As a final and dramatic case, consider a situation in July 1942 during World War II, as described by the historian Christopher Browning in his seminal book *Ordinary Men*.[31] Brought to the outskirts of a small Polish village, around 500 German men belonging to the German Reserve Police Batallion 101 were informed by their commander Major Trapp that they had been given a most unpleasant order from the highest authorities. There were some 1,800 Jews in the village, and the males of working age were to be brought to a work camp. The elderly, women, and children were to be shot. At this point, Trapp made an extraordinary offer: If any men did not feel up to the task, they could step out.

The men had only seconds to decide. A dozen stepped forward; the rest participated in the massacre. Why then did only 12 men decline to participate in mass murder?

Browning considered the obvious explanations. First, Nazi anti-Semitism. Yet, these men were mostly middle-aged family men considered too old to be drafted into the army, who had been educated in the pre-Nazi era with different moral values, and who came from a social class that was anti-Nazi in its political culture and from Hamburg, which was by

---

[30] Tomasello (2019). [31] Browning (1998).

reputation one of the least nazified cities in Germany. A second possible explanation is conformity with authority. But the extensive court interviews indicate that this was not the primary reason either. Moreover, Trapp had explicitly allowed for nonconformity. After taking several more explanations into account, including the lack of forewarning and concern about career advancement, Browning posited a different explanation, based on how men in uniforms identify with their comrades. Many of the policemen seem to have followed a social heuristic:

Don't break ranks.

According to Browning, the men felt "the strong urge not to separate themselves from the group by stepping out,"[32] even if that meant violating the moral imperative of not killing innocent people. Stepping out meant leaving one's comrades more than their share of the ugly task and losing face by doing so. Don't break ranks is a social heuristic that can lead to bravery in combat, such as risking one's life for one's comrades, but it can also lead to atrocities.

Trapp could have framed his offer the other way round, so that the social heuristic would not conflict with the Judeo-Christian commandment "don't murder." Browning suggested that if Trapp had asked that those men should step forward *who felt up to the task*, that is, to "opt in," the conflict would have been partially eliminated and the number of men who participated in the killing might have been considerably smaller. That is a thought experiment, no longer an analysis of the historical record. But it illustrates the ecological nature of moral behavior. Moreover, it indicates that by understanding the conflict between two moral intuitions – don't break ranks and don't kill innocent people – one can find solutions in the environment that can change what people do.

Systematic Inconsistencies

Inconsistencies between moral intuition and behavior are a surprise for virtue ethics. Virtues are believed to be character traits: A virtue makes a person a good one, a vice a bad one. For instance, for centuries, courage was a virtue for men and chastity was a virtue for women (see Chapter 2). Because these traits are considered to be stable, the resulting behavior should be consistently moral or immoral. From an ecological view of morality, consistency is not to be expected. In contrast, one can predict

---

[32] Ibid., p. 71.

in what situation inconsistencies are likely to arise. For instance, a survey asked citizens whether they would be willing to donate an organ after they had died; 69 percent and 81 percent of Danish and Swedish citizens, respectively, answered "yes," compared with about 4 percent and 86 percent who are actually potential donors.[33] The Danish citizens appear to behave inconsistently; the Swedish citizens do not. Yet, the apparent inconsistency of the Danish citizens is due to a mismatch between people's willingness and their government's default rule: Nobody is a potential donor unless they opt in. In the Swedish case, the government's default is presumed consent (opt-out); thus, no such conflict arises.

Similar inconsistencies and only moderate correlations between moral intuition and behavior have been reported in studies that both elicited people's moral intuitions and observed their behavior in the same situation.[34] Consider premarital sexual relations and American teenagers who publicly take a vow of abstinence. These teenagers typically come from religious backgrounds and have revived virginity as a moral virtue. One would expect that their moral intentions, particularly after having been declared in public, would guide their behavior. Yet, teenagers who made a virginity pledge were just as likely to have premarital sex as their peers who did not.[35] The only difference was that, when those who made the pledge had sex, they were less likely to use condoms or other forms of contraception. As mentioned, teenagers' behavior is often guided by a social coordination heuristic: imitate-your-peers – do what the majority of your peers do. If my friends make a virginity pledge, I will too; if my friends get drunk, I will too; if my friends already have sex at age 16, I will too; and so on. If behavior is guided by peer imitation, a pledge in itself plays little part. The social environment is what makes the difference.

Most importantly, if teenagers are not aware of the role that this heuristic plays in guiding part of their behavior, but, instead, believe they make their decisions themselves, this would explain why they were not prepared for the event of acting against their stated moral values. Similarly, the US Government has spent nearly $2 billion since the 1990s on the abstinence-promotion programs, which not only has turned out to be ineffective in preventing adolescent birth rates, but has actually increased these in conservative states.[36] One possible explanation of this failure is that adolescents' behavior is guided by social heuristics, which these governmental programs have not targeted.

---

[33] Commission of the European Communities (2007).
[34] See, for example, Narvaez & Lapsley (2005).   [35] Rosenbaum (2009).   [36] Fox et al. (2019).

Moral Luck

Philosopher Thomas Nagel defined moral luck as follows: "Where a significant aspect of what someone does depends on factors beyond his control, yet we continue to treat him in that respect as an object of moral judgment, it can be called moral luck."[37] The destiny of men who are enlisted for war is an issue of moral luck. Nagel observed that we frequently make moral judgments about people based on factors out of their control, despite our intuition that they cannot be morally assessed for what is not their fault. Moral luck arises from the fact that moral behavior is, in part, determined by our environment and, thus, not entirely controllable by the individual. It concerns the question of whether behavior should be evaluated as right or wrong depending on its result shaped by situational circumstances.[38]

Moral luck is a direct consequence of ecological morality. The teenager who desires to be accepted and imitates what peers do is lucky if the peer group is prosocial rather than criminal. The middle-aged family father who is confronted with choosing between breaking ranks and killing is unlucky to find himself in that situation. Moral luck, like ecological morality in general, expands normative questions such as "What is our duty?" and "What is a good character?" into interactive questions such as "How to create a virtuous environment for humans?"

Virtuous Environments

In this chapter, I have argued that moral intuitions are guided by social heuristics, which are not distinctive from other heuristics in the adaptive toolbox. One and the same heuristic can solve problems that we call moral and those we do not. That perspective helps explain the processes underlying moral intuition rather than taking intuition as an unexplained primitive. While moral psychologists debate over whether our moral sense is reflective and rational, as in Lawrence Kohlberg's theory, or intuitive and nonrational, as in Jonathan Haidt's theory, I believe that any assumed opposition and ranking is a misleading start.[39] Both intuition and deliberation are involved in moral behavior, as they are in decision-making in general. The result of deliberation may become automatic and intuitive over a lifetime or generations, or intuitive judgments may be justified post hoc by reason to save face. If Darwin is right that the function of morality

---

[37] Nagel (1993), p. 59.   [38] Williams (1981).   [39] See also Narvaez (2010).

is to create and maintain the coherence of groups, then social heuristics are the tools toward that goal.

The ecological view of morality emphasizes that behavior is a function of both heuristics and the environment in which they operate. Yet many theories continue to assume a simple causal arrow from an inner process – be it virtues, traits, moral reasoning, or utility calculations – to behavior. In contrast, the adaptive view that is inspired by Simon's scissors (see Chapter 5) explains apparent systematic inconsistencies in moral behavior and takes the phenomenon of moral luck seriously. Virtue is found not only in people but also in environments.

Virtuous environments can support people not only with respect to moral behavior. Chapter 8, the final chapter, deals with the question of how to set up and maintain a research environment that enables innovation through an open culture of intense, critical, but respectful discussion.

CHAPTER 8

Simple Heuristics to Run a Research Group[*]

> If I have seen further, it is by standing on the shoulders of giants.
> *Isaac Newton*[1]

> As enticing as the prospect of unruffled consensus in the workplace may be, when leaders dissuade dissent and divergent thinking, they create an environment that may allow disasters to materialize.
> *Micah Zenko*[2]

Collaboration between researchers has become increasingly common in psychology and other social sciences. Between 1980 and 2013, for instance, the average number of authors on a paper roughly doubled in psychological journals.[3] This positions the social sciences between the humanities, where single-authored publications remain the ideal, and the natural sciences, where the number of authors can be huge: An article on the Higgs boson in 2015 listed 5,153 authors.[4] Collaboration occurs between institutes worldwide, a practice that goes back to 1887 when observatories from Helsinki to Sydney began to map millions of stars.[5] But, it also occurs on a smaller scale when the members of a research group work and publish together instead of pursuing a career individually. The steady increase in collaboration requires reflection about how to make it productive. In this chapter, I focus on a question that is rarely asked: How can one establish and maintain an environment that fosters successful collaboration in a research group? I will use my own experience as a case study. For 22 years, I directed the ABC Research Group at the Max Planck Institute for Human Development in Berlin and before that at the Max Planck Institute for Psychological Research in Munich.[6]

---

[*] This chapter is based on Gigerenzer (2022b).
[1] Letter from Sir Isaac Newton to Robert Hooke (1675). See Merton (1965).   [2] Zenko (2015).
[3] Henriksen (2016).   [4] Aad et al. (2015).   [5] Daston (2017).
[6] ABC is short for Center for *Adaptive Behavior and Cognition*. The initialism also reflects the fact that we were exploring the ABCs of heuristic decision-making under uncertainty.

I begin with a remark on the philosophy of the institutes of the Max Planck Society. It is embodied in a set of heuristic principles that any institution could implement if they are open to rethinking their methods and willing to imitate good models. In short, there are three principles. First, research is built up solely around the world's leading researchers, that is, around a person, not a field. The person is absolutely free to develop a research agenda. It is called the *Harnack Principle*, named after the first president of the Society in 1911.[7] Academies and universities, in contrast, typically select a field and then hire the best person they can find in this area. The second principle is to take risks and ideally create new fields rather than merely excelling in the existing fields. If a research group succeeds in creating a new field that eventually becomes established worldwide, the research group has done its job and may be closed down. The idea is not to invest in what is established and everyone else is doing, but rather to stay at the forefront of innovation and invest resources in risky new projects. To enable such risk-taking, directors are provided with the necessary resources until they retire, which makes them independent from short-term grants. This long-term funding reflects an unusual amount of trust in the directors, compared with the widespread system of distrust that invites playing it safe. Third, because new ideas do not respect the borders of established disciplines, a premium is placed on interdisciplinary research. To facilitate this, the directors are free to select the research staff, agenda, and composition of the group. These three principles – the focus on eminent researchers rather than established fields, guaranteed funding to encourage risk-taking, and an interdisciplinary approach – are the pillars of the Max Planck institutes' success.

These principles enable innovation, but do not specify the details of running a research group. Given the amount of trust that directors enjoy, they can take the time and effort to develop a healthy working culture or not and use their freedom in different ways. Therefore, what follows should not be generalized to how other directors or institutes have set up their research groups. I will simply describe the heuristics that I used to set up the research group and how the group maintained its open culture over the years with a fluctuating set of members.

---

[7] Adolf von Harnack was the first president of the Kaiser Wilhelm Society, founded in 1911, which in 1948 was renamed the Max Planck Society.

How to Start a Research Group

When offered the directorship of the Max Planck Institute for Psychological Research, I was teaching at the University of Chicago. The offer allowed me to create an initial group of about 20 members at the level of associate and assistant professors, postdocs and predocs, as well as IT and support staff. The topic I chose is discussed in this book, decision-making under uncertainty, then a largely uncharted territory given the preoccupation of most psychological, statistical, and economic theories with calculable risk. Taking up Herbert A. Simon's widely neglected question of how people make decisions when the future is uncertain and the assumptions necessary for the expected utility maximization or Bayesian models do not hold, the research program extended this descriptive question to a new, prescriptive one that had not been asked before: How *should* decisions be made under uncertainty? This led to many further exciting questions, such as: In what situations can smart heuristics lead to more accurate decisions than complex strategies? How can the findings be implemented to help doctors, judges, and other experts make better decisions under uncertainty? And, finally, how can heuristics be implemented to create better artificial intelligence (AI)?

Principle 1: Common Topic, Multiple Disciplines

There are two ways to do science. One is *discipline-oriented research*, where researchers identify with a discipline or subdiscipline and work on various topics within its conventions. I have seen this in quite a few psychology departments and also in other social science departments, where subdepartments rarely collaborate with another, let alone interact with other disciplines, even if these are relevant. The other is *problem-oriented research*, where researchers identify with a problem and work on it with colleagues, theories, and methods from various disciplines. Problem-oriented research is more common in the natural sciences, where large numbers of people with diverse backgrounds work together. Discipline-oriented research is a closed system. In problem-oriented research, other disciplines are welcomed as a toolbox containing further useful tools to make progress. Here, the challenge is greater, but so is the satisfaction.

As I have stated, most interesting topics do not respect the fences that have been set up to demark the territory of a discipline and keep strangers out. Decision-making under uncertainty is no exception. Progress requires cooperation between researchers from various disciplines. The initial ABC

Research Group consisted of researchers from cognitive and evolutionary psychology, behavioral economics, empirical sociology, mathematics, engineering, and computer science. Over the years, we also hired anthropologists, animal biologists, neuroscientists, machine-learning researchers, historians of science, philosophers, and medical researchers. Heterogeneity enables studying a topic from multiple perspectives and exploring what is known in fields that rarely seek contact with others.

Hiring researchers from different disciplines, however, is not enough. I have visited research centers bearing the qualifier *interdisciplinary* in their name, but not in their spirit. The psychologists huddled together, pursued their own topics, and published in psychology journals, while the economists stuck with other members of their tribe and published in economic journals. I worried that this state of separation could also happen to our group. The first countermeasure was to establish a common topic. The second was to establish the rule that each researcher must collaborate (and publish) with at least one person from another field. Otherwise, there is not much point in employing researchers from different fields.

Yet, one problem remains. Engaging in interdisciplinary research means taking a risk regarding one's career, given the disappointing state of estrangement and ignorance between many fields. If a young economist publishes in premier psychological journals, that may not count much when applying for a position in an economics department. Similarly, a psychologist who succeeds in publishing in a premier medical journal may be treated as an outsider by other psychologists. I warned all new researchers of the risk they were taking when joining the group. But, I was proven wrong. In my recollection, in not a single case did departmental tunnel vision prevent a group member from finding a good position.

Finally, there is another obstacle. The principle of taking high risks implies that a number of projects will fail; otherwise they would not be so risky. This creates a dilemma for young researchers who need publications on their curriculum vitae to succeed in academia. My advice was to work on two projects, a high-risk project that enables true innovation and a low-risk one consisting of excellent, but standard, research, which provides a safety net if the high-risk project does not pan out.

Principle 2: Create an Open Culture

My greatest fear was that, as a director, I would end up intellectually isolated at the top of a hierarchy. Nobody would dare to criticize my ideas openly. To make sure this did not happen, I asked three of my best American graduate students at the University of Chicago and two of my former German postdocs – all of whom I knew would not hesitate to debate my thoughts if they spotted a flaw – whether they would be willing to take a risk and embark with me into the unknown. They all agreed. These young researchers set the example of an open culture for the rest of the group, a culture of intense, critical, but respectful and fact-oriented discussion.

Yet, this was not what other researchers were used to. Some newcomers were frightened by the passionate discussions, mistaking them for aggressiveness, until they realized that the critique was directed at ideas, not persons, and that a culture open to dissent is actually a "bodyguard" that protects everyone from running into harsh criticism outside the safe environment of the group. To further this protection, we put in place a rule that members preparing a talk for a conference or a job opening first had the opportunity to give their talk to the group (on top of regular weekly talks that all group members were required to give in succession). Attending everyone's practice talk is a time-consuming service but also an opportunity for the listeners to learn how to improve their own talks. The combination of an open culture, a common topic, and interdisciplinarity creates the space for a sparkling intellectual atmosphere.

Principle 3: Spatial Proximity

An open culture can work only if everyone feels accepted and trusts the others. Trust is facilitated by an environment that makes it natural for people to meet. The key features are:

- **Everyone on the same floor:** In my experience, a group that is spread over different floors interacts half as much as when located on the same floor. If the members work in different buildings, the loss is even greater.
- **Open doors:** These set a sign that visitors are welcome and opens up the space.
- **Tea and coffee at 4 pm every day:** This may appear a waste of time, but it is not. When researchers chat over personal things, that helps create trust, and when they discuss research, that helps increase the flow of information. It also provides a relaxed situation in which people can educate others on the basics of their own discipline. To make this work, the director should not demand participation, but simply set a

model by showing up regularly. There was also an element of suspense attached to the tea and coffee hour, as everyone was eager to find out whether cake would be served that day – the *cake rule* is described in the section "Set Collective Goals."

Principle 4: Temporal Proximity

One problem I had encountered in other research groups was that the first people who joined the group tended to look down on or even patronize those who came later as if these were their younger siblings. To avoid such a "birth-order problem," I made sure that all members of the initial group started on the same day. This created a level playing field from the beginning. The downside of this rule is that the administration can be overwhelmed for a short time by the simultaneous appearance of so many new people. But arriving at the same time and figuring out together how things work in an unfamiliar environment fosters bonding.

How to Maintain the Culture

Once an open culture is established, a new challenge emerges: How can one maintain the culture in the ever-changing composition of a research group? Postdocs and graduate students typically leave after 3 or 4 years, while researchers may stay longer, for 5 to 10 years. In addition, research groups tend to grow if successful. In the ABC Research Group, more than 150 predocs, postdocs, researchers, senior researchers, and guests participated over the years. For me, the struggle was finding a balance between giving direction and not directing too much. With too little direction, the group would lose sight of the common topic; with too much direction, I would become oblivious to new ideas that the group developed. I had no experience with running such a large group, but did have experience in running a band before entering academia. So, I decided to run the group as a jam session, not as a conductor that directs from a podium.

Set Collective Goals

A collective goal requires the collaboration of many researchers; it cannot be achieved by a single person. In the case of our group, the first goal was to write a book together that laid out the research program and the first results. We wrote *Simple Heuristics That Make Us Smart* in the first 3 years of the group's existence.[8] The unique feature of *Simple Heuristics* was its intense collaborative nature, written by a highly motivated and efficient group of 18 researchers, all of whom were familiar with the others' research. Each chapter had between two and five authors, but most authors had their hands (and writing) in many other chapters. In numerous meetings and retreats and over games of ping-pong, we collectively went through each sentence of the book.

The next collective goals were two follow-up books, *Ecological Rationality: Intelligence in the World*[9] and *Simple Heuristics in a Social World*.[10] Each was authored by two of us along with the entire research group. This emphasized the collaborative nature of these books, but posed a challenge for librarians as it generated a new genre of books. Previously, only edited books had individually authored chapters, but, here, there were no editors and the entire ABC Research Group was named as the collective coauthor of the book.

While trying to complete these two follow-up books, we ran into a problem. Many of the original team of authors had left to take up professorships around the world, so spatial proximity was no longer a possibility for everyone. These books had to be written without the advantage of everyone being on the same floor, open doors, and daily tea and coffee together. We tried to counteract this physical separation by inviting coauthors abroad to join us in retreats, such as at the beautiful Ringberg castle in Bavaria, owned by the Max Planck Society, where we could discuss research face-to-face. Nevertheless, these books took much longer to complete than *Simple Heuristics*.

We also set goals about publishing articles, but in terms of quality rather than quantity. The premier journals in a field are one marker of quality. For instance, we aimed to publish one paper a year in the *Psychological Review*. Indeed, we published 20 papers in the journal over the first 20 years of the group's existence, which turned out to be more than any psychological department worldwide in terms of papers per capita. At the same time, we published in the top journals of medicine, economics, management, philosophy, and other fields, as well as in prestigious interdisciplinary journals such as *Science*.

Some university departments pay researchers a cash bonus for publishing in a top journal or pay a sum that increases with the impact factor of the journal. This economic view of research is a matter of taste; it replaces

---

[8] Gigerenzer et al. (1999).   [9] Todd et al. (2012).   [10] Hertwig et al. (2013).

scientific curiosity with monetary calculation and encourages individualistic competition and a focus on metrics. In our research group, we introduced the *cake rule* that takes the opposite approach: If a paper is accepted or published, the first author brings cake for the entire group. This rule respects the fact that most ideas have been inspired by the entire group over tea and coffee or in other discussions. It violates the theory of economic incentives because the author does not receive the reinforcement, but, instead, rewards everyone else. Nevertheless, the cake rule worked well and increased our publication record.

How to Deal With Growth

Successful research groups tend to increase magically, by attracting guest researchers and visitors. And unexpected events happen. In the case of our group, the London investment banker David Harding, after reading my book *Reckoning with Risk* (US title: *Calculated Risk*), gave us a generous private donation that enabled us to found the Harding Center for Risk Literacy, which focuses on risk communication in health and beyond. The second unexpected fact was that many of the researchers who had left for a professorship at a university or a job in a tech company kept coming back home to their "family" for days or weeks. As a result, the group grew to about 35 members plus a dozen student assistants and about 10 IT and support staff, not counting the guest researchers and homecoming members. The floor became overly crowded, which required new heuristics to deal with growth.

- **Maintain spatial proximity:** When we ran out of space, the architect proposed constructing a new building for the newcomers. I vetoed the proposal because that would have split the group. Instead, we extended the existing building horizontally, so that everyone could still be on the same floor.
- **Avoid temporal proximity:** The culture of a research group is handed on to newcomers by explicit rules, but, equally important, by implicit learning, through the imitation of how things are done. This illustrates a successful application of the imitate-your-peers heuristic (see Chapter 7). In that way, the open culture lives on even if none of the initial group is still present. This implicit learning process would end abruptly if all or most members were to leave at the same time and be replaced by new people. An entire working culture would be lost.
A good rule is never to hire more people at one point in time than there

are old members. Temporal proximity – starting all members of the group at the same point in time – is ideal for setting up a new group, but fatal later on. Only if the existing group were no longer operating well would it be a smart strategy.

- **Introduce a tutorial system:** In a small group, members learn by doing, and more spontaneity is possible, such as announcing a spontaneous talk in order to present a new discovery or asking for advice on an issue. The larger the group is, the more structural measures it requires to support the learning process. In our group, these measures included a schedule of talks where each member presented the current research at regular intervals, a 1-year course for newcomers that covered *Simple Heuristics* and other classics, a 4-day retreat for the entire group every year, and an annual Summer Institute on Bounded Rationality.

- **Side-by-side writing:** Most young researchers who entered our group had never been taught how to write an article. One of the key heuristics we introduced to fill this void was that a more experienced researcher sat side-by-side with a younger one in front of the computer screen. They discussed the design of the article together as well as the wording of every sentence. Useful questions include: What do we really want to say with this sentence? Do we need this sentence at all? Do we need all the words in it? Did we define the concepts, and are we using different words for the same concept? Side-by-side writing also benefits experienced researchers. It is simultaneous and interactive, and many new ideas can emerge from it. Creativity happens less often if one researcher writes a draft alone, sends it to a coauthor who then revises it alone, and so on. Side-by-side writing is a much more enjoyable and profitable process.

- **Exploit cultural diversity:** A benefit of growth is that it allows for more cultural diversity. It adds to the disciplinary diversity of a research group, but in a different way. Being in close contact with researchers from other countries facilitates the insight that one's own views about work, life, and science are not carved into stone, but a matter of one's cultural upbringing. Thus, they can be changed. Most important, experiencing the cultural contingency directly – in what others fear, what risks they take, and how they make (or avoid) decisions – helps develop a critical view about theories that assume a universal being, from Homo economicus to Western, educated, industrialized, rich, and democratic (WEIRD) societies, which comprise only about 12 percent of the world's population. Sharing space, cake, and an open culture enabled the group members to become good friends who helped each other in research and nonresearch activities and, even after leaving the group, maintained contact and collaboration across continents.

Growth provides benefits but also problems. I will never forget the day when I realized that I could no longer precisely describe what every predoc and postdoc in the group was working on. For me, that illuminating moment was one of extreme discomfort. The lesson is: Let the group grow, but not by too much and not too fast.

Distribute Responsibility

Collective research requires not only an intellectually open culture but also a group spirit, that is, an identification with a group's culture. Identification is facilitated when each member takes on a task that serves the entire group. This is why we distributed the tasks of running the group so that everyone was allocated one task for which they alone were responsible, including the power to make related decisions. These tasks ranged from organizing and running the talks, retreats, the Summer Institute, and the tutorial system for newcomers to purchasing tea and coffee. Distributing tasks so that everyone has full responsibility in one area ensures that no one remains simply a passive member, and it enhances transparency. Everyone knows whom to congratulate or blame – all decisions are made within the group. Responsibility can thus be distributed in the form of a division of labor but also by means of collective decisions, as in hiring.

To maintain the intellectual spirit in a research group, carefully selecting and hiring new members is important. In many institutions, the director makes the decision based on a set of candidates preselected by someone else. This may lead to sensible choices, but the group is left out and does not share any responsibility. At the other extreme, letting every member vote and using the majority rule would install shared responsibility, but introduce a quality problem because beginners may not be aware of what qualities more senior positions require. To avoid this drawback, we introduced a majority rule system with *equal votes for those who were at least at the same level in the academic hierarchy* as the advertised positions. That is, when hiring predocs, everyone in the group has a vote; when hiring postdocs, everyone except the predocs vote, and, when hiring researchers, only the other researchers vote. At the same time, all can participate in the discussion before the votes are taken. In this way, everyone is included and held accountable, shares responsibility, and is motivated to engage actively in the hiring process. The downside is that I was outvoted from time to time, but that is the price for distributed responsibility.

To make the hiring process transparent not only to the group but also to the applicants, an unusual rule is to invite applicants to be present during all job talks. In our group, these typically lasted over 1 or 2 days, and we hired more than one person. The applicants were surprised to be invited to stay with us and listen to the other job talks. This openness makes the hiring process more transparent and provides a unique opportunity for applicants to learn from the other applicants – and for us to see how they interact with competitors.

For support staff, the procedure was similar. When we hired a new office assistant, the other assistants had the freedom to read all applications and select 5–10 candidates for an interview. To the applicants' surprise, they were exclusively interviewed by their potential future colleagues, who also gave them practical tests. It is only rational to rely on the office assistants' judgment; they know better than myself or the other researchers who is competent, they want someone whose chemistry fits with theirs and the group, and they certainly do not want someone who would do less work than they do. Only after the number of candidates had been reduced to two or three final candidates, did I enter the picture and make the choice. This relieved the office staff from responsibility if something went wrong. Once, at the insistence of some researchers who were impressed by an applicant's academic record, I violated this procedure and hired their preferred candidate rather than the one preferred by the office staff. It turned out to be a poor decision.

Secure Open Culture

An open culture of intense, but respectful and fact-orientated, discussion is an asset that needs to be secured. We introduced measures to protect this culture.

- **Be sure to include a contrarian:** Every research group can benefit from (at least) one contrarian, that is, a person who dares to question the group's and the director's wisdom, plays devil's advocate, insists on evidence, and questions what others take for granted. Such a person is sometimes frustrating, but actually provides a great service by protecting the group from falling prey to groupthink. For that reason, when selecting new group members, we preferred those who found some fault or disagreement with our research findings in their application letter, rather than those who politely praised our research. Moreover, if external scholars had a strong disagreement with the group, we flew them in for a visit to discuss the issue in person. When the *Times Higher Education* approached me to write a piece on the importance of devil's advocates for better science, I asked about a hundred former members of my research group for their recollections.[11] To my surprise, many of them perceived themselves as having been the contrarian, and one long-term member countered: "You were the contrarian."

- **Make bets:** Arguments and disagreements often lead to people going on and on and repeating what they have already said. An efficient heuristic is to stop this process early and offer the other side a bet. This forces both sides to state their arguments or predictions precisely so that the bet can be resolved. Some are easy to decide, such as who wrote what, while others may require running a simulation. On some days, I had several bets going on. The prize was mostly cake for the entire group, which turned the disagreement into a social event and the person who lost the bet into a benefactor to everyone else.

Heuristics Shape Research Culture

The principles I have outlined in this chapter can be thought of as heuristic rules that create and maintain the culture of a research group. These rules are partly created intuitively, revised deliberately, and eventually develop into a group's collective intuition. They are called heuristic rather than optimal because there is no single way to create the best of all groups.[12] Heuristics include higher level principles, such as those of the Max Planck institutes for hiring directors, as mentioned, which can be rephrased as "Hire well, and let them to their job." "Hire well" establishes quality; "let them do their job" creates a climate of trust. I applied this policy to my entire staff too, so that it was not an exclusive privilege for me. Other heuristics are meant for the micromanaging level, such as to resolve an argument by offering a bet. These can be further distinguished into heuristics that shape the research environment, such as spatial proximity,

---

[11] Gigerenzer (2022d). [12] Gigerenzer (2006).

and heuristics for dealing with other people. This repertoire needs to be adapted to the specific goals and environments. Together, the repertoire of heuristics molds the intellectual and social climate. The toolbox of an institution, a director, or a group influences whether the culture will become more or less formal, more or less inclusive, and more or less open.

References

Aad, G., Abbott, B., Abdallah, J., Abdinov, O., Aben, R., Abolins, M., ... Zwalinski, L. (2015). Combined measurement of the Higgs boson mass in pp collisions at root s=7 and 8 TeV with the ATLAS and CMS experiments. *Physical Review Letters, 114*, 191803.

Abrahamsen, D. (1946). *The mind and death of a genius*. New York: Columbia University Press.

Admati, A., & Hellwig, M. (2013). *The bankers' new clothes*. Princeton, NJ: Princeton University Press.

Arie, S. (2013, March 21). Uruguay's mandatory breast cancer screening for working women aged 40–59 challenged. *British Medical Journal, 346*.

Ariely, D. (2008). *Predictably irrational: The hidden forces that shape our decisions* (1st ed.). New York: Harper Collins.

Aristotle. (350 BCE/1984). History of animals. In J. Barnes (Ed.), *The complete works of Aristotle* (Vol. 1, rev. Oxford transl.). Princeton, NJ: Princeton University Press.

Arkes, H. R., Gigerenzer, G., & Hertwig, R. (2016). How bad is incoherence? *Decision, 3*, 20–39.

Arshad, A., Anderson, B., & Sharif, A. (2019). Comparison of organ donation and transplantation rates between opt-out and opt-in systems. *Clinical Investigation, 95*, 1453–1460.

Artinger, F. M., Artinger, S., & Gigerenzer, G. (2019). C.Y.A.: Frequency and causes of defensive decisions in public administration. *Business Research, 12*, 9–25.

Artinger, F. M., & Gigerenzer, G. (2016). The cheap twin: From the ecological rationality of heuristic pricing to the aggregate market. *Academy of Management Proceedings, 2016*, 13915.

Artinger, F. M., Gigerenzer, G., & Jacobs, P. (2022). Satisficing: Integrating two traditions. *Journal of Economic Literature, 60*(2), 598–635.

Bago, B., & De Neys, W. (2019). The smart System 1: Evidence for the intuitive nature of correct responding on the bat-and-ball problem. *Thinking & Reasoning, 25*, 257–299.

Bargh, J. A., & Morsella, E. (2008). The unconscious mind. *Perspectives on Psychological Science, 3*, 73–79.

Bastick, T. (1982). *Intuition: How we think and act*. New York: Wiley.

Becker, G. S. (1995). *The essence of Becker*. Stanford, CA: Hoover Institution Press.

Beilock, S. L., Bertenthal, B. I., McCoy, A. M., & Carr, T. H. (2004). Haste does not always make waste: Expertise, direction of attention, and speed versus accuracy in performing sensorimotor skills. *Psychonomic Bulletin & Review*, *11*(2), 373–379.

Berg, N., & Gigerenzer, G. (2007). Psychology implies paternalism? Bounded rationality may reduce the rationale to regulate risk-taking. *Social Choice and Welfare*, *28*, 337–359.

(2010). As-if behavioral economics: Neoclassical economics in disguise? *History of Economic Ideas*, *18*, 133–165.

Berlin, I. (1969). *Four essays on liberty*. New York: Oxford University Press.

Binet, A. (1911). Nouvelles recherches sur la mesure du niveau intellectuel chez les enfants d'école [New studies on the measurement of schoolchildren's intellectual levels]. *L'Année Psychologique*, *17*, 145–201. (Cited in Wolf, Trans., 1973, pp. 209–210)

Binet, A., & Simon, T. (1914). *Mentally defective children* (W. B. Drummond, Trans.). London: Edward Arnold.

(1905/1973). *The development of intelligence in children* (E. S. Kite, Trans.). New York: Arno Press. (Original work published 1905; English translation first published 1916)

Blum, J. (1978). *Pseudoscience and mental ability: The origins and fallacies of the IQ controversy*. New York: Monthly Review Press.

Bond, M. (2009, October). Risk school. *Nature*, *461*(29), 1189–1192.

Bramhall, S. (2011). Presumed consent for organ donation: A case against. *Annals of the Royal College of Surgeons of England*, *93*, 268–272.

Brennen, J. S., Howard, P. N., & Nielsen, R. K. (2018, December). An industry-led debate: How UK media cover artificial intelligence. Factsheet. London: Reuters Institute for the Study of Journalism. Retrieved October 25, 2022, https://reutersinstitute.politics.ox.ac.uk/sites/default/files/2018-12/Brennen_UK_Media_Coverage_of_AI_FINAL.pdf

Brighton, H., & Gigerenzer, G. (2015). The bias bias. *Journal of Business Research*, *68*, 1772–1784.

Browning, C. R. (1998). *Ordinary men: Reserve Battalion 101 and the final solution in Poland*. New York: Harper Perennial.

Bruch, E. E., & Newman, M. E. J. (2018). Aspirational pursuit of mates in online dating markets. *Science Advances*, *4*(8), eaap9815.

Bruner, J. S. (1973). *Beyond the information given: Studies on the psychology of knowing*. New York: Norton.

Brunswik, E. (1955). Representative design and probabilistic theory in a functional psychology. *Psychological Review*, *62*, 193–217.

Burger, J. M. (2009). Replicating Milgram: Would people still obey today? *American Psychologist*, *64*, 1–11.

Byron, M. (Ed.). (2004). *Satisficing and maximizing: Moral theorists on practical reason*. Cambridge, UK: Cambridge University Press.

Calaprice, A. (2011). *The ultimate quotable Einstein*. Princeton, NJ: Princeton University Press.
Carey, S. (2009). *The origin of concepts*. New York: Oxford University Press.
Carson, J. (2007). *The measure of merit: Talents, intelligence, and inequality in the French and American republics*. Princeton, NJ: Princeton University Press.
Chater, N., & Oaksford, M. (Eds.). (2008). *The probabilistic mind: Prospects for Bayesian cognitive science*. Oxford: Oxford University Press.
Chater, N., Tenenbaum, J. B., & Yuille, A. (2006). Probabilistic models of cognition: Conceptual foundations. *Trends in Cognitive Sciences, 10*, 335–344.
Christensen-Szalanski, J. J., & Beach, L. R. (1984). The citation bias: Fad and fashion in the judgment and decision literature. *American Psychologist, 39*(1), 75–78.
Cicero, M. T. (45 BC/2012). *De finibus bonorum et malorum libri quinque*. Vol. 3. Rev. by J. S. Reid. Nabu Press.
Cokely, E. T., & Felz, A. (2014). Expert intuition. In L. M. Osbeck & B. S. Held (Eds.). *Rational intuition*. Cambridge, UK: Cambridge University Press.
Collett, T. S., & Land, M. F. (1975). Visual control of flight behavior in the hoverfly, Syritta pipiens L. *Journal of Comparative Physiology, 99*, 1–66.
Commission of the European Communities (2007, May 30). *Organ donation and transplantation: Policy actions at EU level. Impact assessment*. Press Release No. IP/07/718. Retrieved October 25, 2022, http://europa.eu/rapid/pressReleasesAction.do?reference=IP/07/718&format=HTML&aged=1&language=EN&guiLanguage=en
Conly, S. (2013). *Against autonomy*. Cambridge, UK: Cambridge University Press.
Cosmides, L. (1989). The logic of social exchange: Has natural selection shaped how humans reason? Studies with the Wason selection task. *Cognition, 31*, 187–276.
Cosmides, L., & Tooby, J. (2008). Can deontic logic capture the facts of human moral reasoning? In W. Sinnott-Armstrong (Ed.), *Moral psychology: Vol 1. The evolution of morality: Adaptations and innateness* (pp. 53–119). Cambridge, MA: MIT Press.
Csikszentmihalyi, M. (2008). *Flow: The psychology of optimal experience*. New York: Harper Perennial.
Daniel, C., & Palmer, M. (2007, May 27). Google's goal: To organise your daily life. *Financial Times*. Retrieved October 24, 2022, www.ft.com/content/c3e49548-088e-11dc-b11e-000b5df10621
Darwin, C. (1871/1981). *The descent of man*. Princeton, NJ: Princeton University Press.
  (1893). *The variation of animal and plants under domestication* (Vol. I, 2nd ed.). London: Murray.
Daston, L. (1992). The naturalized female intellect. *Science in Context, 5*, 209–235.
  (2017). The immortal archive: Nineteenth-century science imagines the future. In L. Daston (Ed.), *Science in the archives: Pasts, presents, futures* (pp. 159–182). Chicago, IL: University of Chicago Press.

Daston, L., & Park, K. (1998). *Wonders and the order of nature*. New York: Zone Books.
Dawes, R. M., & Mulford, M. (1996). The false consensus effect and overconfidence: Flaws in judgment, or flaws in how we study judgment? *Organizational Behavior and Human Decision Processes, 65*, 201–211.
Dawkins, R. (1989). *The selfish gene* (2nd ed.). Oxford: Oxford University Press.
Deary, I. J., Whalley, L. J., & Starr, J. M. (2009). *A lifetime of intelligence. Follow-up studies of the Scottish mental survey of 1932 and 1947*. Washington, DC: American Psychological Association.
DeMiguel, V., Garlappi, L., & Uppal, R. (2009). Optimal versus naive diversification: How inefficient is the 1/N portfolio strategy? *Review of Financial Studies, 22*, 1915–1953.
Denny, M. (2004). The physics of bat echolocation: Signal processing techniques. *American Journal of Physics, 72*, 1465–1477.
Dhami, M. K. (2003). Psychological models of professional decision-making. *Psychological Science, 14*, 175–180.
Diehl, L. A. (1986). The paradox of G. Stanley Hall: Foe of coeducation and educator of women. *American Psychologist, 41*(8), 868–878.
Dörfler, V., & Eden, C. (2019). Understanding "expert" scientists: Implications for management and organizational research. *Management Learning, 50*, 534–555.
Dury, M. O'C. (1984). *Some notes on conversations with Wittgenstein: Recollections of Wittgenstein*. Oxford: Oxford University Press.
Easton, C. (2018). Women and "the philosophical personality": Evaluating whether gender differences in the Cognitive Reflection Test have significance for explaining the gender gap in philosophy. *Synthese, 198*, 1–29.
Edwards, W., Lindman, H., & Phillips, L. D. (1965). Emerging technologies for making decisions. In *New directions in psychology II* (pp. 261–325). New York: Holt, Rinehart and Winston.
Egidi, M., & Marengo, L. (2004). Near-decomposability, organization, and evolution: Some notes on Herbert Simon's contribution. In M. Augier & J. J. March (Eds.), *Models of a man: Essays in memory of Herbert A. Simon* (pp. 335–350). Cambridge, MA: MIT Press.
Ellis, H. (1894). *Man and woman*. Newcastle, UK: Walter Scott.
Erev, I., Wallsten, T. S., & Budescu, D. V. (1994). Simultaneous over- and underconfidence: The role of error in judgment processes. *Psychological Review, 101*, 519–527.
Ericsson, K. A., Krampe, R. T., & Tesch-Römer, C. (1993). The role of deliberate practice in the acquisition of expert performance. *Psychological Review, 100*, 363–406.
Evans, J. St. B. T., & Stanovich, K. E. (2013). Dual-process theories of higher cognition: Advancing the debate. *Perspectives on Psychological Science, 8*, 223–241.
Eysenck, H.-J., & Kamin, L. (1981). *The intelligence controversy*. New York: Wiley.

Feynman, R. P. (1967). *The character of physical law*. Cambridge, MA: MIT Press.
Fischer, A. H., Kret, M. E., & Broekens, J. (2018). Gender differences in emotion perception and self-reported emotional intelligence. *PLoS ONE, 13*, e0190712.
Fiske, A. P. (1992). The four elementary forms of sociality: Framework for a unified theory of social relations. *Psychological Review, 99*(4), 689–723.
Ford, D., Easton, D. F., Bishop, D. T., Narod, S. A., & Goldgar, D. E. (1994). Risk of cancer in BRCA1-mutation carriers. *Lancet, 343*, 692–695.
Fox, A. M., Himmelstein, G., Khalid, H., & Howell, E. A. (2019). Funding of abstinence-only education and adolescent pregnancy prevention: Does state ideology affect outcomes? *American Journal of Public Health, 109*, 497–504.
Frederick, S. (2005). Cognitive reflection and decision making. *Journal of Economic Perspectives, 19*, 25–42.
Friston, K. (2010). The free-energy principle: A unified brain theory? *Nature Reviews Neuroscience, 11*(2), 127–138.
Gal, D., & Rucker, D. D. (2018). The loss of loss aversion: Will it loom larger than its gain? *Journal of Consumer Psychology, 28*, 497–516.
Galton, F. (1869/1979). *Hereditary genius*. Julian Friedman.
Gambetta, D. (1996). *The Sicilian Mafia: The business of private protection*. Cambridge, MA: Harvard University Press.
Geddes, P., & Thomson, J. A. (1890). *The evolution of sex*. New York: Scribner & Welford.
German Federal Government (Bundesregierung). (n.d.). Retrieved October 24, 2022, www.bundesregierung.de/breg-de/themen/wirksam-regieren
Gigerenzer, G. (1996). On narrow norms and vague heuristics: A reply to Kahneman and Tversky. *Psychological Review, 103*, 592–596.
  (2002). *Calculated risks: How to know when numbers deceive you*. New York: Simon & Schuster. (UK edition: *Reckoning with risk: Learning to live with uncertainty*. London: Penguin, 2002.)
  (2004a). The irrationality paradox. *Behavioral and Brain Sciences, 27*, 336–338.
  (2004b). Striking a blow for sanity in theories of rationality. In M. Augier & J. G. March (Eds.), *Models of a man: Essays in memory of Herbert A. Simon* (pp. 389–409). Cambridge, MA: MIT Press.
  (2006). Follow the leader. *Harvard Business Review, 84*, 58–59.
  (2007). *Gut feelings: The intelligence of the unconscious*. London: Penguin.
  (2008). Moral intuition = Fast and frugal heuristics? In W. Sinnott-Armstrong (Ed.), *Moral psychology: Vol 2. The cognitive science of morality: Intuition and diversity* (pp. 1–26). Cambridge, MA: MIT Press.
  (2010). Moral satisficing: Rethinking moral behavior as bounded rationality. *Topics in Cognitive Science, 2*, 528–554.
  (2014a). *Risk savvy: How to make good decisions*. London: Penguin.
  (2014b). Breast cancer screening pamphlets mislead women: All women and women's organisations should tear up the pink ribbons and campaign for honest information. *British Medical Journal, 348*, g2636.

(2015). On the supposed evidence for libertarian paternalism. *Review of Philosophy and Psychology*, 6, 363–383.

(2018). The bias bias in behavioral economics. *Review of Behavioral Economics*, 5(3–4), 303–336.

(2019). Expert intuition is not rational choice. Review of *Sources of Power* by Gary Klein, 20th Anniversary Edition. *American Psychologist*, 132, 475–480.

(2021a). What is bounded rationality? In R. Viale (Ed.), *Routledge handbook of bounded rationality* (pp. 55–69). London: Routledge.

(2021b). Embodied heuristics. *Frontiers in Psychology*, 12, 711289.

(2022a). *How to stay smart in a smart world: Why human intelligence still beats algorithms*. Cambridge, MA: MIT Press.

(2022b). Simple heuristics to run a research group. *PsyCH Journal*, 11, 275–280.

(2022c). The idea of a peculiarly female intelligence: A brief history of bias masked as science. In R. Sternberg & D. Preiss (Eds.), *Intelligence in context: The cultural and historical foundations of human intelligence*. New York: Palgrave-Macmillan.

(2022d, June 23). A devil's advocate in every lab would drive better science. *Times Higher Education*, www.timeshighereducation.com/opinion/devils-advocate-every-lab-would-drive-better-science

Gigerenzer, G., & Brighton, H. (2009). Homo heuristicus: Why biased minds make better inferences. *Topics in Cognitive Science*, 1, 107–143.

Gigerenzer, G., Fiedler, K., & Olsson, H. (2012). Rethinking cognitive biases as environmental consequences. In P. M. Todd, G. Gigerenzer, & the ABC Research Group, *Ecological rationality: Intelligence in the world* (pp. 80–110). Oxford: Oxford University Press.

Gigerenzer, G., & Gaissmaier, W. (2011). Heuristic decision making. *Annual Review of Psychology*, 62, 451–482.

Gigerenzer, G., Gaissmaier, W., Kurz-Milcke, E., Schwartz, L. M., & Woloshin, S. (2007). Helping doctors and patients to make sense of health statistics. *Psychological Science in the Public Interest*, 8, 53–96.

Gigerenzer, G., Galesic, M., & Garcia-Retamero, R. (2014). Stereotypes about men's and women's intuitions: A study of two nations. *Journal of Cross-Cultural Psychology*, 45, 62–81.

Gigerenzer, G., & Goldstein, D. G. (2011). The recognition heuristic: A decade of research. *Judgment and Decision Making*, 6, 100–121.

Gigerenzer, G., Hertwig, R., & Pachur, T. (Eds.). (2011). *Heuristics: The foundations of adaptive behavior*. Oxford, UK: Oxford University Press.

Gigerenzer, G., & Hoffrage, U. (1995). How to improve Bayesian reasoning without instruction: Frequency formats. *Psychological Review*, 102, 684–704.

Gigerenzer, G., Hoffrage, U., & Kleinbölting, H. (1991). Probabilistic mental models: A Brunswikian theory of confidence. *Psychological Review*, 98, 506–528.

Gigerenzer, G., & Hug, K. (1992). Domain-specific reasoning: Social contracts, cheating, and perspective change. *Cognition*, 42, 127–171.

Gigerenzer, G., Mata, J., & Frank, R. (2009). Public knowledge of benefits of breast and prostate cancer screening in Europe. *Journal of the National Cancer Institute, 101,* 1216–1220.

Gigerenzer, G., Multmeier, J., Föhring, A., & Wegwarth, O. (2021). Do children have Bayesian intuitions? *Journal of Experimental Psychology: General, 50,* 1041–1070. doi:10.1037/xge0000979

Gigerenzer, G., Reb, J., & Luan, S. (2022). Smart heuristics for individuals, teams, and organizations. *Annual Review of Organizational Psychology and Organizational Behavior, 9*(1), 171–198.

Gigerenzer, G., & Regier, T. (1996). How do we tell an association from a rule? Comment on Sloman (1996). *Psychological Bulletin, 119,* 23–26.

Gigerenzer, G., Todd, P. M., & the ABC Research Group. (1999). *Simple heuristics that make us smart.* Oxford: Oxford University Press.

Gilovich, T., Vallone, R., & Tversky, A. (1985). The hot hand in basketball: On the misperception of random sequences. *Cognitive Psychology, 17,* 295–314.

Gladwell, M. (2007). *Blink: The power of thinking without thinking.* New York: Back Bay Books.

Godfrey-Smith, P. (2016). *Other minds: The octopus and the evolution of intelligent life.* New York: Harper Collins.

Goldstein, D. G., & Gigerenzer, G. (2002). Models of ecological rationality: The recognition heuristic. *Psychological Review, 109,* 75–90.

Goris, H. (2012). Angelic knowledge in Aquinas and Bonaventure. In T. Hoffmann, (Ed.), *A companion to angels in medieval philosophy* (pp. 149–185). Leiden: Brill.

Gøtzsche, P. C., & Jørgensen, K. J. (2013). Screening for breast cancer with mammography. *Cochrane Database of Systematic Reviews* (6), CD001877.

Gould, S. J., & Vrba, E. S. (1982). Exaptation – a missing term in the science of form. *Paleobiology, 8,* 4–15.

Grant, R. A., Mitchinson, B., Fox, C., & Prescott, T. J. (2009). Active touch sensing in the rat: Anticipatory and regulatory control of whisker movements during surface exploration. *Journal of Neurophysiology, 10*(2), 862–874.

Gray, J. (1992). *Men are from Mars, women are from Venus.* New York: Harper Collins.

Grice, H. P. (1989). *Studies in the way of words.* Cambridge, MA: Harvard University Press.

Grill, M., & Hackenbroch, V. (2014, July 20). Unsinn in bester Qualität [Highest-quality nonsense]. *Der Spiegel,* 100–104.

Grosskurth, P. (1980). *Havelock Ellis: A biography.* New York: Knopf.

Gruber, H. E., & Vonèche, J. J. (1977). *The essential Piaget.* New York: Basic Books.

Hahn, U., & Warren, P. A. (2009). Perceptions of randomness: Why three heads are better than four. *Psychological Review, 116,* 454–461.

(2010). Why three heads are better than four: A reply to Sun, Tweney, and Wang (2010). *Psychological Review, 117,* 706–711.

Haidt, J. (2001). The emotional dog and its rational tail: A social intuitionist approach to moral judgment. *Psychological Review, 108*, 814–834.
   (2008). Morality. *Perspectives on Psychological Science, 3*, 65–72.
   (2013). *The righteous mind: Why good people are divided by politics and religion*. London: Penguin.
Haidt, J., & Kesebir, S. (2008). In the forest of value: Why moral intuitions are different from other kinds. In H. Plessner, C. Betsch, & T. Betsch (Eds.), *Intuition in judgment and decision making*. New York: Erlbaum.
Haldane, A. G., & Madouros, V. (2012). The dog and the Frisbee. *Proceedings of the 36th Economic Policy Symposium, Jackson Hole, Wyoming* (pp. 109–159). Federal Reserve Bank of Kansas City.
Hall, G. S. (1904/1976). Biological and anthropological differences between the sexes. In P. C. Lee & R. S. Stewart (Eds.), *Sex differences* (pp. 371–379). New York: Urizen Books.
Halpern, D. F. (2012). *Sex differences in cognitive abilities* (4th ed.). Hillsdale, NJ: Erlbaum.
Halpern, D. F., & Wai, J. (2020). Sex differences in intelligence. In R. J. Sternberg (Ed.), *The Cambridge handbook of intelligence* (2nd ed., pp. 253–272). Cambridge, UK: Cambridge University Press.
Hamann, H. (2022), On getting it right by being wrong: A case study of how flawed research may become self-fulfilling at last. *Proceedings of the National Academy of Sciences, 119*(15), e2122274119.
Hamlin, R. P. (2017). "The gaze heuristic": Biography of an adaptively rational decision process. *Topics in Cognitive Science, 9*, 264–288.
Harari, Y. N. (2017). *Homo Deus*. London: Vintage.
Hauser, M. (2006). *Moral minds: How nature designed our universal sense of right and wrong*. New York: Ecco.
Henriksen, D. (2016). The rise of co-authorship in the social sciences (1980–2013). *Scientometrics, 107*, 455–476.
Hertwig, R., Davis, J. N., & Sulloway, F. J. (2002). Parental investment: How an equity motive can produce inequality. *Psychological Bulletin, 128*(5), 728–745.
Hertwig, R., & Gigerenzer, G. (1999). The "conjunction fallacy" revisited: How intelligent inferences look like reasoning errors. *Journal of Behavioral Decision Making, 12*, 275–305.
Hertwig, R., & Grüne-Yanoff, T. (2017). Nudging and boosting: Steering or empowering good decisions. *Perspectives on Psychological Science, 12*, 973–986.
Hertwig, R., Herzog, S. M., Schooler, L. J., & Reimer, T. (2008). Fluency heuristic: A model of how the mind exploits a by-product of information retrieval. *Journal of Experimental Psychology: Learning, Memory, and Cognition, 34*, 1191–1206.
Hertwig, R., Hoffrage, U., & the ABC Research Group. (2013). *Simple heuristics in a social world*. Oxford: Oxford University Press.

Hertwig, R., Pachur, T., & Kurzenhäuser, S. (2005). Judgments of risk frequencies: Tests of possible mechanisms. *Journal of Experimental Psychology: Learning, Memory & Cognition, 31*, 621–642.

Herzog, S. M., & Hertwig, R. (2013). The ecological validity of fluency. In C. Unkelbach & R. Greifeneder (Eds.), *The experience of thinking: How the fluency of mental processes influences cognition and behaviour* (pp. 190–219). New York: Psychology Press.

Hirsch, S., & Hirsch, A. (2011). *The beauty of short hops: How chance and circumstance confound the moneyball approach to baseball.* Jefferson, NC: McFarland & Co.

Hoffman, J. R., & Kanzaria, H. K. (2014). Intolerance of error and culture of blame drive medical excess. *British Medical Journal, 349*, g5702.

Hoffmann, H., Kessler, H., Eppel, T., Rukavini, S., & Traue, H. C. (2010). Expression intensity, gender and facial emotion recognition: Women recognize only subtle facial emotions better than men. *Acta Psychologica, 135*, 278–283.

Hofstadter, D. (2022, June 9). Are today's neural networks conscious? *The Economist*.

Hofstede, H., & Ratcliffe, J. M. (2016). Evolutionary escalation: The bat–moth arms race. *Journal of Experimental Biology, 219*(11), 1589–1602.

Hogarth, R. M. (2001). *Educating intuition.* Chicago, IL: University of Chicago Press.

Hollingworth, L. S. (1914). Variability as related to sex differences in achievement. *American Journal of Sociology, 19*, 510–530.

House of Lords Science and Technology Select Committee. (2011). *2nd Report of Session 2010–12: Behaviour Change.* Authority of the House of Lords.

Hutchinson, J. M. C., & Gigerenzer, G. (2005). Simple heuristics and rules of thumb: Where psychologists and behavioural biologists might meet. *Behavioural Processes, 69*, 97–124.

Isaacson, W. (2011). *Steve Jobs.* London: Little, Brown.

Johnson, E. J., & Goldstein, D. G. (2003). Do defaults save lives? *Science, 302*, 1338–1339.

Johnson, J. G., & Raab, M. (2003). Take the first: Option-generation and resulting choices. *Organizational Behavior and Human Decision Processes, 91*(2), 215–229.

Johnson, W., Carothers, A., & Deary, I. J. (2009). A role for the X chromosome in sex differences in variability in general intelligence? *Perspectives on Psychological Science, 4*, 589–611.

Jonsson, B., & von Hofsten, C. (2003). Infants' ability to track and reach for temporarily occluded objects. *Developmental Science, 6*, 86–99.

Juslin, P., Winman, A., & Hansson, P. (2007). The naïve intuitive statistician: A naïve sampling model of intuitive confidence intervals. *Psychological Review, 114*, 678–703.

Juslin, P., Winman, A., & Olsson, H. (2000). Naive empiricism and dogmatism in confidence research: A critical examination of the hard-easy effect. *Psychological Review, 107*, 384–396.

Kahneman, D. (2002, December 8). *Maps of bounded rationality: A perspective on intuitive judgment and choice*. Prize Lecture, 449–489.

(2003). Maps of bounded rationality: A perspective on intuitive judgment and choice. In T. Frangsmyr (Ed.), *Les Prix Nobel: The Nobel prizes 2002* (pp. 1449–1489). Nobel Foundation.

(2011a). *Thinking, fast and slow*. London: Allen Lane.

(2011b, September 12). The marvels and the flaws of intuitive thinking. *Edge*. Retrieved October 24, 2022, www.edge.org/conversation/daniel_kahneman-the-marvels-and-the-flaws-of-intuitive-thinking-edge-master-class-2011

(2019). Comment on artificial intelligence and behavioral economics. In A. Agrawal, J. Gans, & A. Goldfarb (Eds.), *The economics of artificial intelligence: An agenda*. Chicago, IL: University of Chicago Press.

Kahneman, D., & Frederick, S. (2005). A model of heuristic judgment. In K. J. Holyoak & R. G. Morrison (Eds.), *The Cambridge handbook of thinking and reasoning* (pp. 267–293). Cambridge: Cambridge University Press.

Kahneman, D., & Tversky, A. (1972). Subjective probability: A judgment of representativeness. *Cognitive Psychology, 3*, 430–454. (Reprinted in D. Kahneman, P. Slovic, & A. Tversky (1982) (Eds.), *Judgment under uncertainty: Heuristics and biases* (pp. 1932–1947). Cambridge, UK: Cambridge University Press).

(1973). On the psychology of prediction. *Psychological Review, 80*, 237–251.

(1984). Choice, values, and frames. *American Psychologist, 39*, 341–350.

(1996). On the reality of cognitive illusions. *Psychological Review, 103*, 582–591.

Kam, C. D., & Zechmeister, E. J. (2013). Name recognition and candidate support. *American Journal of Political Science, 57*, 971–986.

Kane, S. A., Fulton A. H., & Rosenthal, L. J. (2015). When hawks attack: Animal-borne video studies of goshawk pursuit and prey-evasion strategies. *Journal of Experimental Biology, 218*, 212–222.

Kant, I. (1764/2011). *Observations on the feelings of the beautiful and sublime* (P. Frierson & P. Guyer, Trans.). Cambridge, UK: Cambridge University Press.

(1784). Beantwortung der Frage: Was ist Aufklärung? *Berlinische Monatsschrift*, December, 481–494.

Katsikopoulos, K. V., Şimşek, Ö., Buckmann, M., & Gigerenzer, G. (2020). *Classification in the wild*. Cambridge, MA: MIT Press.

Katsikopoulos, K., Şimşek, Ö., Buckmann, M., & Gigerenzer, G. (2021). Transparent modelling of influenza incidence: Big data or a single data point from psychological theory? *International Journal of Forecasting, 38*(2), 613–619.

Kay, J., & King, M. (2020). *Radical uncertainty*. London: Bridge Street Press.

Keren, G., & Schul, Y. (2009). Two is not always better than one: A critical evaluation of two-systems theories. *Perspectives on Psychological Science, 4*, 533–550.

Khamsi, R. (2005, February 1). Bacteria show signs of ageing. *Nature*. Retrieved October 25, 2022, www.nature.com/news/2005/050131/full/news050131-6.htm

Kitcher, P. (1992). The naturalists return. *Philosophical Review, 101,* 53–114.
Klein, G. (1998/2017). *Sources of power: How people make decisions* (20th anniversary ed.). Cambridge, MA: MIT Press.
  (2015). A naturalistic decision making perspective on studying intuitive decision making. *Journal of Applied Research in Memory and Cognition, 4,* 164–168.
Knight, F. (1921). *Risk, uncertainty, and profit* (Vol. XXXI). Boston, MA: Houghton Mifflin.
Kohlberg, L. (1984). *Essays on moral development – Vol. 2. The psychology of moral development: The nature and validity of moral stages.* San Francisco, CA: Harper & Row.
Kösters, J. P., & Gøtzsche, P. C. (2003). Regular self-examination or clinical examination for early detection of breast cancer. *Cochrane Database of Systematic Reviews* (2), CD003373.
Kristal, A. S., & Whillans, A. V. (2020). What we can learn from five naturalistic field experiments that failed to shift commuter behaviour. *Nature Human Behaviour, 4,* 169–176.
Kruglanski, A. W., & Gigerenzer, G. (2011). Intuitive and deliberative judgments are based on common principles. *Psychological Review, 118,* 97–109.
Kühberger, A. (1995). The framing of decisions: A new look at old problems. *Organizational Behavior and Human Decision Processes, 62,* 230–240.
Kühberger, A., & Tanner, C. (2010). Risky choice framing: Task versions and a comparison of prospect theory and fuzzy-trace theory. *Journal of Behavioral Decision Making, 23*(3), 314–329.
Kurzweil, R. (2012). *How to create a mind.* New York: Penguin.
Lehrke, R. G. (1978). Sex linkage: A biological basis for greater male variability in intelligence. In R. T. Osborne, C. E. Noble, & N. Weyl (Eds.), *Human variation: The biopsychology of age, race, and sex* (pp. 171–198). New York: Academic Press.
Lejarraga, T., & Hertwig, R. (2021). How experimental methods shaped views on human competence and rationality. *Psychological Bulletin, 147*(6), 535–564.
Lewis, M. (2003). *Moneyball.* New York: Norton.
  (2017). *The undoing project.* New York: Norton.
Libet, B. (2004). *Mind time: The temporal factor in consciousness.* Cambridge, MA: Harvard University Press.
Luan, S., Schooler, L., & Gigerenzer, G. (2011). A signal detection analysis of fast-and-frugal trees. *Psychological Review, 118,* 316–338.
Maier, M., Bartos, F., Stanley, T. D., Shanks, D. R., Harris, A. J. L., & Wagenmakers, E.-J. (2022). No evidence for nudging after adjusting for publication bias. *Proceedings of the National Academy of Sciences, 119* (31), e2200300119.
Mallon, E. B., & Franks, N. R. (2000). Ants estimate area using Buffon's needle. *Proceedings of the Royal Society B, 267,* 765–770.
Mandel, D. R. (2001). Gain-loss framing and choice: Separating outcome formulations from descriptor formulations. *Organizational Behavior and Human Decision Processes, 85*(1), 56–76.

(2014). Do framing effects reveal irrational choice? *Journal of Experimental Psychology: General*, *143*, 1185–1198.

Marewski, J. N., Gaissmaier, W., Schooler, L. J., Goldstein, D. G., & Gigerenzer, G. (2010). From recognition to decisions: Extending and testing recognition-based models for multi-alternative inference. *Psychonomic Bulletin & Review*, *17*, 287–309.

Martignon, L., & Hoffrage, U. (2002). Fast, frugal, and fit: Lexicographic heuristics for paired comparison. *Theory and Decision*, *52*, 29–71.

Masters, B. A. (1986, April 18). When the Cliffies finally conquered Lamont. *The Harvard Crimson*. Retrieved October 25, 2022, www.thecrimson.com/article/1986/4/18/when-the-cliffies-finally-conquered-lamont

Matesanz, R. (2003). Factors influencing the adaptation of the Spanish Model of organ donation. *Transplant International*, *16*, 736–741.

McBeath, M. K., Shaffer, D. M., & Kaiser, M. K. (1995). How baseball outfielders determine where to run to catch fly balls. *Science*, *268*, 569–573.

McDowell, M., & Jacobs, P. (2017). Meta-analysis of the effect of natural frequencies on Bayesian reasoning. *Psychological Bulletin*, *143*, 1273–1312.

McKenzie, C. R. M., & Nelson, J. D. (2003). What a speaker's choice of frame reveals: Reference points, frame selection, and framing effects. *Psychonomic Bulletin and Review*, *10*, 596–602.

McNemar, Q., & Terman, L. M. (1936). Sex differences in variational tendency. *Genetic Psychology Monographs*, *18*, 1–66.

Medvegy, Z., Raab, M., Tóth, K., Csurilla, G., & Sterbenz, T. (2022). When do expert decision makers trust their intuition? *Applied Cognitive Psychology*, *36*(4).

Melnikoff, D. E., & Bargh, J. A. (2018). The mythical number two. *Trends in Cognitive Sciences*, *22*, 280–293.

Mercier, H., & Sperber, D. (2011). Why do humans reason? Arguments for an argumentative theory. *Behavioral & Brain Sciences*, *34*, 57–74.

(2018). *The enigma of reason*. London: Penguin Books.

Mertens, S., Herberz, M., Hahnel, U. J. J., & Brosch, T. (2022). The effectiveness of nudging: A meta-analysis of choice architecture interventions across behavioral domains. *Proceedings of the National Academy of Sciences*, *119*(1), e2107346118.

Merton, R. K. (1965). *On the shoulders of giants*. New York: Free Press.

Meyerowitz, B. E., & Chaiken, S. (1987). The effect of message framing on breast self-examination attitudes, intentions, and behavior. *Journal of Personality and Social Psychology*, *52*(3), 509–510.

Meyers-Levy, J., & Loken, B. (2015). Revisiting gender differences: What we know and what lies ahead. *Journal of Consumer Science*, *25*, 129–149.

Miller, J. B., & Sanjuro, A. (2018). Surprised by the hot hand fallacy? A truth in the law of small numbers. *Econometrica*, *86*, 2019–2047.

Minton, H. L. (1988). *Lewis M. Terman: Pioneer in psychological testing*. New York: New York University Press.

Montagne, B., Kessels, R. P., Frigerio, E., de Haan, E. H. F., & Perrett, D. I. (2005). Sex differences in the perception of affective facial expressions: Do men really lack emotional sensitivity? *Cognitive Processing*, *6*(2), 136–141.

Moxey, A., O'Connell, D., McGettigan, P., & Henry, D. (2003). Describing treatment effects to patients: How they are expressed makes a difference. *Journal of General Internal Medicine, 18*, 948–959.

Mugford, S. T., Mallon, E. B., & Franks, N. R. (2001). The accuracy of Buffon's needle: A rule of thumb used by ants to estimate area. *Behavioral Ecology, 12*, 655–658.

Nagel, T. (1993). Moral luck. In D. Statman (Ed.), *Moral luck* (pp. 57–71). Albany, NY: State University of New York Press.

Narvaez, D. (2010). Moral complexity: The fatal attraction of truthiness and the importance of mature moral functioning. *Perspectives on Psychological Science, 5*, 163–181.

Narvaez, D., & Lapsley, D. (2005). The psychological foundations of everyday morality and moral expertise. In D. Lapsley & C. Power (Eds.), *Character psychology and character education* (pp. 140–165). Notre Dame, IN: University of Notre Dame Press.

Neiman, S. (2008). *Moral clarity: A guide for grownup idealists*. New York: Harcourt.

Newell, A. (1973). You can't play 20 questions with nature and win: Projective comments on the papers of this symposium. In W. G. Chase (Ed.), *Visual information processing: Proceedings of the Eighth Annual Carnegie Symposium on Cognition* (pp. 283–308). New York: Academic Press.

Newell, A., & Simon, H. A. (1972). *Human problem solving*. Englewood Cliffs, NJ: Prentice-Hall.

OECD. The Organisation for Economic Co-operation and Development. (2017). *Behavioral insights and public policy: Lessons from around the world*. OECD Publishing.

(2019), *PISA 2018 results: Vol. III. What school life means for students' lives*. OECD Publishing.

Ortmann, A., Gigerenzer, G., Borges, B., & Goldstein, D. G. (2008). The recognition heuristic: A fast and frugal way to investment choice? In C. R. Plott & V. L. Smith (Eds.), *Handbook of experimental economics results: Vol. 1. Handbooks in Economics No. 28* (pp. 993–1003). Amsterdam: North-Holland.

Osbeck, L. M., & Held, B. S. (Eds.). (2014). *Rational intuition*. Cambridge, UK: Cambridge University Press.

Pachur, T., & Marinello, G. (2013). Expert intuitions: How to model the decision strategies of airport customs officers? *Acta Psychologica, 144*, 97–103.

Pachur, T., Mata, R., & Schooler, L. J. (2009). Cognitive aging and the adaptive use of recognition in decision making. *Psychology and Aging, 24*, 901–915.

Pascal, B. (1669/1995). *Pensées*. London: Penguin Classics.

Pashler, H., Coburn, N., & Harris, C. R. (2012). Priming of social distance? Failure to replicate effects on social and food judgments. *PLoS ONE, 7*(8), e42510.

Pearson, K. (1897). *The chances of death and other studies in evolution* (Vol. I). London: Edward Arnold.

Pearson, K., & Lee, A. (1903). On the laws of inheritance in man: Inheritance of physical characters. *Biometrica*, 2, 357–462.

Pessoa, F. (1996). *The book of disquiet* (Richard Zenth, Trans.). London: Penguin Classics.

Peterson, C. R., & Beach, L. R. (1967). Man as an intuitive statistician. *Psychological Bulletin*, 68, 29–46.

Petracca, E. (2021). On the origins and consequences of Simon's modular approach to bounded rationality in economics. *The European Journal of the History of Economic Thought*, 28(5), 708–732.

Pfeifer, P. E. (1994). Are we overconfident in the belief that probability forecasters are overconfident? *Organizational Behavior and Human Decision Processes*, 58, 203–213.

Piaget, J., & Inhelder, B. (1951/1975). *The origin of the idea of chance in children* (L. Leake, P. Burrell, & H. D. Fishbein, Trans.). New York: Norton.

Pippin, R. B. (2009). Natural & normative. *Daedalus*, Summer, 35–43.

Pohl, R. F. (2006). Empirical tests of the recognition heuristic. *Journal of Behavioral Decision Making*, 19, 251–271.

Polanyi, M. (1966/2009). *The tacit dimension*. Chicago, IL: University of Chicago Press.

Pólya, G. (1945/1988). *How to solve it* (2nd ed.). Princeton, NJ: Princeton University Press.

Popomaronis, T. (2020, October 22). Jeff Bezos's 3-question rule for hiring new Amazon employees – and how to answer them right. *CNBC make it*. Retrieved October 25, 2022, www.cnbc.com/2020/10/20/jeff-bezos-3-question-rule-for-hiring-new-amazon-employees.html

(2021, January 26). Elon Musk asks this question at every interview to spot a liar: Why science says it actually works. *CNBC make it*. Retrieved October 25, 2022, www.cnbc.com/2021/01/26/elon-musk-favorite-job-interview-question-to-ask-to-spot-a-liar-science-says-it-actually-works.html

Raab, M., Gula, B., & Gigerenzer, G. (2012). The hot hand exists in volleyball and is used for allocation decisions. *Journal of Experimental Psychology: Applied*, 18, 81–94.

Reber, A. S. (1989). Implicit learning and tacit knowledge. *Journal of Experimental Psychology: General*, 118, 317–327.

Rebonato, R. (2012). *Taking liberties: A critical examination of libertarian paternalism*. New York: Palgrave Macmillan.

Richardson, H. S. (2004). Satisficing: Not good enough. In M. Byron (Ed.), *Satisficing and maximizing: Moral theorists on practical reason* (pp. 106–130). Cambridge, UK: Cambridge University Press.

Rifkin, J. (2002). *Science in the age of sensibility: The sentimental empiricists of the French Enlightenment*. Chicago, IL: University of Chicago Press.

Rizzo, J. M., & Whitman, G. (2020). *Escaping paternalism*. Cambridge, UK: Cambridge University Press.

Rose, C. (Executive producer). (2009, February 11). *The Charlie Rose show* [television broadcast]. Public Broadcasting System (PBS).

Rosenbaum, J. (2009). Patient teenagers? A comparison of the sexual behavior of virginity pledgers and matched nonpledgers. *Pediatrics, 123*, 110–120. doi: 10.1542/peds.2008-0407

Rosenbaum, S. E., Glenton C., & Oxman, A. D. (2010). Summary-of-findings tables in Cochrane reviews improved understanding and rapid retrieval of key information. *Journal of Clinical Epidemiology, 63*, 620–626.

Ross, C. (2022, January 21). Once billed as a revolution in medicine, IBM's Watson Health is sold off in parts. www.statnews.com/2022/01/21/ibm-watson-health-sale-equity

Salovey, P., & Williams-Piehota, P. (2004). Field experiments in social psychology: Message framing and the promotion of health protective behaviors. *American Behavioral Scientist, 47*, 488–505.

Santayana, G. (1905). *The life of reason*. New York: Scribners.

Savage, L. J. (1954/1972). *The foundations of statistics* (2nd ed.). New York: Wiley.

Scheibehenne, B., & Bröder, A. (2007). Predicting Wimbledon 2005 tennis results by mere player name recognition. *International Journal of Forecasting, 23*, 415–426.

Schneider, S. (2010, June 29). *Homo economicus – or more like Homer Simpson?* Deutsche Bank Research.

Schofer, G. (1976). G. Stanley Hall: Male chauvinist educator. *The Journal of Educational Thought, 10*, 194–200.

Schooler, L. J., & Hertwig, R. (2005). How forgetting aids heuristic inference. *Psychological Review, 112*, 610–628.

Schüll, N. D. (2012). *Addiction by design: Machine gambling in Las Vegas*. Princeton, NJ: Princeton University Press.

Scottish Council for Research in Education. (1933). *The intelligence of Scottish children: A national survey of an age group*. (Publications of the Scottish Council for Research in Education V). London: University of London Press.

(1939). *The intelligence of a representative group of Scottish children* (Vol. VX). London: University of London Press.

(1949). *The trend of Scottish intelligence* (Vol. XXX). London: University of London Press.

(1958). *Eleven-year-olds grow up* (Vol. XLII). London: University of London Press.

Sedlmeier, P., & Gigerenzer, G. (2001). Teaching Bayesian reasoning in less than two hours. *Journal of Experimental Psychology: General, 130*, 380–400.

Serwe, S., & Frings, C. (2006). Who will win Wimbledon? The recognition heuristic in predicting sports events. *Journal of Behavioral Decision Making, 19*, 321–322.

Shaffer, D. M., Krauchunas, S. M., Eddy, M., & McBeath, M. K. (2004). How dogs navigate to catch frisbees. *Psychological Science, 15*, 437–441.

Shaffer, D. M., & McBeath, M. K. (2002). Baseball outfielders maintain a linear optical trajectory when tracking uncatchable flyballs. *Journal of Experimental Psychology: Human, 28*, 335–348.

(2005). Naïve beliefs in baseball: Systematic distortions in perceived time of apex for fly balls. *Journal of Experimental Psychology: Learning, 31,* 1492–1501.

Sher, S., & McKenzie, C. R. M. (2006). Information leakage from logically equivalent frames. *Cognition, 101,* 467–494.

Shields, S. A. (1982). The variability hypothesis: The history of a biological model of sex differences in intelligence. *Signs: Journal of Women in Culture and Society, 7,* 769–797.

Simon, H. A. (1988). Nobel laureate Simon "looks back": A low-frequency mode. *Public Administration Quarterly, 12,* 275–300.

——— (1990). Invariants of human behavior. *Annual Review of Psychology, 41,* 1–19.

——— (1992). What is an "explanation" of behavior? *Psychological Science, 3,* 150–161.

——— (1997). *Models of bounded rationality: Vol. 3. Empirically grounded economic reason.* Cambridge, MA: MIT Press.

Şimşek, Ö. (2013). Linear decision rule as aspiration for simple decision heuristics. In C. J. C. Burges, L. Bottou, M. Welling, Z. Ghahramani, & K. Q. Weinberger (Eds.), *Advances in neural information processing systems: Vol. 26. 27th Annual Conference on Neural Information Processing Systems 2013 [online version]* (pp. 2904–2912). New York: Curran Associates.

Sinnott-Armstrong, W. (Ed.). (2008). *Moral psychology.* (2 Vols.). Cambridge, MA: MIT Press.

Sloman, S. A. (1996). The empirical case for two systems of reasoning. *Psychological Bulletin, 119,* 3–22.

Smith, V. L. (2003). Constructivist and ecological rationality in economics. *American Economic Review, 93,* 465–508.

——— (2008). *Discovery: A memoir.* Bloomington, IL: AuthorHouse.

Snowden, E. (2019). *Permanent record.* London: Macmillan.

Spearman, C. (1904). General intelligence, objectively determined and measured. *American Journal of Psychology, 15,* 201–293.

Sperber, D. (1994). The modularity of thought and the epidemiology of representations. In A. Hirschfeld & S. A. Gelman (Eds.), *Mapping the mind* (pp. 39–67). Cambridge, UK: Cambridge University Press.

Sperber, D., & Wilson, D. (1986). *Relevance: Communication and cognition.* Oxford: Blackwell.

Standing, L. (1973). Learning 10,000 pictures. *Quarterly Journal of Experimental Psychology, 25,* 207–222.

Stanovich, K., West, R., & Toplak, M. (2011). *The great rationality debate: The science of reason.* New York: Psychology Press.

Stephens, D. W., & Krebs, J. R. (1986). *Foraging theory.* Princeton, NJ: Princeton University Press.

Sternberg, R. J. (1990). *Metaphors of mind: Conceptions of the nature of intelligence.* Cambridge, UK: Cambridge University Press.

Strickland, E. (2019, April 2). How IBM Watson overpromised and underdelivered on AI health care. *IEEE Spectrum.* https://spectrum.ieee.org/

biomedical/diagnostics/how-ibm-watson-overpromised-and-underdelivered-on-ai-health-care

Sturm, T. (2012). The "rationality wars" in psychology: Where they are and where they could go. *Inquiry, 55*(1), 66–81.

Summers, L. H. (2005, January 14). *Remarks at NBER Conference on diversifying the science & engineering workforce.* Retrieved October 25, 2022, http://web.archive.org/web/20080130023006/http:/www.president.harvard.edu/speeches/2005/nber.html

Sunstein, C. R. (2005). *Laws of fear: Beyond the precautionary principle.* Cambridge, UK: Cambridge University Press.

(2020, February 28). The cognitive bias that makes us panic about coronavirus. Opinion. *Bloomberg.* Retrieved October 25, 2022, www.bloomberg.com/opinion/articles/2020-02-28/coronavirus-panic-caused-by-probability-neglect

Terman, L. M. (1916). *The measurement of intelligence.* Boston, MA: Houghton Mifflin.

Terman, L. M., & Merrill, M. A. (1937). *Measuring intelligence.* Boston, MA: Houghton Mifflin.

Terman, L. M. & Miles, C. C. (1936). *Sex and personality.* New York: McGraw-Hill.

Terman, L. M., & Oden, M. H. (1947). *The gifted child grows up: Vol. IV. Genetic studies of genius.* Redwood City, CA: Stanford University Press.

Tetlock, P. E., & Mellers, B. (2002) The great rationality debate. *Psychological Science, 13,* 94–99.

Thaler, R. H. (1991). *Quasi rational economics.* New York: Russell Sage Foundation.

Thaler, R. H., & Sunstein, C. R. (2003). Libertarian paternalism. *American Economic Review, 93*(2), 175–179.

(2008). *Nudge: Improving decisions about health, wealth, and happiness.* New Haven, CT: Yale University Press.

Thompson, H. B. (1903). *The mental traits of sex.* Chicago, IL: University of Chicago Press.

Todd, P. M., & Gigerenzer, G. (2001). Putting naturalistic decision making into the adaptive toolbox. *Journal of Behavioral Decision Making, 14,* 381–383.

Todd, P. M., Gigerenzer, G., & the ABC Research Group. (2012). *Ecological rationality: Intelligence in the world.* Oxford: Oxford University Press.

Tomasello, M. (2019). *Becoming human: A theory of ontogeny.* Cambridge, MA: Belknap.

Tombu, M., & Jolicoeur, P. (2004). Virtually no evidence for virtually perfect time-sharing. *Journal of Experimental Psychology: Human Perception & Performance, 30,* 795–810.

Tombu, M., & Mandel, D. R. (2015). When does framing influence preferences, risk perceptions, and risk attitudes? The explicated valence account. *Journal of Behavioral Decision Making, 28*(5), 464–476.

Tooby, J., & Cosmides, L. (1992). The psychological foundations of culture. In J. H. Barkow, L. Cosmides, & J. Tooby (Eds.), *The adapted mind* (pp. 19–138). Oxford: Oxford University Press.

Tripodi, V. (2015). Intuition, gender, and the underrepresentation of women in philosophy. *Architettura, 58*, 136–146.

Trout, J. D. (2005). Paternalism and cognitive bias. *Law and Philosophy, 24*, 393–434.

Tuckett, D. (2011). *Minding the markets*. London: Palgrave Macmillan.

Tversky, A., & Kahneman, D. (1974). Judgment under uncertainty: Heuristics and biases. *Science, 185*, 1124–1131.

 (1981). The framing of decisions and the psychology of choice. *Science, 211*, 453–458.

 (1986). Rational choice and the framing of decisions. *The Journal of Business, 59*(4), S251–S278.

United States Department of Justice.(n.d.). Retrieved October 24, 2022, www.justice.gov/opa/pr/deutsche-bank-agrees-pay-72-billion-misleading-investors-its-sale-residential-mortgage-backed

Volz, K. G., Schubotz, R. I., Raab, M., Schooler, L. J., Gigerenzer, G., & von Cramon, D. Y. (2006). Why you think Milan is larger than Modena: Neural correlates of the recognition heuristic. *Journal of Cognitive Neuroscience, 18*, 1924–1936.

Wang, Y., Highhouse, S., Lake, C. J., Petersen, N. L., & Rada, T. B. (2017). Meta-analytic investigations of the relation between intuition and analysis. *Journal of Behavioral Decision Making, 30*, 15–25.

Weber, M. (1930/1992). *The Protestant ethic and the spirit of capitalism*. Abingdon, UK: Routledge.

Weininger, O. (1903/1906). *Sex & character*. Portsmouth, NH: William Heinemann.

Wellman, B. (1933). Sex differences. In C. Murchison (Ed.), *Handbook of child psychology* (2nd rev. ed., pp. 626–649). Worcester, MA: Clark University Press.

Williams, B. (1981). *Moral luck*. Cambridge, UK: Cambridge University Press.

Wilson, M. (2002). Six views of embodied cognition. *Psychonomic Bulletin & Review, 9*, 625–636.

Wissler, C. (1901). The correlation of mental and physical tests. *Psychological Review, Monograph Supplement, 3*(6), 1–62.

Wolf, T. H. (1973). *Alfred Binet*. Chicago, IL: University of Chicago Press.

Zarembo, A. (2003, December 3). Funding studies to suit need. *Los Angeles Times*. Retrieved October 25, 2022, www.latimes.com/nation/la-na-valdez3-2003dec03-story.html

Zenko, M. (2015). *Red team: How to succeed by thinking like the enemy*. New York: Basic Books.

Zimbardo, P. (2007). *The Lucifer effect: Understanding how good people turn to evil*. New York: Random House.

Index

1/N, 112
ABC Research Group, 141–152
adaptive toolbox, of heuristics, 40, 91–103
Administrative Behavior (Simon), 93
Against Autonomy (Conly), 75
algorithms
  intuition and, 15, 82–85
  misrepresentation of, 82–85
  technological paternalism and, 81, 82–85
Animal and Plants Under Domestication (Darwin), 34
Aquinas, Thomas, 2
Ariely, Dan, 11, 45
Aristotle
  gender bias and, 21
  on paternalism, 69
  view of peculiar female intelligence and, 22
  on women's memory, 24
Arkes, Hal, 64
artificial intelligence (AI)
  intuition and, 80–82
  intuition as challenge to, 85–86
as-if model, 115–117
Asian disease problem, 49–51
aspiration level, 106–107, 129–130
authority ranking, 130
Automatic System. *See* System 1 thinking

Bacon, Francis, 14
Bayes' theorem, 45, 61, 63–64
Bayesian reasoning, 159, 165, 168
Beach, Lee Roy, 60
Becker, Gary, 57, 130
Berlin, Isaiah, 70
Bezos, Jeff, 97–99
bias. *See also* gender bias
  citation, 59–61
  exponential growth, 16
  racial, 30–32
bias bias, 11–14, 16, 47
  dual-process theory and, 67

framing effect and, 47–51
general principles of, 59
governmental paternalism and, 12–14
hot hand fallacy and, 56–58
intelligent inference and, 51–52
irregular sequences and, 55
law of small numbers and, 52–55
logical rationality and, 44–45
randomness and, 52–55
stubborness and, 61–64
biased sample estimators, 56
Binet, Alfred, 27–30
boosting, 73–75
  paternalism and, 69, 71
Boring, Edwin, 38
Browning, Christopher, 135–137
Bruegel, Pieter, 125
Buffon's needle algorithm, 111–112

Carlson, Magnus, 1
Catholic doctrine, 128–130
Cattell, James McKeen, 27
certainty, 2–3, 47
cheap twin paradox, 107
Chomsky, Noam, 133
cognition, embodied, 109
collaboration, 141
Common Sense (Paine), 14
communal sharing, 130
comradeship, 136–137
Conly, Sarah, 75
coordination, predator–prey, 119–121
coordination problems, 117–118
correlation, surrogate, 104
Covid-19, 16
Csikszentmihalyi, Mike, 56

Darwin, Charles, 26–27, 132–133
Dawkins, Richard, 113
decision theory, 110
default choices, 76–78

Descartes, René, 2–3, 107
descriptive invariance, 50, 59
direct pursuit heuristic, 120
dominant cue condition, 100
dual-system theory, 11, 43, 65–67
   gaze heuristics and, 118

echolocation, 121
ecological morality, 140
   comradeship and, 136–137
   fairness and, 135
   imitation and, 135
   moral luck and, 139
   social heuristics and, 134–139
ecological rationality, 54–55, 58, 80, 92–93, 96–106, 129
   adaptive toolbox and, 40, 97, 103–108
   fluency heuristic and, 92–93
   moral intuition and, 127–128
   one-good-reason heuristics and, 100
   recognition heuristic and, 104–105
   Vernon Smith and, 107–108
Ecological Rationality: Intelligence in the World, 147
Edwards, Ward, 61, 64
Einstein, Albert, 2, 10
Ellis, Havelock, 23, 34–36
embodied heuristics
   ants as illustration of, 111–112
   gaze heuristic and, 115, 123–124
equality heuristic, 135
equality matching, 130, 131
equivalence, logical, 52
evolutionary theory, 96
   development of intuition and, 109–111
   intelligence and, 26–27
   moral intuition and, 132–133
exaptation, 118–119
expected utility maximization, 94–96, 143
experience, 3–6
Eysenck, Hans-Jürgen, 32

fairness, 135
fast-and-frugal heuristic, 98, 101–103, 112, 139
fast-and-frugal trees, 99, 101–103
Feynman, Richard, 51
The Fight Between Carnival and Lent (Bruegel), 125
Fiske, Alan, 130
flow, 1, 56
fluency
   intuition and, 4–5
fluency heuristic, 4, 17, 92–93, 103
framing effect, 44–45, 47–51
Franklin, Benjamin, 126

French ministerial commission on the education of "abnormal" children, 27
frequencies, natural, 63
Freud, Sigmund, 6

Galton, Francis, 23, 26–27
gambler's fallacy, 55
gaze heuristic, 113–124
   as embodied heuristic, 115, 123–124
   as-if model and, 115–117
   coordination problems and, 117–118
   dual-system theories and, 118
   echolocation and, 121
   exaptation and, 118–119
   Royal Air Force (RAF) and, 121–123
   Tizzy Angle and, 122
   whiskers and, 121
gender bias
   Aristotle and, 21
   female intuition and, 23–25
   Hall and, 22
   intelligence and, 26–27, 30–34
   intuition and, 10–11
   Kant and, 21
   male reason and, 23–25
   moral virtue and, 24–25
   in popular psychology, 39
   theories of female intelligence and, 22–23
   variability hypothesis and, 34–37
   view of peculiar female intelligence and, 38–40
Gödel, Escher, Bach (Hofstadter), 85
Goldstein, Daniel, 76
GPT-3, 85–86
great rationality debate, the, 12

Haidt, Jonathan, 127, 139
Hall, G. Stanley, 21–22, 24, 38
Halpern, Diane, 39
Harari, Yuval, 82, 83–85
Harding Center for Risk Literacy, 148
Harding, David, 148
Helmholtz, Hermann von, 2–3, 47, 110
Hereditary Genius (Galton), 26
Hertwig, Ralph, 64
heuristics
   1/N, 112
   adaptive, 103–108
   AI and, 40
   biases and, 15
   conscious and unconscious use of, 67, 98, 107, 113, 118
   deliberate use of, 97–99
   direct pursuit, 120, 122

heuristics (cont.)
  ecological rationality and, 93, 96–106
  embodied, 111–112, 115
  equality, 135
  fast-and-frugal, 98, 103, 139
  fast-and-frugal trees, 99, 101–103
  fluency, 17, 92–93, 103
  gaze, 113–124
  intuitive use of, 97–99
  Max Planck Society and, 142
  one-good-reason, 98, 100
  recognition, 103–106
  research culture and, 152
  satisficing, 106–107
  social, 41, 127–128, 132–139
  social narratives and, 128–132
Hofstadter, Douglas, 85
Homo Deus (Harari), 83
homo economicus, 44
hot hand fallacy, 56–58
Hug, Klaus, 131
Hume, David, 2, 128

imitation, 135
inference, intelligent, 51–52
inferences, invited, 47
inferences, unconscious, 47, 110
Inhelder, Bärbel, 11, 60
instincts, social, 132
intelligence
  evolutionary theory and, 25
  failures to measure, 27
  gender bias and, 26–27, 30–34
  general, 25, 27, 30, 38
  genetic ability and, 29–30
  invention of, 23, 26, 38
  measurement of, 27–30
  peculiar female, 38–40
  personality and, 32–33
  racial bias and, 30–32
  theories of female, 22–23
  variability hypothesis and, 34–37
The Intelligence Controversy (Eysenck and Kamin), 32
intuition, 3
  algorithms and, 15, 82–85
  artificial intelligence (AI) and, 80–82
  Bayesian, 63–64
  blame for political failure and, 76
  certainty and, 2–3
  as challenge to AI, 85–86
  chess and, 1
  cognitive biases and, 11
  defining features of, 2–7
  dichotomy with reason, 15–17
  evolutionary development of, 109–111
  experience and, 3–6
  explicit learning and, 9
  fluency and, 4–5
  gender bias and, 10–11
  growth of psychology and, 42–43
  heuristic use of, 97–99
  implicit learning and, 8–9
  irrationality and, 2, 76
  logic and, 44–45
  mistrust of, 2, 7
  myth of female, 41
  myth of substantial costs and, 64–65
  post hoc justications of, 8
  randomness and, 52–55
  rationality and, 10–11, 45–46
  reason and, 1–2
  scientific view of, 15–17
  stubborness and, 61–64
  as unconscious inferences, 3, 6–7
  war on, 10–14
invariance, description, 50, 51
IQ tests, 23, 28–34, 36–41, 155
irrationality argument, 45, 76
irrationality paradox, 59

Johnson, Eric, 76
Judgment under Uncertainty (Kahneman and Tversky), 60–61
Juslin, Peter, 61

Kahan, Dan, 63
Kahneman, Daniel, 11, 44–45, 50, 60–61, 64, 66–67
Kamin, Leon, 32
Kant, Immanuel, 2, 21
Klein, Gary, 91
Knight, Frank, 95
Kohlberg, Lawrence, 127, 139
Kühberger, Anton, 50–51
Kurzweil, Ray, 81

law of small numbers, 52–55
learning, explicit, 9
learning, frequency, 64
learning, implicit, 8–9
Lewin, Kurt, 107
Lewis, Michael, 83
liberty, negative, 70
liberty, positive, 70. *See* boosting
Libet, Benjamin, 9
logic
  intuition and, 44–45
logical rationality, 44–46, 64, 80
Loken, Barbara, 41

Man and Women (Ellis), 34–35
Man as an Intuitive Statistician (Peterson and Beach), 60–61
market pricing, 131
masculinity-femininity scale, 33
Max Planck Institute, 141–143. *See also* research program
McKenzie, Craig, 61
The Measurement of Intelligence (Terman), 39
McNemar, Quinn, 36
Merrill, Maude, 31
Meyers-Levy, Joan, 41
Miles, Catherine Cox, 32–33
Miller, Joshua, 57
Moneyball (Lewis), 83
moral intuition
　changes over time, 133–134
　defined, 125–126
　evolutionary theory and, 132–133
　fast-and-frugal heuristic and, 139
　moral reasoning and, 126
　principles of, 127
　satisficing and, 127–128
　social heuristics and, 127–128, 132–134, 137–138
　social instincts and, 132
　systemic inconsistencies in, 137–138
　virtue ethics and, 137–138
moral luck, 139
moral reasoning, 126
Morey House Test, 36
multitasking, 6
Musk, Elon, 97–99, 100

Nagel, Thomas, 139
naturalism, 128
neoclassical economics, 47, 75
　bounded rationality and, 94
Newell, Alan, 40
Newell, Allen, 67
Nudge (Thaler and Sunstein), 11
nudging, 45, 68, 69, 71–72
　default choice and, 76–78
　effectiveness of, 79–80

Oden, Melita, 31
one-good-reason heuristic, 98, 99–100
optimization, doctrine of, 93
Ordinary Men (Browning), 136–137
organ donation, 76–79, 137–138

Pascal, Blaise, 1, 6
paternalism, 68
　boosting and, 69, 71
　default choices and, 76–78

governmental, 12–14, 64–65
hard, 69, 71, 75
libertarian, 68, 69, 75, 80
neoclassical economic theory and, 75
nudging and, 71–72, 76–78
technological, 15, 80–86
"Paternalism and Cognitive Bias" (Trout), 75
Pearson, Karl, 35–36
personality, 32–33
Pessoa, Fernando, 6
Peterson, Cameron, 60
Piaget, Jean, 11, 43, 60, 109
Polgár, Judith, 1
Pólya, George, 15
preadaptation, 118
Predictably Irrational (Ariely), 11
prospect theory, 50
Protestant work ethic, 125–126
　satisficing and, 128–130

randomness
　intuition and, 52–55
rational choice theory, 4, 11, 92. *See also* logical rationality
rationality
　bounded, 93–96
　constructivist, 107
　ecological, 40, 54–56, 80, 92–93, 96–106, 129, *See also* ecological rationality
　intuition and, 45–46
　logical, 44–46, 64, 80
rationality war, 12
reason
　dichotomy with intuition, 15–17
　intuition and, 1–2
　morality and, 24
Reckoning with Risk, 148
recognition heuristic, 103–106
　brain activity and, 106
　ecological rationality of, 104–105
Rehow, Pierre, 133
relevance maxim, 49
research
　discipline-oriented, 143
　interdisciplinary, 144
　problem-oriented, 143
research program
　collective goals and, 146–148
　culture of, 146–152
　dealing with growth and, 148–150
　distribution of responsibility and, 150–151
　open culture and, 144–145, 151–152
　spatial proximity and, 145–146
　temporal proximity and, 146

Royal Air Force (RAF), 121–123
Russell, Betrand, 9

Sanjuro, Adam, 57
satisficing, 129
   moral, 128
   moral intuition and, 127–128
   naturalism and, 128
satisficing heuristic, 106–107
   Catholic doctrine and, 130
   Protestant work ethic and, 128–130
Savage, Jimmy, 95–96
Schneider, Olive, 36
The Selfish Gene (Dawkins), 113
sensibility
   as precursor to intelligence, 24
sequences, irregular, 55–56
Sex & Character (Weininger), 24
Sex and Personality (Terman and Miles), 32
Simon, Herbert, 40, 65, 93–96
Simon, Théodore, 27–30
Simple Heuristics in a Social World, 147
Simple Heuristics That Make Us Smart, 147
small worlds, 46, 94–96
Smith, Vernon, 107–108
social heuristics, 127–128
   ecological morality and, 134–139
   moral intuition and, 132–134, 137–138
Spearman, Charles, 27
speed-accuracy trade-off, 5
Sperber, Dan, 118
stable-world principle, 82
Stanford-Binet Intelligence Scales, 23, 29, 30–31, 36
Suicide Killers (Rehow), 133
Summers, Larry, 33
Sunstein, Cass, 11, 44, 56

System 1 thinking, 11, 43, 65–67
System 2 thinking, 11, 43, 65–67

Terman, Louis, 23, 29–33, 36, 38
Thaler, Richard, 11, 44, 56
Thinking, Fast and Slow (Kahneman), 11
Tizzy Angle, 122
Tomasello, Michael, 136
Trout, J. D., 75
Tversky, Amos, 44–45, 50, 60–61, 64
two-system theories. *See* dual-system theory

uncertainty, 17, 94–96, 99, 143–144
   framing and, 47
   fundamental (radical), 95
   moral intuitions and, 127–128
   risk versus, 46, 59, 94–96, 108
   stable-world principle and, 82
unconscious, 6–7
   inferences, 2–3, 47, 110
   intelligence, 3
   moral intuition and, 125
   use of heuristics, 67, 113

variability hypothesis, 34–37, 38
virtue ethics, 137–138

Wason selection task, 131–132
Weber, Max, 125–126, 128–130
Weininger, Otto, 24
Whitehead, Alfred, 9–10
Winterfeldt, Detley von, 64
Wissler, Clark, 27

Yerkes, Robert, 30
"You Can't Play 20 Questions with Nature and Win" (Newell), 65

Printed in the USA
CPSIA information can be obtained
at www.ICGtesting.com
LVHW010041281223
767563LV00002B/189